SPIRIT FRUIT

John M. Drescher

HERALD PRESS, SCOTTDALE, PENNSYLVANIA

1974

Library of Congress Cataloging in Publication Data

Drescher, John M
  Spirit fruit

  Bibliography: p. 348
  1. Meditations.   I. Title.
  BV4832.2.D74   242   73-21660
  ISBN 0-8361-1730-1

SPIRIT FRUIT
Copyright © 1974 by Herald Press, Scottdale, Pa. 15683
Library of Congress Catalog Card Number: 73-21660
International Standard Book Number: 0-8361-1730-1
Printed in the United States of America

To my wife Betty who, more than any other person I know, demonstrates the fruit of love, joy, peace, patience, kindness, goodness, fidelity, gentleness, and self-control.

Preface

During the past decade dozens of books and an abundance of articles have appeared dealing with the gifts of the Holy Spirit. Before this time a definite dearth of material on this dimension of the work of the Spirit existed. However, interest began to grow. The charismatic movement cut across denominational lines and became a spiritual dynamic among young and old, Catholic and Protestant.

Without a doubt the church was overdue in reviving interest in the gifts of the Spirit. No gift of the Spirit dare be despised or disposed of as for the first century only. The church needs each gift of the Spirit now as much as then.

In comparison to the emphases on spiritual gifts, we find little written during the same decade on the fruit of the Spirit. This is a serious lack. We need both gifts and fruit and we must keep both in their proper place for effective Christian work and witness. The gifts without the fruit are bare. We need also return to a careful consideration of the fruit of the Spirit. Otherwise our spiritual growth will be stifled.

Absence of material on the fruit of the Spirit became evident to me in preparation for teaching a minister's course on the work of the Holy Spirit. Out of concern for a study on the fruit of the Spirit this book was written.

These chapters, dealing with the fruit of the Spirit, are primarily devotional. Meditations are short with the hope that the reader will carry the book along and read a chapter or two in his spare minutes. The length of the chapters also lends itself to daily devotional reading.

Two emphases appear throughout the book. The first points out that the fruit is singular because every Christian has the Holy Spirit and demonstrates to one degree or another all the fruit. The fruit is like the petals of a beautiful rose. Every petal is necessary to make up the whole. So each fruit is necessary to make up the Christian life.

A second emphasis is that the fruit of the Spirit is produced only in relation to other people. It cannot be produced or practiced between God and us alone.

In the discussion of each fruit the pattern is first to give the meaning of the fruit, then to show how that fruit is illustrated in the life of Christ, and finally to show how the fruit characterizes our lives as Christ's followers.

To give credit for many of the ideas shared here is impossible. Dozens of commentaries on the Book of Galatians and other relevant passages on the fruit of the Spirit were studied. Hundreds of articles dealing with the Christian's experience in the Holy Spirit were read with ideas and illustrations incorporated into this book. In addition many books, written about the Holy Spirit's work, were read. A list of some of these is at the close of the book.

Numerous books coming out of the recent charismatic movement might also be added. However, these books discuss little on the fruit of the Holy Spirit. Their focus is primarily on the gifts. For that reason not many of these are included in the bibliography.

This book goes forth with the earnest prayer that it may be used by the Holy Spirit to make the lives of those who read it radiant with love, joy, peace, patience, kindness, goodness, faithfulness, gentleness, and self-control.

Contents

Spirit Fruit

1. The Spirit's Orchard

An orchard stands next to our backyard. Different kinds of fruit trees are planted there. Each spring and summer we look for signs of life and we expect fruit.

Growing fruit does not suggest a lot of noise and excitement. In the spring we do not say, "Fruit is growing in the orchard because we hear noise and because the trees are starting to jump around." We know fruit is being produced because we see steady, silent growth of buds, fragrant flowers, and finally luscious fruit. It is all so silent yet all so evident.

Spiritually we are not assured that the Holy Spirit is present simply because there is shouting, speaking, singing, or jumping. We look for other evidence. The Scripture says this evidence is the fruit of the Spirit. When the fruit of love, joy, peace, patience, gentleness, goodness, faithfulness, humility, and self-control are apparent to all who look, we know the Holy Spirit is in the life of a person and He is at work in them.

Quiet, Steady Growth

The Holy Spirit works quietly in our lives just as the fruit grows on trees. As a tree responds to new life in the spring, so we, who are in Christ, respond to the new life in the Spirit.

Fruit grows and ripens steadily and slowly as a result of refreshing rain, sunshine, nourishment, and pruning. So also the fruit of the Spirit grows with refreshing spiritual showers of God's blessing, the sunshine of God's love and the love of God's people, the nourishment of the Scripture and prayer, and the pruning of our lives by God, the great Caretaker. We must allow Him to cut away the dead branches and the wayward sprouts, all that is not Christlike.

Careful Cultivation

We must cultivate the ground if we want fruit to grow. Alexander Maclaren wrote, "These fruits, though they are the direct result of the indwelling Holy Spirit and will never be produced without His presence, are none the less truly dependent upon our manner of receiving that Spirit and on our own faithfulness and diligence in the use of His gifts. It is, alas! sadly too true, and a mother of tragically common experience that instead of 'trees of righteousness, the planting of the Lord,' heavy with ruddy clusters, there are but dwarfed and scrubby bushes which have scarcely life enough to keep up a little show of green leaves and 'bring no fruit to perfection.' Would that so-called Christian people would more earnestly and searchingly ask themselves why it is that, with such possibilities offered to them, their actual attainments should be so small."

The church provides the best conditions for the growth of the fruit of the Spirit. A Christian cannot bear the fruit of the Spirit without the fellowship of believers.

The fruit of the Spirit grows only as we relate to others who also are growing in the graces of Christ. One cannot grow as a Christian for ten to twenty years and not show evidence of the fruit of the Spirit.

Christ wants us to bear not only some fruit, but much fruit. John 15:1-18. He says we can do this if we abide in

14

Him: "Abide in me, and I in you. As the branch cannot bear fruit by itself, unless it abides in the vine, neither can you, unless you abide in me. I am the vine, you are the branches. He who abides in me, and I in him, he it is that bears much fruit, for apart from me you can do nothing."

Pleasant Variety

Archbishop Harrington Lees spoke of the fruit of the Spirit as a flower garden. In it grew the honeysuckle of love, the rose of joy, the lily of peace, the snowdrop of long-suffering, the mignonette of kindliness, the daisy of goodness, the forget-me-not of faithfulness, the violet of meekness, and the wallflower of self-control.

We see the beauty of the fruit of the Spirit against the garden of wickedness, which Paul catalogued as works of the flesh, naming fifteen examples. Galatians 5:19-21.

Someone has described the fruit of the Spirit as the eight elements of love. Joy is love's cheerfulness, peace love's confidence, long-suffering love's composure, kindness love's consideration, goodness love's character, faithfulness love's constancy, meekness love's comeliness, and self-control love's conquest.

Still another pictures joy as the gladness of love; peace, the quietness of love; long-suffering, the patience of love; gentleness, the graciousness of love; goodness, the character of love; faith, the confidence of love; meekness, the humility of love; and temperance, the self-control of love.

Others see in the fruit of the Spirit three groups of three. The first three show the Christian's relation to God; the second three, the Christian's relation to others; the third three, the Christian's relation to himself.

Some see the triad of experience: love, joy, peace; the triad of conduct: long-suffering, gentleness, goodness; and the triad of character: faith, meekness, and self-control.

Samuel Chadwick paraphrased Paul's passage on the fruit of the Spirit as follows: "The fruit of the Spirit is an affectionate, lovable disposition, a radiant spirit and cheerful temper, a tranquil mind and a quiet manner, a forbearing patience in provoking circumstances and with trying people, a sympathetic insight and tactful helpfulness, generous judgment, loyalty and reliableness under all circumstances, humility that forgets self in the joy of others, in all things self-mastery and self-control which is the final work of perfection."

I believe the fruit of the Spirit pictures for us the person of Christ and the pattern for the Christian life. The early followers of Christ were called "Christians" because they were like Christ. Our lives today should remind people of Jesus. Being like Jesus becomes the supreme miracle of being filled with the Holy Spirit.

2. The Threefold Ministry of the Spirit

In his fine book, *A Life Full of Surprises*, Lloyd John Ogilvie tells of attending a meeting on human relations before which a priest, a Methodist layman, and others talked about the inability of many Christians to do much about the urgent needs of the modern world.

One person said he had gone to church for years before he had an experience that showed him what Christianity really meant and made his spiritual life vital.

The priest responded, "My friend, you have received the Holy Spirit!" The Holy Spirit makes Christ real, the Bible relevant, and our expression radiant.

He Makes Christ Real

First the Holy Spirit testifies to the reality of Jesus Christ. "He will bear witness to me," Jesus said. Again He said, "He will glorify me." At every stage of leading us to Christ the Holy Spirit is active. He bears witness to Christ, opening our eyes to see the truth as it is in Jesus and the absolute sufficiency of Christ for our salvation. He convicts us of sin and leads us from our sins to trust in Jesus who came to save us out of our sins.

The Holy Spirit effects the new birth and gives us a

17

consciousness of Christ's presence in our lives. He gives us the inner assurance that we are God's dear children. The Holy Spirit leads us into the knowledge and understanding of the truth.

The Spirit unshackles Christ from the pages of ancient history and makes Him "God with us," our contemporary. The Holy Spirit is the available, immediately accessible Jesus. The Spirit shows us Christ. Walter Hylton wrote near the close of the thirteenth century, "The Holy Ghost openeth the eye of the soul and showeth to the soul the sight of Jesus wonderfully, and the knowledge of Him as well as the soul can suffer it little by little."

And J. Oswald Sanders says in his book, *The Holy Spirit of Promise,* "The ministry of the Spirit is Christo-centric. Just as the work of the telescope is to reveal, not itself, but the glories which it brings within the range of vision, so the congenial ministry of the Holy Spirit is to stand behind the scenes and reveal Christ to those who are united to Him by faith."

A profound humility of the Trinity precludes any exaltation of the Holy Spirit over Jesus Christ. Jesus said the "Spirit of truth . . . will bear witness to me" (John 15:26). The Son magnifies the Father (John 17:4) while the Father honors the Son (Philippians 2:9-11) and the Holy Spirit reveals and glorifies Him (John 16:14, 15).

So also the gifts of the Spirit bring about, not the fullness of the Spirit, but the "fulness of Christ" (Ephesians 4:11-13) in the believer. The Apostle Paul's admonition to "be filled with the Spirit" is an imperative plea for the appropriation of the Spirit's presence, not a reference to His gifts.

Exaltation of the gifts and manifestations of the Holy Spirit quenches His power. Christ and His redeeming work, not the Holy Spirit and His giving of gifts, are to be lifted up. The Giver, not the gifts, must be uppermost.

He Transforms Us

A second function of the Holy Spirit is to transform us from one glory to another into the likeness of Christ — to help us grow in Christlike character. His purpose is to reproduce the character of Christ in each one of us. The Spirit is not satisfied until Christ is formed in us. Paul said that God's purpose for him, even before he was born, was for Christ to be revealed in him. The same is true of each Christian.

So the Holy Spirit's love for Christ is such that He shows us Christ and seeks to lead us in the way of Christ until "Christ be formed" in us (Galatians 4:19). But the Holy Spirit will not operate in unsurrendered territory. Only as we yield to His leading and surrender to His power will He begin His work so that the Christ-life will become more and more evident.

Perhaps the Christian should hang a sign on himself which says, "God at work here." The Holy Spirit, in His transforming work, keeps rebuilding and renewing rather than accomplishing a once-for-all remodeling job. "We . . . are being changed" (2 Corinthians 3:18) by the Spirit of God. And the complete meaning of this continues far beyond conversion even until after death when we shall see Him and be like Him in a fullness never known here. But even now Christ is personally present in our being by His indwelling Spirit (Ephesians 2:22; 3:17) so that He sanctifies every nook and cranny of our being.

"One can have convictions that are Christlike, but if his desires or his actions are not Christlike, he is not worthy to be called a Christian," says Paul Quillian, reminding us that we are no more Christian than our lives are Christlike. And the work of the Holy Spirit is to make us Christlike.

Beatrice Cleland's poem, "Indwelt," describes the naturalness of this experience.

19

Not merely by the words you say,
Not only in your deed confessed,
But in the most unconscious way
   Is Christ expressed.

Is it a beautiful smile?
A holy light upon your brow?
Oh, no — I felt His presence while
   You laughed just now.

For me 'twas not the truth you taught,
To you so clear, to me still dim,
But when you came to me you brought
   A sense of Him.

And from your eyes He beckons me,
And from your heart His love is shed,
Till I lose sight of you and see
   The Christ instead.

He Equips Us

A third function of the Holy Spirit is to equip us for Christ's service in the world. He gives us the needed gifts to make His mission complete. We see our mission in the light of Christ's mission, for Jesus said, "As my Father hath sent me, even so send I you" (John 20:21, KJV). The Holy Spirit gives us gifts necessary for the task and empowers us for the task.

In 1 Corinthians 12:4-6 Paul points out that there are different gifts, different administrations or services, and different ways of working. He says that each person receives some gift of the Spirit for the good of the brotherhood and for the witness in the world. To one He gives wisdom, to another knowledge, to another faith, to another healing, to another the working of miracles, to another prophecy, to another discerning of spirits, to another tongues, and to another the interpretation of tongues.

Peter underscores the same truth when he says, "As every man hath received the gift, even so minister the same one to another, as good stewards of the manifold grace of God" (1 Pet. 4:10, KJV).

3. The Relationship of Gifts and Fruit

Centuries ago a king called to his side his most trusted herald. He handed him a letter and commanded him to read it throughout the entire empire. The king longed to improve the level of living for his people and to promote great happiness in the homes of the land.

In the letter the king offered special benefits to each subject. The one stipulation said that to collect the benefits each person needed to appear at the nearest village square on the day the king's representative came to that village. All the benefits the king promised would be received only through a personal appearance before the king's representative.

So also, it can be said, that all the benefits and blessings God has for us to experience come through His Holy Spirit. All God has for us is made a reality through the Holy Spirit. The indwelling Spirit enables and equips us to live Christ's own life through us. By His graces and His gifts we are prepared to fulfill His purpose for us.

John Wesley wrote, "Every good gift is from God, and is given to men by the Holy Ghost. By nature there is in us no good thing. And there can be none: but so far as it is wrought in us by that good Spirit."

This leads to several observations.

Fruit Is the Best Evidence of the Holy Spirit

Possession of any spiritual gift is never the only or even the primary evidence that a person has received the gift of the Holy Spirit. In the New Testament the primary evidence of the Holy Spirit is not in some charismatic, spectacular, or ecstatic gift or expression. The evidence of the Holy Spirit is moral and ethical. It is in whether the life and spirit is Christlike. That is why the Apostle Paul says, "Anyone who does not have the Spirit of Christ does not belong to him" (Romans 8:9).

Jesus and Paul warn against thinking that working great miracles or displaying gifts of healing or speaking in tongues are sure signs of the Holy Spirit at work. Jesus, in Matthew 24:24, tells us that in the last times false christs shall come showing great signs and wonders. Because of these many shall be deceived and depart from the truth. We are told not to follow such because they do not have the Christ-Spirit.

All the gifts, in some sense and to a remarkable degree, can be duplicated. But the fruit of the Spirit cannot be copied or counterfeited. They, at times, may seem similar to the characteristics exemplified by some who do not know Christ, but when the test comes the true gifts stand — in persecution, war, or death itself.

The darkest hours of history were those when men sought to demonstrate Christianity by the spectacular rather than living the Christlike life — be it in crusades or by building great cathedrals, in fighting holy wars or establishing holy places, in working mighty miracles or crowning powerful kings.

People have sought to show loyalty and love for Christ in every way imaginable as a substitute for following Christ and letting the Holy Spirit live through them the life of Christ Himself. Desiderius Erasmus wrote in 1503, "Nor shall I believe that you are in the Spirit except I behold in

23

you the fruits of the Spirit."

To discern the fruit of the Spirit in its true dimension is to see that the production of fruit is no less a miraculous work of the Spirit than is the performance of some gift of the Spirit. And though the fruit may seem less spectacular than the gifts it is just as supernatural and striking a witness of what God, through His Spirit, can do in the life of one led by Him.

If Christianity is to be radiant and relevant, equal stress must be put on the fruit and gifts of the Spirit. For unless the fruit of love, joy, peace, and the other fruit characterize our lives Christianity can claim very little that is unique from any other faith. And unless the gifts of the Spirit are present in our lives we lack the power which makes Christianity different from any other religion.

Basically the inner need of the church is twofold. It needs the fruit of the Spirit to live effectively for Christ and the gifts of the Spirit to serve effectively for Him. By the fruit of the Spirit the life of Christ is manifest and by the gifts of the Spirit the ministry of Christ is continued. So the purpose of the Spirit is to produce people who portray the divine image and have the power for divine work.

A second observation is that the Holy Spirit is sovereign to share His gifts as He wills, to whom He wills, and when He wills. 1 Corinthians 12:11. To demand any one gift is to usurp the sovereignty of the Spirit. To make any one gift a test of whether one has the Spirit is contrary to the Scripture.

Receiving any gift is a serious responsibility as well as a precious privilege since it affords first of all an opportunity for self-giving in sacrificial service to others. Every gift of the Spirit is for the good of the total church and not a personal privilege or a hoarded spiritual treasure. "To each is given the manifestation of the Spirit for the common good" (1 Corinthians 12:7).

Fruit Keeps Gifts from Being Disruptive

When the Spirit's ministry in the area of gifts is perverted by being kept separate from the fruit of the Spirit, the work of Christ is hindered and gifts often become disruptive in the life of the church.

Possessing and exercising spiritual gifts does not necessarily make us more gracious and easy to live with. In fact, without the fruit of the Spirit, a gift may cause us to be more difficult to live with. It is possible to have a gift of the Spirit yet retain the same old cantankerous attitudes in relation to others. Some who have the gift of prophecy and are the greatest preachers are hard to live with. Some who exercise the gift of tongues are touchy and proud. So also with any other gift of the Spirit.

What is missing? The fruit of the Spirit! Growing in the fruit of the Spirit makes one a loving person. He is patient, helpful, and constructive; he is not possessive or self-assertive; he has good manners and does not take advantage of others. He is not touchy and does not keep a list of the failings of others. 1 Corinthians 13:4-6.

Spiritual maturity then is measured, not so much by the presence of spiritual gifts, as by the presence of a Christlike spirit. The relevant question in relation to the reality of the Holy Spirit's work within one is not, "do I possess a special spiritual gift? Rather the question is whether in daily life the fruit of the Spirit — love, joy, peace, long-suffering, kindness, goodness, faithfulness, meekness, and self-control — are manifest in relation to people who rub me the wrong way. The "fruit test" is the valid test of spiritual experience. Jesus says, "You will know them by their fruit."

Fruit Is Demonstrated in Relation to Others

In contrast to the works of the flesh in Galatians 5 and

in contrast to the gifts of the Spirit in 1 Corinthians 12 and 14, the fruit of the Spirit is singular. Why? While the works of the flesh are conflicting and confusing the fruit of the Spirit shows great unity. Each grace contributes to the complete witness and beauty of the whole.

Fruit is singular also because each Christian demonstrates, to some degree, all the graces.

Gifts of the Spirit are plural because the Spirit does not give all the gifts to one person. In 1 Corinthians 12:4-6 Paul points out there are different gifts and the Spirit gives each person a gift "individually as he [the Spirit] wills."

Now notice that the fruit of the Spirit is demonstrated and put to the test in relation to other people. The fruit cannot be practiced between us and God. Real religion is Christlike living in relationship to others.

4. Walking in the Spirit

Howard Hageman's Irish grandmother said concerning the minister of her church, "I believe everything he says, but he says it in a way that makes me wish I didn't believe it."

The Holy Spirit deals with our dispositions as well as our dispensations, with our attitudes as well as our actions, with our behavior as well as our beliefs.

The Holy Spirit's work is to produce the life of Christ in us. We can no more live the life of Christ without the Holy Spirit's enabling power than we can become God's children without His energizing purpose.

Andrew Murray concludes a discussion on Galatians 3:3 with the comment, "Beloved believers, having begun in the Spirit, continue, go on, persevere in the Spirit. Beware of, for a single moment, continuing or perfecting the work of the Spirit in the flesh. Let 'no confidence in the flesh' be your battle cry, let a deep distrust of the flesh, and fear of grieving the Spirit by walking after the flesh, keep you very low and humble before God. Pray God for the Spirit of revelation, that you may see how Jesus is all, and does all, and how by the Holy Spirit a divine life indeed takes place in your life, and Jesus is enthroned as the Keeper and Guardian and life of your soul."

The Apostle Paul's discussion on the works of the flesh and the fruit of the Spirit begins and ends with "Walk in the Spirit." He shows what the walk in the Spirit excludes — the works of the flesh. He shows what the walk in the Spirit includes — the fruit of the Spirit. The Galatian Christians forgot the fact that the Christ-life is lived only by yielding to the Spirit. We also often forget it. We try to live the Christ-life in our own strength. We seek to make ourselves mature spiritually in our own strength. No wonder we fail. No wonder we produce little more than the fruit of the flesh rather than the fruit of the Spirit.

To become a Christian one must accept Christ in faith. To live the Christian life means to walk by faith step by step. In faith we accept God's forgiveness. In faith we receive God's forgiveness. In faith we know the glorious hope of the future is certain.

The Holy Spirit who brought us to faith also gives us victory in our battle against evil. The Spirit purifies us from sin by applying the Word of God to our lives. The Holy Spirit reveals the righteousness of Christ and the forgiveness of sin. The difference between the convicting of the Holy Spirit and the condemnation of the devil is that when the Holy Spirit reveals our sin and unworthiness He always shows us Christ's cleansing blood and Christ's accomplishment on our behalf. Satan shows us only discouragement, defeat, and death. Instead of removing guilt, Satan adds to our guilt.

A New Kind of Living

To walk in the Spirit means that in going about our daily duties, we seek to remain under the Spirit's control. We obey His leading. To walk in the Spirit means to open our lives to God's will for us each moment and in each decision. The only way He can lead is if we repent and turn from all which the Holy Spirit shows us is unchristlike and "put on" all which the Holy Spirit shows us we need.

To walk in the Spirit is to take the next step the Holy Spirit shows us. We cannot take more than one step at a time physically. So also spiritually. The Spirit leads us one step at a time in our walk with God. When He reveals that which is unchristlike in our lives we say, "By God's grace and help I will repent and put it off." When He shows us a Christlike quality absent from our lives we say, "By God's grace and help we shall take whatever He desires and add it to our lives."

This means a willingness to clear up any dishonesty, to repair any broken relationship, and to die to any evil habit the Holy Spirit shows us. It means also doing those Christlike things which we have left undone, freely forgiving those who have wronged us, and speaking the word the Spirit prompts us to say. It means thinking Christlike thoughts, to "take every thought captive to obey Christ."

This is really a new kind of living, based not in our own strength but in the power of the Spirit. For as Paul says in Timothy, God gives all we need to know to do His will if we have the desire to do it.

Henry Drummond wrote, "In the New Testament alone the Spirit is referred to nearly three hundred times. And the one word with which He is constantly associated is power." Samuel Shoemaker observed, "Something comes into our own energies and capacities and expands them. We are laid hold of by Something greater than ourselves. We can face things, create things, accept things that in our own strength would have been impossible."

Think what a difference it would make in the average home if the fruit of the Spirit were really in evidence. Think of the experience in the average church if the fruit of the Spirit, love, joy, peace, patience, and all the rest were really present. Think what would happen in the country, in the marketplace, at the workbench, and the schoolroom.

Holy Spirit Leadership

The New Testament contains the recurring account of the wonderful leadership of the Holy Spirit in the lives of people. They did not manipulate or use the Holy Spirit. Instead He owned and empowered them. This is always true of the Holy Spirit's leadership in our lives. He dare not be dictated to. Instead we surrender ourselves, our lives, to His wonderful control. Then He possesses, directs, and transforms us.

What a wonderful experience to be under His control, not always certain where the next step may lead, yet with confidence and trust we allow Him to control, assured that He leads unerringly through every unknown experience.

Christ wants, through His Holy Spirit, to do far greater things in our lives than we ever dreamed. He is capable of doing more than we can ask or think through the power working in us. He longs to pour out His Spirit on us, to produce His own life in us. In another sense we alone allow Him to do His work. We may hold back His work through our refusals. Only as we surrender to the Holy Spirit and let go of ourselves will we experience the radiant, joyous, and real living we so much need and which Christ desires to give us.

Gordon Glegg in his book, A Scientist and His Faith, tells of the opening of an exhibition in England by the Queen. When all was in readiness, the Queen declared the exhibition open and made a tour of the various presentations. She found one exhibitor slouched in his chair, sound asleep. Glegg writes: "There was a moment of consternation while everyone watched to see what the Queen would do. She paused a moment, and then, with a smile, passed on to the next exhibit, for Royalty does not force itself on anyone."

How like the Holy Spirit! Tender and sensitive, He enters where invited and does not intrude uninvited. He awaits our welcome. Only as we yield to the Holy Spirit is fruit produced. The Holy Spirit wants to make our lives Christlike but we must respond. He will not do His good and gracious work against our will.

5. Agape — Love's

William Barclay of Scotland says
lass the Gaulic language has twenty
her so. The English language limits us
love. Today the word "love" means
serves too many purposes. It can refer
one taking her fourth husband or it ca
pens when a father gives his life for his

In order to understand the word "
of the Spirit found in Galatians 5:22, 23
er. Four Greek words describe as many
are: *eros* (sensual love), *storge* (don
(friendship love), and *agape* (a good-will-

Four Kinds of Love

Eros refers to love between man an
ual or physical love based on passion.
reject sexual or physical love. It places it
points out its goodness in the sanctity of
we associate *eros* with lust rather than with

Philia describes the highest kind of
warm, close relationship of body, mind, a
of the highest level of friendship. Since it
level, this love can fade as the friendship
or its beauty begins to fade. In friendship t
in contrast to the all-encircling character of (

torge is the family love, the love of the parent for the
and the child's love for the parent. We love those of
wn family. There is a closeness of kinship. As brothers
isters we love each other because of our family ties.

The Christians took *agape,* a word both small and weak
assical Greek, and made it strong. They needed a word
escribe the incredible concern of God for undeserving
as portrayed in Romans 5:8. "God shows his love for us
at while we were yet sinners Christ died for us."

William Barclay says, "*Agape* is the spirit in the heart
will never seek anything but the highest good of its
wmen." It is love, not mere emotion. Emotion, at times,
be totally absent. *Agape* is the love that gives, sacrifices,
has compassion. The will controls this love. *Agape* love
to love not only when people deserve love but when
do not deserve it. *Agape* love wills to build good re-
nships and helps regardless of the cost.

Dependent on Emotion

This fruit of love becomes more than mere emotion.
ther does not depend on feeling or emotion to do her dut
n her baby cries at night. Even though she is tired, lov
here. So she gets out of bed, feeds her little one, an
ks him to sleep. Really, when we say we cannot lov
ther we are saying that we no longer want to love tha
son.

Because Christian love is a matter of the will, God ca
us the command, "Love one another." We follow th
mand not because of sentiment or feeling but becaus
will to do so. Christian love becomes the response of
lded will to the clear command of God who "is love."

Paul Ramsey wrote, "Christian love . . . has nothing
with feelings, emotions, taste, preference, temperamen
any of the qualities in other people which arouse feelin

34

Love Fruit

of revulsion or attraction, negative or positive preferences. Christian love depends on the direction of the will . . . not on stirring emotion."

Aarlie J. Hull in an article, "Love Is Deed," describes her struggle to love. She was continually frustrated because she thought a Christian must always feel genuine love for everyone everywhere. She relied too heavily on human emotion. She likened love to a warm feeling. Then she came to see that simply doing what Christ's love dictated changed her whole life. She says, "The realization that Christian love is not always a warm feeling but is more often the performance of a deed has simply revolutionized my Christian life. I cannot govern my emotion but I can govern my action and that is exciting. . . . Oh, I welcome warm feelings whenever they happen along (sometimes coming when I least expect them), but I don't need them to experience Christian love because that love has taken on a new dimension . . . love is in deed." John 3:18).

C. H. Dodd defines love as "energetic and beneficent good will which stops at nothing to secure the good of the beloved subject. It is not primarily an emotion or an affection; it is primarily an active determination of the will."

Christian love, however, is not simply a product of the human heart when one wills it. Rather it is a divine gift made real to us and through us to others by the Holy Spirit (Romans 5:5; Galatians 5:22).

Love Is What One Does

Love is more what you do than what you feel. The Apostle Paul in 1 Corinthians 13 tells what love does. A husband and wife in the wedding vows promise, not how they will feel together the next year, but what they will do for each other. When one does a deed of love the feeling of love follows, not the other way around. As we find happiness when we share it, so love becomes real when we express it in something we do.

A lady wrote: "I have one besetting sin. There is a certain person who is a thorn in my flesh, and I just cannot love that person. Is this love of God which I have for another person a feeling that I can turn on and off like an electric light?"

The answer is no! Love showers good things on others even as God showered His love upon us while we were His enemies. Christ came to die for us when we did not love Him. *Agape* love is Christ living in us through His Spirit and letting Him live and reach out through us.

Christian love differs from mere human love. It includes the entire person — the heart, mind, feelings, and will. We do not fall into it but we choose to exercise it even toward the unlovely. It triumphs over self. We experience it only through the power of God through the Holy Spirit. The unregenerate cannot experience the love of which the Bible speaks. Only the Spirit-filled Christian can exemplify true Christian love.

"The differentia of the Christian," said C. Anderson Scott years ago, "is that, in the Christian sense, he loves." He simply says in another way what Jesus said centuries ago: "By this all men will know that you are my disciples, if you have love for one another" (John 13:35).

6. Christ — Love's Example

Five-year-old Mary underwent a serious operation. She had lost considerable blood and needed a transfusion. After checking the rest of Mary's family the test showed that the blood of her brother matched hers.

"Will you give your sister some of your blood, Jimmy?" asked the doctor.

Jimmy set his teeth and said, "Yes sir, if she needs it."

At once they prepared Jimmy for the transfusion. In taking the blood the doctor noticed Jimmy getting pale. Yet there was no apparent reason.

"Are you feeling ill, Jimmy?" asked the doctor.

"No sir!" said Jimmy, "but I'm just wondering when I will die."

"Die!" gasped the doctor. "Do you think people die when they give blood to someone else?"

"Yes sir!" replied Jimmy.

"And you were going to give your life for Mary?"

"Yes sir!" replied the boy simply.

The Scripture says, "Greater love has no man than this, that a man lay down his life for his friends" (John 15:13). "In this is love, not that we loved God but that he loved us and sent his Son to be the expiation for our sins" (1 John 4:10).

To show the love of God the Scripture takes us back to Bethlehem and the cross of Calvary. In the twin wonders of the incarnation and the crucifixion we see God's love. In giving His only Son, God demonstrated His love to us. The death of Jesus Christ on the cross and the shedding of His blood for our sins have become the center of the Christian message. "By this we know love, that he laid down his life for us." No wonder the poet wrote: "Oh! the love that drew salvation's plan, oh! the grace that brought it down to man, oh! the mighty gulf that God did span at Calvary."

But the Scripture not only says that God is the fountainhead of love but also that Jesus Christ is the manifestation of perfect love. The love of Christ is the pattern for the Christian life. We are to walk in love as Christ loved us (Ephesians 5:2). Love so characterized His life that He could say, "By this all men will know that you are my disciples, if you have love for one another."

Selflessness, Service, and Sacrifice

What is Christ's example? Read Philippians, chapter two. He is the example of selflessness. He left glory and came to earth to save us. Though He was God He became man. Christ is the example of service. Though He was Lord of all He became the Servant of all.

A missionary doctor friend told me how he sometimes walks the sands of Ethiopia, after a busy day at the clinic and hospital, to relax, rest, and be recreated. He tries to imagine how Christ felt as He walked the sands of Galilee, after all those busy days when the crowds pushed on Him for help and healing all day long. Yet Christ was never too busy to stoop and help another.

Christ's love did not stop with selflessness and service. His love was the love of sacrifice. Though it meant death in order to save us He willingly laid down His life for us. We must be willing to die for the people we seek to save. Christian love does not shy away from sacrifice or

38

suffering to help another.

Jesus could have stopped at any place along His earthly life and said, "If that is the way people are going to treat me, I'm through. I don't need to suffer such things. I will not take their spit in my face, their false accusations, their mad treatment, their denials. I'll not die to save them. They are unappreciative. They don't value my sacrifice. Why should I suffer?" Jesus could have said all this a thousand times over.

But He didn't. He continued to forget Himself for others, to stoop to serve, and finally one day the Lord of glory climbed a cruel cross on Calvary. He spread His arms on the cross, opening Himself up to all man's meanness and madness and said, "If dying is necessary to save man from his downward way, if the cross is the only way to demonstrate my love, I'm willing to die." And in dying He prayed, "Father, forgive them; for they know not what they do."

As He Is, So Are We

The Scripture says in 1 John 4:17, "As he is so are we in this world." Alexander Maclaren wrote, "Large truths may be spoken in little words." The Christian should become the living likeness of his Lord. "As he is, so are we."

This statement says what we are rather than what we believe. It describes our nature rather than our knowledge. The likeness to Christ, according to the context, is in love. Love reveals us as believers in Christ, as His representatives, disciples, and followers. This love moves toward others in the spirit of self-giving and self-sacrifice. Fear shrinks from others in the spirit of self-preservation.

We show our likeness to Christ first by our love for God. We are like Christ in being joined to God, in holding fellowship with God, in joyful submission and obedience to God, in walking as Christ walked, in being filled by Christ's Spirit, and in being concerned about that which concerns Him.

We show our likeness to Christ also in our love for others. His compassion and concern for others become ours. Like Christ we willingly suffer and sacrifice for others and desire to live for them rather than for ourselves.

Christ entrusted His reputation and honor to us, His disciples. As we portray Christ, our lives reveal Him to unbelievers.

Christ sent His Holy Spirit to us so that the true life of Christ might be manifest in our bodies. We grow into His likeness as we give ourselves to the Holy Spirit's control. He molds us into His image and conforms us to His likeness by His Spirit. Christ reproduces Himself in our lives by His Spirit. "Christ in you, the hope of glory." Christ manifests Himself in our mortal bodies.

What Is Christ's Spirit?

A friend and I were traveling together. We talked about the new interest in the ministry of the Holy Spirit. He talked of the new surging of the Spirit's work at all levels and in all places. Suddenly my friend stopped me and said, "But many times I wonder what kind of Spirit we are asking for when we ask for the Holy Spirit. The Scripture says, 'If any man have not the Spirit of Christ, he is none of his.' What kind of Spirit is the Spirit of Jesus? I'm not sure," he said, "that people are asking for Christ's Spirit."

What is the Spirit of Christ? The Holy Spirit and the Spirit of Jesus are the same. What kind of Spirit did Jesus have? We must go to the Gospel for our portrait of Christ.

Certain things become apparent immediately. We read in Luke 4:18, "The Spirit of the Lord is upon me, because he has anointed me to preach good news to the poor. He has sent me to proclaim release to the captives and recovering of sight to the blind, to set at liberty those who are oppressed, to proclaim the acceptable year of the Lord."

The Spirit of Jesus identified with the helpless, hopeless, and homeless; the poor, the prisoner, the oppressed, and the outcast. Is that the Spirit we are praying for? We dare not spiritualize Luke 4:18. Christ's mission was first to the poor and needy.

In Luke 7 when John the Baptist was in prison for his preaching he sent word to Christ asking if He was the Messiah or should he expect someone else. John was not sure in the despondency of the prison. Jesus did not answer in the way expected. The disciples returned and told John that He was doing the things spoken of in Luke 4:18. When the blind see, the lame walk, the prisoners are ministered to, and the poor have the gospel preached to them, there the Spirit of the Lord is.

Are we asking for that kind of Spirit? Unless we are concerned about the kind of person Christ was concerned about and the kind of person He was, we do not have the Spirit of Christ. In every revival we thus find an accompanying intense concern for the oppressed, the prisoner, and the poor.

Go through the Gospels and notice Christ's Spirit is one of love and compassion for persons in need. His Spirit says, "Return good for evil"; "Pray for them who persecute you"; "Bless those who speak evil of you"; and "Love your enemy," rather than take up the sword against him.

Christ's Spirit is one of obedience, the denial of our will for the Father's will. When we have Christ's Spirit, the Holy Spirit, our chief joy is to do God's will. To learn to know the Holy Spirit and what He will do in our lives we must go to the New Testament and see what He did in the life of Jesus and in the lives of the early disciples.

41

7. God — Love's Source

A college student writes about the Holy Spirit infilling his life: "One of the first things to change was my prayer life. It became a whole new thing to me. I began praising and thanking God more and more. My prayer life was changed from one of meager repetition to one of praise and more praise, petition and confession. . . .

"Many other things changed in my life. I began to have a strong desire to read and study Scripture. And when I did read the Bible, it came alive and spoke to me. I was also able to witness with a power that I hadn't known before. I began to see that what I told people about Jesus Christ was bearing fruit. The worship service in my own church took on new meaning. My whole attitude toward the church changed from one of bitterness to one of loving concern. But there was one thing that really made the difference.

"That difference was love. For the first time in my life I began to realize just what Christ's love was like. And because of that understanding a great burden was lifted from me. A burden of guilt and sin that I had been struggling with for a long time was lifted from my shoulders.

"By the power of the Holy Spirit I was able to see and win the victory of the cross. I finally knew what it meant to be a free person. I was and am free of the burden of guilt and sin that had been a part of my life. My life was transformed from a striving to follow the Ten Commandments to a living in the love of Jesus Christ, which became possible through the indwelling of the Holy Spirit. I began to experience the fruit of the Spirit more and more in my life — love, joy, peace.

"I have a lot to thank and praise God for. I really thank Him for the purpose in life I have because of His great love for me. 'For I am convinced that nothing can ever separate us from his love. Death can't and life can't. The angels won't, and all the powers of hell itself cannot keep God's love away. Our fears for today, our worries about tomorrow, or where we are — high above the sky, or in the deepest ocean — nothing will ever be able to separate us from the love of God demonstrated by our Lord Jesus Christ' (Romans 8:38, 39, *Living Bible*)."

Love Is of God

In 1 John the apostle says, "Love is of God." What a beautiful expression of the source of love. In verse 8 he writes, "God is love." He does not describe what produces love. The closer we come to the heart of God, the more we know God's love.

God's love for us is where our love begins. "We love, because he first loved us" (1 John 4:19). Psychologists tell us that babies are born not knowing how to love, but with a capacity to receive and experience love. In other words they learn to love by feeling and seeing how their parents love them and each other. This human example though imperfect shows how God's love works.

Long before the child knows of love, even before birth itself, the mother loves the child. Long before the child can respond to love, the mother pours out her love on the child without thought of the child's response. During the days of total dependence when the child demands constant attention, yet doesn't so much as return a smile, the mother's love remains strong.

43

Finally the child matures and begins to respond. He smiles, then takes the mother's hand, does what she says, and gives tokens of his love. The child's love responds to the mother's love. The child loves the mother because she first loved him.

How descriptive of our spiritual life! God loved us long before we were aware of it. Even from the foundation of the world He loved us. When helpless, homeless, or unwilling to respond to His love, He loved us. His love is everlasting.

Through the message of the gospel and through the love of God's people we now see God's love. As we see that love in Christ, our hearts and minds respond. Today "We love, because he first loved us." In the words of the well-known hymn, we say:

Saviour, teach me day by day
Love's sweet lesson to obey;
Sweeter lesson cannot be:
Loving Him who first loved me.

Thus may I rejoice to show
That I feel the love I owe;
Singing till Thy face I see,
Of His love who first loved me.

By the quality of our love we reveal God's love to others. 1 John 4:20. Our love for others depends on our love for God. We apply Christian love by doing for others what God does for us. We learn to love by receiving God's love and then by practicing it. As God takes us and loves us so we ought to accept and love others. A person cannot feel loved and accepted by God until he has experienced acceptance and love by one of God's children.

Do you remember the song from the musical, *Oliver*

which asks, "Where is love? Does it fall from the sky above?" The answer is, "No!" It grows out of relationship with God. But one cannot maintain an intimate, vital relationship with God, the source of love, and not be progressively filled with love for others.

How Is Love Achieved?

Everything begins with the love of God, for He is the God of love. This love is a transforming love. When poured into human hearts, it produces the great qualities of the Christian life and character. Romans 5:3-5. Endless stories tell of the change in people's lives when they experience the happiness and glory of God's love. Love makes us alive and responsive to God's Holy Spirit in us.

George Sweete writes, "A great many people make the mistake of struggling to get the fruit of the Spirit without ever opening themselves up to the Spirit Himself. This kind of effort is in vain. The secret of the fullness of love is the fullness of the Spirit of God. Paul the apostle tells us plainly, 'The love of God is shed abroad in our hearts by the Holy Ghost which is given unto us' (Romans 5:5, KJV). We cannot just decide to start loving. That is why the problem of love cannot be solved by slogans, placards, and songs alone. We all vote for love, but without the Holy Spirit within and giving ourselves to the Spirit's control we cannot achieve love."

The love of which God is the source is not normal or natural. Human nature does not sacrifice and suffer for others. Only through the Spirit of God do love and sacrifice spring spontaneously to life.

"Love is of God." God gave us the capacity to receive His love. To be God's children means that His Spirit lives within us to make us channels of God's love.

Love Is the Spring of Action

Paul in 2 Corinthians 5:14, 15 says that Christ's love becomes the spring of our actions. It compels us to live differently in that we no longer live for ourselves but for Him who loved us and gave Himself for us. It compels us to judge differently in that we no longer judge according to the flesh. We no longer judge people by their possessions, position, popularity, race, religion, riches, color, creed, or country. Now we think first not about human characteristics but whether or not the person knows Jesus Christ, for we know that if anyone is in Christ he is a new creation. The old life has passed away and an entire new life has begun. We know that if a person does not know Jesus Christ he still lives in darkness and does not know the true way of life. The love of Christ also compels us to serve as Christians. We are ambassadors for Christ, God draws others through us to Him. When we really experience the new life in Christ, we know we have a new work for God, to represent Him to others.

8. Redemption — Love's Purpose

O. W. S. McCall in his book, *The Hand of God,* pictures himself standing by the cross asking, "How much should a man give?" Christ does not answer but in the awful stillness he demonstrates His love when His head sinks to His breast and He dies. "There was no more to give." Redemptive love never stops giving. We see it clearly on the cross.

Reuel Howe illustrates redemptive love in the story of a mother and her eight-year-old daughter. The girl did something which caused her to feel alienated from her mother. Although her mother tried her best to help, the daughter finally ran out of the room in anger and went upstairs. Seeing her mother's new dress laid out for a party that evening, she found scissors and vented her hostility by ruining her mother's new dress, seeking to injure her mother.

Later the mother came upstairs, saw the dress, threw herself on the bed, and wept. Soon the small daughter came into the room and whispered, "Mother." But there was no reply.

"Mother, Mother," she repeated. Still no reply.

"Mother, Mother, please," she continued.

Finally the mother responded, "Please what?"

"Please take me back, please take me back," pleaded the girl.

That is what love does; it takes people back. "Love never ends." It reaches out until redemption is realized.

Redemptive Love Is Costly

Fear of death is so deep within us that we need a greater power to overcome it. That power is love. Love casts out fear of every kind — fear of failure, fear of reputation, fear of persons, yes, fear of death itself.

Love causes a mother to rescue her child though it means her death. Love drives a father to rescue his drowning son though it may mean his own life. Whenever a person dies for another we speak of a love stronger than life or death. We know that only love can make such demands for the good of others.

Tom Skinner, black evangelist, gave a passioned message at the United States Congress on Evangelism. He pleaded with his white Christian brothers and sisters to demonstrate their love for the blacks. "I am willing," he said, "to die for you. Are you willing to die for me?"

Skinner, a former gang leader of The Harlem Lords, pleaded for Christians to put into practice a love which will forget self so that regardless of criticism or alienation or even death which might follow they would do what love dictates in standing for God's truth and justice in today's world.

Today demands love, costly Christian love which reaches out in redemption no matter if it may mean life itself.

In the fourth century, an Eastern monk by the name of Telemachus decided to leave the world of men and live alone in the deserts and mountains. By isolation, prayer, meditation, and fasting he strove to save and satisfy his soul.

After a time he knew something was missing. One night on his knees an insight came to him. He saw that the life of solitude was selfish and not selfless. Telemachus decided if he was going to serve God he must serve men. Leaving his desert haunts, he returned to Rome, the capital of the world. To his surprise Christianity had become the official religion. Christians no longer hid in tombs to worship.

Everything seemed changed except for one thing. One awful vestige of pagan Rome remained — the arena. True, Christians were no longer thrown to lions for entertainment, but captives of war were forced to fight and kill each other.

Telemachus followed the swarming crowds to the spectacle. People cried for blood as man fought against man. Suddenly the monk jumped over the wall into the arena and rushed between the gladiators. Surprised, they stopped fighting.

But the crowd cried, "Let the games go on."

He was pushed aside but again he ran back between the two men. Now rocks and curses thundered from the angered spectators. Still he tried to stop the senseless slaughter. Then the commander's voice barked an order, a gladiator's sword rose, flashed in the sunlight, and struck the old man dead.

Suddenly the crowd quieted, shocked that a holy man was killed. The game ended in silence and the audience melted away. Never again did the gladiators fight in the arena. The old man, by dying, ended the brutal games. His death was more valuable to mankind than his life.

Love Finds a Way

Love that redeems continues to reach out. It holds on when every human emotion gives up and says, "All is hopeless." Sympathy and humanitarian desires may carry one a short way. But only love, given by God, can go the second mile.

An old Christian woman, in speaking of a teenage girl who was in serious trouble, said, "We will have to love her out of it." This is the reaction of Christian love. We never drive people to Christ. People are loved into His kingdom.

Leonard Griffith recalls an old legend of a wealthy merchant who heard of Paul as he traveled about the Mediterranean world. Finally the man's business took him to Rome, and he sought out the apostle in prison.

The merchant got in touch with Timothy, who arranged an interview. When the man stepped into the room where the apostle was, he was surprised to find him looking old and physically frail. But about him was a strength, serenity, and magnetism that made itself felt.

They talked for a while, and finally the merchant left. Outside the cell, he turned to Timothy, "What is the secret of this man's power? I have never seen anything like it before."

"Did you not guess?" replied Timothy. "Paul is in love."

The merchant looked puzzled. "In love?" he asked.

"Yes," said Timothy. "Paul is in love with Jesus Christ."

The businessman looked even more bewildered. "Is that all?" he asked.

Timothy smiled and replied, "That is everything."

9. Transformation — Love's Power

In his autobiography, *Missionary to the New Hebrides,*
John G. Paton tells how Christians through love are transformed and become more than conquerors.

Paton tells of a chief who was full of the love of Christ
and who wished to share the gospel with others. He sent
word to an inland chief that he and four other men were
coming to bring them the gospel. The chief received an un-
friendly reply, threatening death when he approached the
village. But the Christian islander said, "We come to you
without weapons of war! We come only to tell you about
Jesus. We believe that He will protect us today."

As they passed on into the village, the chief ordered a
"shower of spears" thrown at the Christians. They picked
them up and returned them kindly. The islanders were so
surprised at these Christians who came without weapons
and even refused to throw the spears back, that they
stopped fighting.

When the five men neared the village public grounds
the Christian chief called out: "Jehovah thus protects us.
Once we would have thrown your spears back at you and
killed you. He has changed our dark hearts. He asks you
now to lay down all these other weapons of war, and to hear
what we can tell you about the love of God, our great
Father, the only living God."

Realizing that an unseen person had protected the

Christians, they listened for the first time to the story of Christ. Later the chief and his whole tribe decided to become Christians.

In the fairy tale, "Beauty and the Beast," Beauty needed to live with the beast to save her father. The beast was a frightful, grotesque, bizarre-looking creature. Yet he was gentle, kind and good. Because of his character he won Beauty's love and her love transformed the beast to a handsome prince. It speaks of the transforming power of love.

At the Center of Creation

The transforming power of love is at the core of creation. Monroe C. Babcock, an American poultry expert, wrote a technical pamphlet on the science of egg production. He learned that hens love people, especially people who love them, and when hens are loved they lay more eggs. So if your hens are holding back on you it may be more important to read the Bible and go to church than read farm bulletins and buy better feed.

Lives of persons are changed only by love. Johns Hopkins University researchers came to the conclusion that one good teacher made the difference. The researchers set out to discover why a group of potential delinquents turned out so well socially and morally.

The study showed these youth well on the road to crime. They found that all were influenced by one teacher, a gentle, white-haired woman. "Those boys," she reminisced. "Yes, I remember them well. I loved every one of them." Transfusions of the love transform lives.

Henry Drummond shared a short, beautiful story. "There lived once a young girl whose perfect grace of character was the wonder of those who knew her. She wore on her neck a gold locket which no one was ever allowed to open. One day, in a moment of unusual confidence, one of her companions was allowed to touch its spring and learn its secret. She saw these words: 'Whom having not seen I love.' That was the secret of her beautiful life. She had been changed into the same image."

Love that transforms us is a love which cares deeply for persons. Although it is not human nature to care deeply, yet the Holy Spirit does His transforming work through persons who love as Christ loved.

How About a Plastic Heart?

"Does a plastic heart have love in it?" This question was sent by seven-year-old Linda Griggs of Pittsburgh to the famed heart surgeon Dr. Michael DeBakey of Houston, Texas. Dr. DeBakey replied:

"Yes, a plastic heart has love in it, a great deal of love.

"The love in a plastic heart comes from many people who love other people, and don't want them to die.

"So these people work all day and often all night to build a heart that will make people live longer.

"If you think of how much love there would be in hundreds of hearts, then that is how much love there is in a plastic heart."

Dolly Madison, wife of the fourth president of the United States, was one of the most popular women in American history. Wherever she went, she charmed and captivated everyone obscure and well-known, rich and poor, men and women alike.

She was once asked to explain the secret of her power over others. Surprised by the question Mrs. Madison exclaimed, "Power over people. I have none. I desire none. I merely love everyone." And those who love are richly rewarded by love returned.

An unknown poet penned a poem telling the truth of transforming love.

I love you
Not only for what you are,
But for what I am
When I am with you.

I love you,
Not only for what
You have made of yourself,
But for what
You are making of me.

I love you
For the part of me
That you bring out
I love you
For putting your hand
Into my heaped-up heart
And passing over
All the foolish, weak things
That you can't help
Dimly seeing there,
And for drawing out
Into the light
All the beautiful belonging
That no one else had looked
Quite far enough to find.

I love you because you
Are helping me to make
Of the lumber of my life
Not a tavern
But a temple;
Out of the works
Of every day
Not a reproach
But a song. . . .

We help people only when we love them the way they are and by loving help them become what God wants them to be.

Reuben Youngdahl in *This Is God's Day* writes, "If but one life is transformed because you lived a life of love, your contribution to the world will be felt."

10. Obedience — Love's Test

A beautiful tradition came down the centuries concerning the last days of the Apostle John. He gathered together his disciples for a final farewell message. As he looked into their faces with all the tenderness of the parting moment, he said to them: "Little children, love one another."

But they said, "We have heard that message before. You have been telling us that from the beginning. Give us some other word."

And again looking down upon them, he said with increasing tenderness, "Little children, that which you heard from the beginning that I say to you, that you love one another."

"Oh," they replied, "but you have given us that message ever since we have known you. Now that you are going away we want some parting word by which to remember you. Give us some other commandment tonight."

Then for the last time John said, "Little children, dear little children, a new commandment I give unto you, that you love one another."

He had no other commandment. All the commandments were bound up in that one bundle of love and obedience, that we love others as Christ loves them. "And this commandment we have from him, that he who loves God should love his brother also."

Message of Obedience

Our love for Christ is gauged not by the measure of our emotion but by the measure of our obedience. Jesus says in John 14:15, "If you love me, you will keep my commandments." Again in John 14:21, 23, "He who has my commandments and keeps them, he it is who loves me; and he who loves me will be loved by my Father, and I will love him and manifest myself to him. . . . If a man loves me, he will keep my word, and my Father will love him, and we will come to him and make our home with him."

So the test of our love for Christ is in our complete obedience to His commandments. He reveals Himself to those who obey Him. The one who does not desire to obey the known will of God will not know Christ. To disobey is to make Christ distant.

Some long for greater spiritual power. They want to know Christ as a living reality. They desire the fullness of the Holy Spirit. All comes only when there is ready and radiant obedience. The Holy Spirit "is given to them that obey Him."

God tests our love by our obedience to Christ's command to love others. Since our love depends on our will rather than our feelings, Christ can command us to love. Enabled by the Holy Spirit we can devote ourselves to love.

Why does lack of love so often characterize religious people? Jesus found this true of the scribes and Pharisees against whom His severest and most scathing denunciations were directed. Because of this we suppose they were especially degenerate. One of the surprises of modern scholars is that the scribes and Pharisees were not so bad. They were the most religious and respected groups of their day. But their religion lacked love. They did not see that, as Jesus says, His followers manifest love to God by loving their fellowmen and this love moves to action in behalf of the needy. 1 John 3:17.

The New Commandment

To abide in love is to incarnate the great law of love, to love others in every detail of our daily life. We are to practice the new commandment.

In the seventeenth century when Presbyterians and Episcopalians were feuding in Scotland, Archbishop James Ussher was traveling incognito through southern Scotland and arrived one Saturday night at the home of the clergyman and mystic Samuel Rutherford. He was received with characteristic hospitality. It was the custom in the Rutherford home on Saturday evening for all the members of the household to gather for catechetical instruction under the direction of the minister. The question addressed to the guest that evening was, "How many commandments are there?" He replied, "Eleven." Those present were amazed at such ignorance.

The next morning Rutherford rose early and went out to a grove of trees to meditate and pray. To his astonishment he discovered in the grove the kneeling figure of his guest. The archbishop, upon disclosing his identity, was asked by his host to conduct the morning service. The preacher took as his text, "A new commandment, I give unto you, That ye love one another." Rutherford, who was sitting with his wife in the pew, whispered in her ear, "There you have the eleventh commandment." He might have added, "The commandment which gathers up in itself all other commandments."

James H. McConkey in *The Three-Fold Secret of the Holy Spirit* says, "We are to make 'Love one another' the touchstone by which we test every thought, word, and deed of our daily lives, until all are brought into conformity to the law which was supreme in the life of Christ Himself. The rebuke you administered yesterday to a brother in Christ, was it done in love or vexation? The counsel you gave, was it proffered in love or pride of opinion? The meeting you led, the address you made, were they in love — to help others — or to add to your own reputation?

"The money you gave, was it in love to the lost or in pride and self-esteem? The remarks you make about others, are they in love? The thought you cherish in your secret heart concerning them, are they too, full of love? . . . This is the supreme test of every detail of your life, by which you may know whether it is 'God that worketh in you' or self."

Jesus makes it clear what this love is in Matthew 5:43-48: "You have heard that it was said, 'You shall love your neighbor and hate your enemy.' But I say to you, Love your enemies and pray for those who persecute you, so that you may be sons of your Father who is in heaven; for he makes his sun rise on the evil and on the good, and sends rain on the just and on the unjust. For if you love those who love you, what reward have you? Do not even the tax collectors do the same? . . . You, therefore, must be perfect, as your heavenly Father is perfect."

In the *Living Bible*, Romans 12:9-12 is paraphrased, "Don't just pretend that you love others: really love them. . . . Stand on the side of the good. Love each other with brotherly affection and take delight in honoring each other. Never be lazy in your work but serve the Lord enthusiastically. Be glad for all God is planning for you. Be patient in trouble, and prayerful always."

11. Visibility — Love's Action

Frightened by the clamor of thunder in the night, a little child cried out. Holding her securely in his arms, her father explained that she needn't fear. God would take care of her because He loved her greatly.

"I know God will take care of me and loves me," she replied. "But right now, Daddy, I want someone with skin on to love me."

We are to be God's love, with skin on. Genuine Christian love must find embodiment in lives and in action or it ceases to exist. 1 John 3:17 ff. First of all it expresses itself to God in response to His love for us. Paul, however, only rarely speaks of the Christian's love to God. Instead he usually speaks of the relationship of faith. Paul, as did Jesus, speaks mostly about the love of the Christian for his fellowmen. And he, along with John, says love for others is the real test as to whether we love God. 1 John 4:20.

"Love must not be a matter of words or talk; it must be genuine, and show itself in action" (1 John 3:18, NEB).

Demonstrated Love

An idea struck me as a retreat for husbands and wives was about to begin. I tried it on this group. I first spoke on how Jesus made love visible. He didn't merely send a word from heaven. He came. He didn't merely discuss God's great love. He demonstrated that love by His life and supremely by His death on our behalf. Prophets spoke of God's love, and Hosea years before dramatized God's love in his own life. Yet only when Christ came did people really see God's love.

Further, Jesus tells us to make our love concrete. "Turn the other cheek"; "give to him who asks of you." "If someone asks you for a coat give him your undershirt as well." "Pray for your persecutors." "Speak blessings on those who do you ill." Jesus asked for a visible love. Upon Christ's authority He gave the world the right to judge us as Christians on the basis of our observable love toward others.

"But how do we make love visible in our families?" I asked. "Or how do we make love visible in our churches, communities, and between nations?" That is a point for take-off in any group which takes Jesus' words seriously.

When the Scripture speaks of the fruit of the Spirit being love it refers to a visible expression, a love demonstrated in relation to other people. Fruit is visible. There is no such thing as invisible fruit on a tree; so there is nothing like invisible love.

In the home words of love and acts of love must become real. Without visible expression of love, love cannot live. In an intriguing little paragraph in *The Virginianians*, Thackeray captures this concept of visible love in a humorous way. "When a man is in love with one woman in a family, it is astonishing how fond he becomes of every other person connected with it. He ingratiates himself with the maids; he is bland with the butler; he interests himself in the footman; he runs errands for the daughters; he gives advice and lends money to the young son at college; he pets little dogs which he would otherwise kick; he smiles at old stories which would make him break out in yawns, were they uttered by anyone but papa. He beats time when darling little Fanny performs her piece on the piano, and smiles when

61

wicked little Bobby upsets the coffee over his shirt."

We can see love in the home when words of love are spoken and acts of love are done. There is no other way. We do not find a wife who is in love with her husband and children complaining about the work she needs to do. Love feeds on the expression of love. Love ceases to be real when expressions of love are not repeated.

Love Is Listening

How else does love become visible in the church, community, and world? Dietrich Bonhoeffer in *Life Together* says, "The first service that one owes the other in the fellowship consists in listening to them. Just as love for God begins with listening to His Word, so the beginning of love for the brethren is learning to listen to them.

"Many people are looking for an ear to listen. They do not find it among Christians, because these Christians are talking when they should be listening. But he who can no longer listen to his brother will soon be no longer listening to God. He will do nothing but prattle in the presence of God. This is the beginning of the death of the spiritual life. . . ."

Christians ought to be the best listeners. It is a test of love. It makes love visible. Jesus was always surrounded by people and I suppose people were then much like people today, looking for someone who listens and ignoring those who don't. I believe Jesus understood what was in man not only because He was divine but also because He listened intently. He heard the heart's cry. He heard the intense inner yearning and the deep need.

Christ's longest recorded sermon can be read in fifteen minutes and some think that it is a combination of several sermons. Let us confess we have a lot to learn in listening to others. The reason our message is sometimes superficial is that we see only the surface instead of stopping long enough to listen to what people are saying. We begin to love others when we learn to listen to them. Listening makes love visible.

Affirming Each Other

Love is visible when we affirm another in his gifts or in what he can and ought to do. We demonstrate love by expressing our expectations in a person. We make love visible by telling another of our love for him. It is meaningless to hear a stranger say, "God loves you," if no accompanying evidence, someone here and now, someone who cares enough to risk a little on your behalf, says, "I love you." Real love must become incarnate in persons rather than in pronouncements and programs.

Kenneth Morse wrote, "We can carry the cross on high banners, preach the cross, sing of its wondrous power until we are hoarse. But it will accomplish little unless the marks of the crucifixion appear in the suffering, the denial, the scorn, the unpopularity we are willing to undergo in behalf of persons. When we Christians are concerned enough to die a little for the sake of persons for whom Christ died, then perhaps we only begin to be evangelists who are worthy of the Christ we serve."

Love must be visible in the church, the community of believers. The New Testament records observable experiences and events. The communities which Jesus visited and to which He sent the disciples saw how He loved the poor and the distressed, gave sight to the blind, cast out devils and set souls free, healed the lame, and cleansed the lepers. They may not have understood Him or always interpreted His love properly, but they saw the power of God's love at work.

When Creeds Become Incarnate

In the community of love creeds become incarnate in

deeds. Otherwise creeds are worthless. People will hear our words but the value of these words and their power for action to change life are in direct proportion to their visibility in performance.

A church may speak much about love and Christian concern. That love becomes visible when someone enters who is different in appearance or beliefs. It becomes visible when the church stops ignoring the hurts and ills of people next door.

The church has long looked at the world and said, "You will know them by their fruits." The world can as well look at the church and say the same.

Jesus in Matthew 18 says that if there is difficulty between us and another person we are to go to the other person and be reconciled. This is visible love. Jesus says in Matthew 5:23, 24 that a right relationship with others is so important that He doesn't want a dime or dollar of our offering or a pretense of worship until we are reconciled. He says, "So if you are offering your gift at the altar, and there remember that your brother has something against you, leave your gift there before the altar and go; first be reconciled to your brother, and then come and offer your gift."

Someone suggested that we follow this literally. Let the pastor stand at the church door with the offering plate and say as people enter, "If you do not have peace with any other person, leave your offering here, and go at once and be reconciled. Then return and worship." Some things would happen if this were carried out. No doubt the congregation would be slim for several weeks. Then the church would overflow in attendance and praise because real Christian love is indeed contagious.

In her excellent book, *Say Yes to Life*, Anna B. Mow comments on Matthew 18. She tells about one "Brother Rufus" whom she calls a skillful apprentice in love. "A misunderstanding developed between him and an old friend.

He was greatly troubled because the friend refused to discuss the matter with him. He felt he had to do something, but he had no idea what to do next. Then to his delight, he found the next step suggested in the eighteenth chapter of Matthew. 'Take someone along and go again' (verse 16). Then he pondered 'Whom shall I take? If I take a friend of mine he will think we are ganging up on him, and then things would be worse than ever. I know what I will do. I will take his best friend along, and I won't tell my side of the story until we are all there.' Brother Rufus' choice of a companion was the shock treatment which opened the way to complete reconciliation." This is visible love.

How often we miss the meaning of this kind of love. Jesus said we are to go with deep desire to win our brother and not win over him. For often we go with the attitude of winning our argument instead of winning our brother. Paul in Galatians 6:1 writes, "Brethren, if a man is overtaken in any trespass, you who are spiritual should restore him in a spirit of gentleness. Look to yourself, lest you too be tempted."

Love for Enemies

One could illustrate in many ways how love can be visible. Jesus says our enemies can see genuine Christian love. What is our reaction against hostility? Do we love only those who are nice to us and treat us kindly?

That is no test of love. Even hippies do as much. Jesus said love means, "Bless them that curse you, do good to them that hate you" (Matthew 5:44, KJV). Christ transformed hostility into love. "It is no matter to live lovingly with good-natured, with humble and meek persons," said Jeremy Taylor, "but he that can do so with the froward, with the willful and the ignorant, with the peevish and perverse, he only hath true charity."

In her book, *Living with Love,* Josephine Robertson tells a story. "In 1883, a youthful clergyman, the Rev. Joe Roberts, arrived by stagecoach in a blizzard to minister to the Indians of Wyoming. This great, wild area had been assigned to the Protestant Episcopal Church by President Grant. Soon after Joe Roberts arrived, the son of the chief was shot by a soldier in a brawl, and Chief Washakie vowed to kill the first white man he met. Since this might mean the start of a long, bloody feud, young Roberts decided to take action. Seeking out the tepee, fifteen miles away in the mountains, he stood outside and called the chief's name. When Washakie appeared, Roberts opened his shirt.

"I have heard of your vow," he said. "I know that the other white men have families, but I am alone. Kill me instead."

The chief was amazed and motioned him into his tent. "How do you have so much courage?" he asked.

Joe Roberts told him about Christ, His death, His teachings. They talked for hours. When Joe left, the chief of the Shoshones had renounced his vow to kill and resolved to become a Christian.

Washakie had seen love in action.

Every group which calls itself Christian would do well to decide what it should do to make love visible in the home, church, community, and world. For unless love becomes visible it is not love at all.

There is an "or else" quality about Christian love. "Love or else." If a man claims to love God and despises his brother, he is a liar and a hypocrite. Either he loves God or he does not. There is no middle ground. The hard test will be something other people can know and see: the attitude toward those for whom Christ died.

12. Inclusiveness — Love's Limits

At supper one evening our daughter, then seven years old, was sharing the day at school. A new student arrived. She was a Catholic.

"But," said Rose, "she doesn't look like a Catholic." At this the other children laughed.

"What does a Catholic look like?" they asked.

Quickly Rose responded, "Catholics have freckles."

This brought more laughter. But Rose stuck to her facts. All the Catholics she knew had freckles. So all Catholics everywhere must have freckles.

On a child's level we can understand such reasoning. But when adults reason in the same way, something is wrong. We call it labeling persons. All Jews are shrewd. All Scotch are stingy. All Irish are quick-tempered. All persons of a faith different from our own are not Christian.

Rose said all Catholics have freckles because her acquaintances were limited. She soon learned this was wrong because she came to know many other Catholics. The broader our acquaintanceship becomes and the more we know of Christian love, the less we will use labels. We see others as persons. Whenever we use a label, we begin to judge another by a standard we have set up, and to our shame we often choose a worse criterion than freckles.

See People as God's Creation

Paul in speaking of the effect of Christ's love on us says, "From now on, therefore, we regard no one from a human point of view" (2 Corinthians 5:16). One way we judge others from a human point of view is to consider them as strangers who must meet our standards of race, education, religion, politics, class, or possessions before we can accept and love them. "But," says the apostle, "we no longer judge that way. The love of Christ impels us to judge differently."

Jesus became involved with others as persons loved by God. All the barriers and standards of today were present then. Yet His love surmounted the deepest and sharpest differences between a Jew and a Samaritan.

So the Spirit of Christ first sees others as persons, those for whom Christ died and He now longs to save. The Christian sees God as Creator of all and therefore he accepts all His creation. He sees the importance of receiving others for what they are. He receives them and then gives them what they need and not what they deserve. Finally only in receiving others as they are do we really see them. As we love others we also understand them.

Jesus receives the nonreceivables: the woman at the well, Zacchaeus, Matthew, Mary, Simon, and others whom Jesus met, accepted, loved, and led to a new life. How often the unacceptable became His point of contact! Christ lived in the creative tension of accepting the unacceptable. "The heathen," He said, "love those who love them." He calls us to love even the unlovely, the unacceptable, and the rejected.

In only one way can we win those who are unacceptable, unlovely, and rejected. J. B. Phillips says, "People can only be loved into the kingdom." Those who are unlovely feel unloved and do not love themselves. Those who feel rejected have also rejected themselves. We suffer the greatest because of the lack of love and acceptance.

The Christian accepts the unacceptable, the unlovely, the rejected person so that he may accept himself and realize the acceptance and love of God. Can anyone understand the love of God who does not know the love and acceptance of one of God's children? The one transformed by Christ accepts and loves whoever is unacceptable and unloving to him.

We need and must remember this Spirit of Christ in all our work in the world, in the church, and in our families. Remember Jesus saw the unacceptable in another person as the signal for action. It was His point of contact. May we make it ours.

A Story of Acceptance

I was stressing this point at a luncheon speech in Denver some time ago. After the luncheon a lady came to me and said, "What you said is right but it's a most difficult thing. It is not easy. Let me illustrate."

Then she told me that she was from three generations of preachers' families, and the church has a certain way of doing its work. But her son is unorthodox in his way of witnessing. Yet her son was winning dozens of persons to Jesus Christ while her own church was doing little or nothing.

One evening her son came to his car and found two young men with long hair and dirty clothes trying to break into it. He asked if he could be of service to them. The young men said they needed to go to a certain city. Because it was quite some distance he invited them to his home overnight and promised to take them in the morning. They came and ate supper. After supper this woman's son told the young men that he and his wife attend a service nearly every evening and they invited them along.

"What kind of service?" they wanted to know.

"It's a service where we share what the Lord has done for us and pray together," he said.

"But we are too dirty. We can't go along," the men said.

"There is the bathroom if you want to wash up but you are welcome as you are."

The young men went to the meeting. When they returned home they were silent for some time. Then one said, "Did you say you have a meeting like that every night?"

"Yes, almost every night."

"Do you have one tomorrow evening?" they asked.

"Yes, we do."

"Would it be possible to stay and go along?"

"Certainly."

"And because my son accepted those hippies the way they were he was able to lead them to new life in Christ," the woman finally said. Her son found out later these young men who had turned off society and the church and whom society and the church had turned off, both had doctors' degrees and great potential.

Do you see Christ's method? We are inclined to say, "If that's the way they want to do, if that's the way they want to look, let them go their way and I'll go mine." But Jesus didn't; neither dare we!

Love's final test, as Erich Fromm points out, is whether we can love the "stranger" who may not share our values or our cultures or even be particularly admirable himself. After all, it was while we were yet sinners that God loved us. Romans 5:8.

We do not love God any more than the person we love the least. We do not love any person lost in sin in some other community or country if we do not love the hippie next door. In fact, one of the best tests that we really have the Spirit of Christ is whether we love those who are next to us at home or on the job who do differently than we desire. Said James F. Meyer, "God never had the problem of finding a person He could not love."

13. Acceptance — Love's Ability

As Dr. Parkes Cadman left a meeting one evening a woman who prided herself in being an unbeliever and anti-religious fanatic met him at the door and said, "Dr. Cadman, may I ask you a question?"

"Certainly," replied the great preacher.

"Do you believe Christ died for your sins?" asked the woman.

Touching the woman gently on the arm and with a gracious smile Dr. Cadman replied, "Yes, my dear, I believe Christ died for my sins, and I believe He died for yours also."

Taken completely off her guard by the gracious answer, the woman could not reply. He had disarmed her by drawing about him a circle of love which included her also.

Controversy cannot hold its own against a genial spirit of love and good will. Neither can love limit itself to a small, selfish world.

How big is our world? In Jesus' day some criticized Him because His world included such persons as Zacchaeus, the woman who brought ointment, and Matthew the tax collector. They could not imagine Him including Samaria in His world. To talk with an immoral Samaritan woman was unheard of. Christ's world was much larger than others of His day.

Edwin Markham, many years ago, wrote a stanza all of us should store in our minds:

He drew a circle that shut me out —
Heretic, rebel, a thing to flout.
But love and I had the wit to win:
We drew a circle that took him in.

That was the Spirit of Christ. He did not stop short of giving all for us. He died for the world. We cannot imagine Christ loving only one group or a certain kind of person. His love reached out to all. His arms encircled all.

When the church closes its circle of love, it loses its likeness to Christ and its mission to the world. When a congregation thinks of any person as being outside its concern, spiritual calamity will follow. When a group of believers thinks it can go it alone, it is blind and becomes a clique rather than Christ's church.

Love does not limit its concern. Love longs to enlarge its circle to include all, even as Christ did.

When Others Differ

One test of true Christian love is that of loving others who may not think or do exactly as you and I do. Can we love each other in spite of these differences? Or will we yield to growing feelings of bitterness and "holier than thou" attitudes?

Satan tempts us to feel inner disgust toward another who may do something differently than we do or believe differently than we believe. Such a spirit of ill feeling can run rampant, especially during times of rapid change. The real test of our Christian love is what the other person's actions or words do to us.

Christian love never despises another. True love deepens for another person when difficulties appear rather than depreciates him. It seems so easy to feel bad against one who we say "should know better." Our lack of love becomes a worse sin than the brother's fault.

Where the other person's opinion or practice differs from our own, Christian love needs to be most redemptive and real. All the graces of the Spirit can be exercised and employed when others differ with us most.

Today we should really love one another even though differences occur in the church. Christian humility helps us believe that the Holy Spirit lives and works in our brothers and sisters. We need always to acknowledge that the Holy Spirit is leading others just as much as we wish others to acknowledge that He is leading us.

When we have this common trust in the Lord, the Holy Spirit, and in our brethren, then our love can abound more and more as Paul prayed.

Christians can spend so much time in correcting another's views that they can really do nothing constructive and positive. Many cannot accept the fact that equally sincere Christians can hold a diametrically opposite view on many things. The judgmental attitude which says regarding another person, "He just doesn't want to obey the plain Scripture," is unchristian in itself. It may be that the one so judged may have searched longer and deeper than we have to find God's will. Sometimes it may be that we should be coming out where he is rather than expecting him to come out with our viewpoint.

Romans 14 may give us some help in dealing with differences. Here Paul deals with different viewpoints. Paul says we are to be persuaded or convinced in our own mind. Verses 5, 22. Further, we should admit that another believer can hold a different view from ours that is equally right for him. Verse 6. Don't attempt to impose your convictions on other Christians. Verse 1. Don't criticize the other Christian's convictions, regardless of whether they are more lenient or more strict than yours. Verse 3. Above all, don't judge others or ruin the work of God by needless arguments over differences. Verse 20.

Less than Perfect

Real love does not demand perfection. How often we limit our love to others because they do not in some way or another conform to our idea. But Christ's love is not dependent on good behavior or certain performance, otherwise He could never love the sinner nor could He ask us to love our enemies.

Christian love does not look for exact returns. Rather, it goes on loving and helping regardless of return. This is another reason why we cannot love in our own strength alone. This is why we need the love of God Himself shed abroad in our hearts by the Holy Spirit.

We hear expressions even among Christians which imply that love cannot be expressed if love is not returned. This attitude implies that unless others reach a certain standard we have no obligation to love or help.

At this point Christian love reveals itself. As long as we base our love on the other's response to us, our love is less than Christian love. As long as our love reaches only those who we feel deserve our love it is not Christian love. If our love helps only those we think are worthy, it is not Christian love. Christian love makes no demands. It only takes the command of the Master — to love.

Do we love only those who agree with us, look like we do, think like we do, and love us? Because a person is different should it make any difference in our concern for him? God loves variety. He created no two persons alike. If the church, then, is to express God's love it must be much more than a club of like-minded people. It must be a community of love where differences are not only tolerated but invited and appreciated. A faith which vitiates the personality of persons is not Christianity. Christianity is not a conforming but a transforming experience together.

Freedom to Accept Anyone

We can so easily do the same things we deplore in others. One of the most damning things about communism is that it demands everyone be alike — politically, socially, and theologically. If persons do not conform they are ostracized or killed. There is no freedom for difference of opinion. That we say is communism.

Yet how often, as Christians, we seek to put everyone in the same straitjacket. Unless everyone agrees with us politically, socially, and theologically we find no room for them in the church.

But the love of Christ frees us to love all kinds of people regardless of relationships and circumstances. If the fellowship of Christ's church cannot hold together people with differences, then its love is not Christ's love. It is not the love the Bible speaks about and which Jesus says tells whether or not we are His disciples. It may be the love which binds cliques together. It may be a commonality which is based on race, riches, religion, creed, country, or color, but it is not Christ's love.

One of the best-known stories Jesus told was about loving people who are different. Jesus met a young lawyer who wanted to justify his lack of love by asking who his neighbor is. The lawyer soon learned his neighbor was anyone in need, no matter how different.

True Christian love leads us to affirm the uniqueness of the other person. To love someone does not drive us to make that person a carbon copy of ourselves. Only insecure, selfish people take this approach. True love not only allows but encourages another to be his unique self. The Apostle Paul says this love has the quality of seeking not its own.

14. Make Love Your Aim

E. Stanley Jones said to Mahatma Gandhi: "I am very anxious to see Christianity nationalized in India, so it will no longer be a foreign thing identified with a foreign people and a foreign government, but be a part of the national life of India, contributing its power to India's uplift and redemption. What would you suggest we do to make this possible?"

Gandhi's penetrating reply was, "I would suggest first, that all of you Christians must begin to live more like Jesus Christ. Second, I would suggest that you must practice your religion without adulterating and toning it down. Third, I would suggest you put your emphasis on love, for love is the center and soul of Christianity."

G. K. Chesterton defined a novel this way. In the first chapter boy meets girl. In the last chapter boy kisses girl. The book tells why it took so long. The Bible tells why it takes so long for love to become a reality in the lives of all men.

We usually stop at the close of the great love chapter of the Bible (1 Corinthians 13) without realizing that Paul's punch line comes at the beginning of the next chapter. It is "Make love your aim." It means to change the center of life from self to others, to seek to heal wherever there is hurt, to bind up wounds rather than slash deeper, and to redeem rather than to reject.

Years ago a young man went to Africa as a missionary. He was capable and brilliant, but he was also critical and harsh with people. He rubbed people the wrong way and aroused hostility because of his hard-nosed approach to problems and persons. Finally the church wrote a letter to the sponsoring board in North America asking that he be brought back. Because of his spirit he could not serve in Africa.

The home board, however, after considerable conversation, decided to give the young man another chance. There was one stipulation. He must promise to read 1 Corinthians 13 every day for the next year. With the reading of this love chapter daily, the young man's life was changed and filled with love. Shortly thereafter the same church which voted to send him home after his first year voted to make him its bishop. He served as a devoted and much loved servant for fifty years in Africa.

A Way of Life

To make love our aim means to adopt it as a way of life. It is a fundamental, responsible approach to all of life. Divine love is not sentiment. It is a disciplined relationship. Kirkegaard points out the difference between these two concepts in *Works of Love,* where he says, "Spontaneous love [or sentiment] can soon be changed into something else." Christian love binds us to others by duty.

So Christian love speaks not so much of how we feel toward others but what we do for them. In one of his folk songs, William Flanders reminds us that love is a verb, something we do. The opposite of love is not hate but selfishness. The more we think of self, the less we can love. This love is the most revolutionary force in the world.

Anatole Lunacharsky, former Commissar of Education in the USSR, wrote in 1935, "We hate Christianity and Christians. Even the best of them must be considered our worst enemies. They preach love of one's neighbor and mercy, which is contrary to our principles. Christian love is an obstacle to the development of the revolution. Down with love of our neighbor! What we want is hatred. We must know how to hate. Only thus will we conquer the universe."

This is quoted not so much to point out the ugliness of communism but to help us think further on several things.

First, if we want to fight communism or any other vice our best instrument is love. "Love," he says, "is an obstacle to the development of revolution." When we hate we join godless forces. How often have we traded hate for hate?

Second, only as we have a burning love or a burning hatred, do we have a cause and a motive greater than ourselves. One or the other can change the world.

Third, those in between, the lukewarm, accomplish little or nothing.

Love for one another was the badge of Christians in the first-century churches. Today we sing the popular folk song, "And They'll Know We Are Christians by Our Love." It catches up our desire and need.

Love Leads to Understanding

To make love our aim means that then we begin to understand other people and help them. Paul in Philippians, chapter one, prays that our "love may abound more and more, with knowledge." We never really understand another person until we love that person. Love alone gives us a correct viewpoint. When we love another, suddenly we see the person as he is, his real needs, and his real possibilities. Only as we love can we take the hand of the helpless and together climb to higher ground.

Only as we love can we avoid a condescending attitude. Only as we love do we see that oftentimes the overcritical person is starved for love and appreciation; the aggressive youth is often unsure of himself; the aloof person is likely fighting inward problems of worthlessness; and the person who continually draws attention to himself wants acceptance. Then the love of Christ becomes real to persons around us.

During a sharing period a woman said, "I know the Bible says God loves me. But my problem is that I can't feel loved by Him. How can I feel God's love?"

The pastor said he was ready to give a quick theological response but restrained himself and asked the group. The next week he met the lady again and asked her how things were going. She told him everything was fine, adding, "So many people expressed concern, support, and understanding toward my situation that I no longer feel alone. I have received visits, phone calls, and letters of encouragement all week. I know God must love me because His people have shown it to me."

Not Skin-Deep

To make love our aim means that we love people with sincerity. Scripture says we are to love one another, not from the skin but from the heart. Yet much of our concern for others is only skin-deep.

Now if our love toward others is only skin-deep it is easily disturbed. The least little scratch draws blood and sends us, like scrapping children, to someone to whom we can cry about every bruise or hurt in order to get back at the person who hurt us. We quickly tell and show what the other person has done to us. We have the proof; look at the scratch.

Skin-deep love does not stand up under adversity or disfavor. It is hurt by every touch of criticism, unkindness, or difference of opinion. Skin-deep love demands a personal apology for about everything from the other person. When love is only skin-deep, we are ready to part paths when someone rubs us the wrong way. Every person who gets against us becomes our enemy. Our skin is hurt.

Heart love is something different. Since it is deep within, it is not affected easily by what happens on the outside, by people rubbing me the wrong way or by scratches and bruises. Heart love, the Christlike grace, endures long and endeavors always to do the best for the other person without thought of reaction or return.

Heart love has a deep concern for the other's good and refuses to think thoughts of ill will toward him. It is not easily hurt or turned away by what is said or done. It absorbs hatred and hostility in order to help. Nestled deep inside, heart love continues to perform its function of nourishing and helping the whole body in spite of the bumps and knocks the body receives. No wonder Scripture says we are to love from the heart fervently.

Love Lets the Good News Through

Make love your aim because it is the only way the good news of Christ can get through. Love not only tests our fellowship and friendship with Christ but also determines whether or not the world will hear our message.

Years ago Pittsburgh built a large, modern million-dollar post office. On the day of dedication a large crowd gathered. Bands played. The governor and mayor gave speeches and the people celebrated. Much money, planning, and muscle went into the building. However, when the time came to send the first letter it was found, to the chagrin of the engineers, that there was no small slot to drop in a letter. No matter how costly, complete, or modern the post office building was it lacked what was necessary for a letter to get mailed.

So also it is true of the Christian and the church. No matter how modern its methods of communication or its organization; no matter how great its endeavor or celebration; no matter how solemn its speeches or how sacred its sanctuary; if love is missing, the message of Christ cannot get through.

Love is not luxury for Christian living; it is an essential. It is the mark of Christ's follower. If there is any time when people need to know we "are Christians by our love" it is now. "Make love your aim." Make it your goal. It is the charm, the crown of all Christian character. Love is the nature and life of God Himself within us. Make love your goal.

One mother felt she had all she could take. During a long winter, sickness and accident had struck just about everyone in her home. Mumps, measles, a broken nose, a broken leg, and four new teeth for the baby made pressures and demands accumulate until she fell on her knees in protest and desperation, "Oh Lord! I have so much to do." To her amazement what came out was quite different. The words she heard herself cry out were these: "Oh Lord! I have so much to love!"

Joy Fruit

15. Joy — Love Smiling

In A.D. 248 Cyprian, the bishop of Carthage, wrote to his friend Donatus, "This seems to be a cheerful world, Donatus, when I view it from this fair garden under the shadow of these vines. But if I climb some great mountain and look out over the wide lands, you know very well what I would see — brigands on the road, pirates on the seas; in the amphitheaters men murdering each other to please the applauding crowds, and under all roofs I see misery and selfishness. It is really a bad world, Donatus, an incredibly bad world.

"Yet in the midst of it, I have found a quiet and holy people. They have discovered a joy which is a thousand times better than any pleasure of the sinful life. They are despised and persecuted but they care not. These people, Donatus, are Christians and I am one of them."

According to the New Testament, joy is one of the characteristics of the Christian. "The fruit of the Spirit is . . . joy." F. R. Maltby said that Christ promised His disciples three things: "They would be absurdly happy, completely fearless, and in constant trouble."

Joy — A Major Theme of New Testament

The word "joy" occurs in the New Testament 60 times; "rejoice," 72 times. The word translated "greetings" in the New Testament literally means "joy be with you." Read such passages as Matthew 28:9; Luke 1:28; Acts 15:23;

85

2 Corinthians 13:11; James 1:1 with the phrase "joy be with you" and see how the pages and life of the New Testament ring with joy.

The gospel is not joyless. Much of the great literature of the ages is sad and pessimistic. Keats could envy the static beauty of figures on a Grecian urn. Contemporary writers also voice the despair to which Aeschylus and Sophocles gave expression in their tragedies. Think of the despair of ancient Greece. Sinclair Lewis calls us a lot of fools, and Ernest Hemingway said that life is futile and cruel. William Faulkner arrives at the opinion that nothing matters anyway.

Not so the gospel. "Joy unspeakable and full of glory" is written to persecuted persons.

The New Testament begins with angels announcing good news of great joy and closes with joy flooding heaven.

God gave us the ability to weep and He also gave the gift of mirth so that we see both the gloom and humor of life.

In 1769 Cruden, the noted author of the *Concordance of the Bible*, wrote "To laugh is to be merry in a sinful manner." Some still feel that way. One psychologist says, "The lack of ability to find humor in life is a sign of poor mental health." The lack of joy which radiates in the Christian's life could be a sign of poor spiritual health. God wants us to be happy, to be full of joy. Joy is the evidence that the Holy Spirit dwells within.

Who has more right to joy than a Christian! All other "joy" is shallow and hollow. But the Christian has a deep fountain of joy which still runs clear and full when the cisterns of the world are dry.

Our Lord in one of the darkest hours of history said, "Be of good cheer, I have overcome the world." He had the sorrows of the world in His heart and the joy of heaven in His soul.

What is joy? Joy is love smiling. It is love exulting, rejoicing, the echo of pleasant words of love we speak to others and the overflow of happiness we give to others because we have happiness deep within. It is dependent upon a relationship to Jesus Christ. It is the inward reality which produces outward radiance.

What is striking about the New Testament concept of joy is that it does not depend on external circumstances. Although Paul's level of joy is determined to some extent by his relation to his fellow laborers (2 Timothy 1:4; Philemon 7), with joy he refers to the churches in which he worked (1 Thessalonians 2:20; Philippians 4:1). The roots of Christian joy lie in One whom the Christians have not seen, yet they love Him and believe in Him and "rejoice with unutterable and exalted joy " (1 Peter 1:8).

Joy in Adversity

Joy does not depend on circumstances for existence nor does it evade adverse circumstances, trials, or sufferings. An example is Jesus Himself "who for the joy that was set before him endured the cross" (Hebrews 12:2). The Christian also can rejoice in suffering. No rosy optimism or flight to the beyond motivate the Christian's joy. The joy of the Christian is the fruit of a conviction that Christ will eventually conquer through suffering. Our relation to Christ is what counts.

In Dickens' *Martin Chuzzlewit,* when Martin learns that the fifty-acre tract in America in which he had invested all his savings, and Mark Tapley's too, turns out to be a hideous swamp, he sinks into a fever. Mark, however, refusing to be overpowered by the calamity takes himself in hand. "Now, Mr. Tapley," said Mark, giving himself a tremendous blow on the chest by way of reviver, "just you attend to what I've got to say. Things is looking as bad as they *can* look, young man. You'll not have such another opportunity for showing your jolly disposition, my fine fellow, as long as you live. And, therefore, now's the time to come out strong, or never!"

Alexander Maclaren wrote, "Joy may grow in the very face of danger, as a slender rosebush flings its bright sprays and fragrant flowers over the top of a cataract." As long as the roots are connected to the soil it is safe and beautiful. When the Christian is connected to Christ, even in danger he has joy.

<u>Jesus then is the source of joy. He said, before leaving His disciples, "These things I have spoken to you, that my joy may be in you, and that your joy may be full."</u> *John 15:11*

A lady missionary was flying home from an overseas assignment after the Korean War and a group of GI's were also on the plane. All during the trip the celebrating soldiers came and offered her a drink and cigarettes. Each time she kindly said, "No, thank you, I don't need it."

Finally some of the boys decided to go talk to her and find out why she wouldn't accept the cigarettes and drink. Two or three went to her and said, "Mrs. Webster, when we offer you a drink or cigarettes you keep saying, 'No, thank you, I don't need it.' Would you tell us why you keep saying that?"

She said, "I would be glad to. When you take a drink of liquor, an alcoholic beverage, or cigarette, you do it because you are seeking joy. It's supposed to bring joy and satisfaction. Isn't that right?"

"Yes," they said.

"Well, you see, I already have joy inside. I don't need the drink or the cigarette."

"Where did you find this joy?"

She said, "At the end of my rope. I found Jesus the Giver of real joy at the end of my rope."

Bernard of Clairvaux wrote:

Jesus, Thou joy of loving hearts!
Thou fount of life! thou light of men!
From the best bliss that earth imparts,
We turn unfilled to Thee again.

We are much like the disciples between Easter and
Pentecost when they kept themselves locked in the upper
room. They had the life, death, and resurrection of Jesus to
preach about, but they remained dumb. So with us. We
know all about the facts of Christmas, Good Friday, and
Easter but we do not have the power of the Spirit within us.
As we face a hostile world we grow despondent.

Salute Life with a Smile

Those early disciples, to the discomfiture of all, listened
to false accusations in council halls while their faces shone
like angels. They left the judgment halls with bleeding backs,
rejoicing that they were counted worthy to suffer for Christ's
name. They rejoiced and praised their way through prisons
and saluted death with a smile. The reason? They knew a
living Savior. Christ had come back. They rejoiced because
they had assurance of victory.

Samuel Dickey Gordon says, "Joy is distinctly a Christian
word and a Christian thing. Happiness is the result of what
happens of an agreeable sort. Joy has its springs deep down
inside. And that spring never runs dry, no matter what happens. Only Jesus gives that joy. He had joy, singing its
music within, even under the shadow of the cross. It is an
unknown word and thing except as He has sway within."

One can understand the plight of the young man who was
given any and everything that his selfish whims desired and
who wrote his obituary in a suicide note: "I'm completely
fed up with being terribly happy."

"Rejoice" is sometimes said to be the standing order of

89

the church. One of the primary objects of John's writing his first epistle is that his readers might experience "fullness of joy." Jesus in the darkest hours of history said, "These things I have spoken to you, that my joy may be in you, and that your joy may be full" (John 15:11). Paul wrote to the Romans, "The kingdom of God is . . . righteousness, and peace, and joy" (Romans 14:17, KJV). The difficulties and delights of the Christian life are described in the context of inner joy. If joy is missing in any circumstance in the Christian's life to that extent it is unchristian. The Apostle Paul says in Colossians 1:24 that he rejoices in his sufferings.

David Redding writes in an article in *Christianity Today*, "After five terrible beatings and two horrible stonings, Christianity's most jubilant apostle got up and dusted off the opposition with a shout, 'Rejoice, and again I say unto you, rejoice!' After wading through inquisition, torture, blood, and hell, the Bible ends with a great host no man could number, singing, 'Hallelujah.' " With all the tragedy in the New Testament, it is still the most joyful book ever written.

Jesus and the apostles preached in order to bring the good news of great joy.

William Barclay writes, "It may be that a preacher has to awake sorrow and penitence in his people; it may be that he has to awaken fear within their hearts; it may be that he has to rouse them to self-loathing, and to humiliation. But no Christian sermon can ever end there.

"The sermon which leaves a man in dark despair is not a Christian sermon, for after the shame and the humiliation of penitence there must be the joy of forgiveness claimed and the love of God experienced. No man can ever rise from a Christian service without the possibility of joy flaming and blazing before him." [1]

---

1. William Barclay, *Flesh and Spirit* (Nashville: Abingdon, 1962), p. 82.

16. Jesus — Man of Joy

Someone asked the radiant Rufus Moseley if he thought Jesus ever laughed. "I don't know," he answered, "but He certainly fixed me up so I can laugh."

A misleading falsehood has come down through the ages. It was reportedly said by Pilate, "Nobody has ever seen Jesus laugh." But Pilate didn't really know Jesus. The Gospels tell a different story. Certainly there were times of sorrow, withdrawal, heavy burdens, tears, and even denunciations, but everywhere Jesus went He spread hope, cheer, and the living reality of joy and happiness.

Jesus displayed joy. Children recognized Him as a person of joy and swarmed around Him. Children are not drawn to the drab, dull, dismal, unhappy person. Throughout His life Jesus spoke much of joy. When He came to the last hours with His disciples He said, "These things have I spoken unto you, that my joy might remain in you, and that your joy might be full" (John 15:11, KJV). These words are meaningless if Jesus was not radiant with joy.

Many songs we hear and sing and books we read seem to pity Jesus for His sufferings. But Jesus spoke of His own life, even with its difficulties and final death, as a joyful life. Consider the exhaustless sources of Jesus' joy: His trust in His Father; His boundless hope for the future; His consciousness that He had found and was doing God's will; His sense of God's approval on His life; and His knowledge that He was doing a great and abiding service for all people.

Joy Wherever He Walked

Yes, Jesus was a man of joy. One can trace Christ's walk through the country by the joy He left behind. He pushed sorrows and shadows aside wherever He went. Burdened souls saw new hope and happiness. One time He spoke to thousands for three days. The people were so excited they ate nothing during that time. Such things do not happen unless joy pervades.

Those who claim Christ was not joyful do not know Him. His gospel is the good news of joy. Angels sang for joy when He was born. His birth announcement introduced the words, "I bring you good news of a great joy which will come to all the people" (Luke 2:10).

John in his Gospel expresses the joyful aspect of Jesus' ministry and reports that John the Baptist already saw this joy. He likens himself to the friend of the bridegroom, who is delighted that finally the bridegroom has arrived. "The friend of the bridegroom, who stands and hears him, rejoices greatly at the bridegroom's voice; therefore this joy of mine is now full" (John 3:29).

Edith Kent Battle imagines Jesus with younger boys and girls thus, "He let them hold His strong, warm hand. He was their friend. He laughed with them . . . isn't that the way we could tell who He was, today?"

Not only did Jesus share fully in that festival of highest human joy, the wedding feast, but He often used the marriage celebration to describe the true character of His kingdom. The kingdom is pictured by Jesus as always happy like a wedding. We do Him and ourselves a wrong to make Christianity seem like a funeral.

Fedor Dostoevski said in 1880, "Cana of Galilee . . . ah, that sweet miracle! It was not men's grief, but their joy Christ visited. He worked His first miracle to help man's gladness." One of the accusations Christ's enemies made was that He drew the crowds of common people and was found sitting down at the banquets of publicans and sinners. He was aglow with joy. People don't want a kill-joy for dinner especially at a wedding feast. Jesus was a "man of sorrows and acquainted with grief." Because He lived so close to people, He sensed their sorrows and knew their sufferings. But people knew Jesus as full of joy.

His Message Was Joy

In His manifesto of the kingdom in Matthew 5, Christ began with the note of happiness. The word "happiness" is a deliberate, vital, inevitable word. Christ came to solve the world's problems and not to gain the world's ear.

Jesus brought a breath of fresh air into piety and religious observances. He rejected all attempts to make religion a sorrowful yoke to bear. Christ was anointed "with the oil of gladness" above His fellows. Wherever He went the atmosphere was described as full of "great joy."

G. K. Chesterton closes one of his greatest books called *Orthodoxy* with these words: "There was something that He hid from all men when He went up a mountain to pray. There was something He covered constantly by abrupt silence or impetuous isolation. There was some one thing that was too great for God to show us when He walked upon our earth; and I have sometimes thought it was His mirth."

Dean Inge wrote in *The Rustic Moralist,* "I have never understood why it should be considered derogatory to the Creator to suppose that He has a sense of humor."

Where did we get the idea that "virtue lies in gravity, and smiles are simply symptoms of depravity." As Christians we ought to be the most joyful and happy persons in the community. In fact, our deep sense of joy in Christ ought to be so evident that all others we meet should be attracted to it. We cannot claim to be a follower of Jesus and not have this joy. Let all who divest themselves of gladness and joy in the name of God know that they are not Jesus' followers. Leon Bloy writing a letter November 3, 1889, said, "For the people who know the Bible and tradition and the complete history of humanity, joy is the most infallible sign of the presence of God."

17. The Missing Ingredient

In listing six essentials enjoyed by early Christians which seem to be possessed by few members of the modern church, George A. Buttrick includes a deep sense of joy, the only, the final answer to our quest for happiness.

The late Bishop Otto Dibelius of Germany, several years before his death, looked over his church conference program and wrote the general secretary, "When I scan the topics you have announced, I wonder if your New Testament hasn't revised Luke 2 to read, 'Behold, I bring you good problems of great moment which shall engage you for the next 2000 years.' "

What bothered the bishop was that the church is too problem conscious. The church lacked joy. He said the image of the church and the modern man should show the power that overcomes the world and the joy of faith and victory. That is a good hint for conference topics and speakers. It is a good reminder to us all.

"Gospel" means good news. How does our average meeting impress an onlooker? Does he think we assemble to mourn a defeat or to celebrate a victory? A tremendous asset for the Christian witness is a personality that radiates joy.

Contrary to Regulation

A Christian wrote a postal card to a friend, and on the side of the card where it said "address only" he wrote the words, "Be of good cheer." When his friend received the card he was compelled to pay extra postage. For this he was not particularly pleased. He looked to see the reason and noticed the message, "Be of good cheer." Underneath the postal authorities had stamped, "Contrary to regulation." Many Christians look as though their religion does not agree with them.

A Christian layman who works with overseas students in American universities makes it a practice to ask those who accompany him to church what their reaction is to Christianity. Many of them respond, he says, with statements like, "The teaching is good, but the people are so grim, so sad. They don't seem very happy about it."

Some time ago a newspaper recorded the reflections of a visitor in our country for six months. He was asked for his impressions of North America. After expressing much appreciation for our country he said, "Something is wrong with the people. They are friendly and helpful, but they appear to be unhappy. In America there is much pleasure but no joy."

Read the advertising pages of newspapers and magazines, and listen to the commercials on radio and TV, and you might get the impression that people today get a great deal more joy out of life than did their parents or grandparents. Never has joy or happiness been sought more consciously. A majority of people believe, and the advertisers know it, that happiness lies in that car which "says something about you" or that house for indoor-outdoor togetherness; or in the needed vacation. The false assumption is that joy is somewhere else, some time other than now, and wrapped around things.

We live in an age of cocktails, advertising smiles on every side, and the craze for pleasure. It seems like the first period in history where joy is unlimited.

The Struggle for Happiness

But it is not a true story. When people struggle so hard for happiness, the struggle itself speaks of its absence. Psychologists tell us that the ceaseless search for happiness is only a frantic attempt to be free from fear. People are awfully afraid. No wonder Jesus' constant call was "fear not," "be of good cheer." It seems Satan is saying, "Give people everything, but take the joy out of it."

Nietzsche once said that the trick today is not to arrange a festival, but to find people capable of enjoying one. "I used to be able to get people to laugh just by falling down," said Coco, the clown, who has performed with Ringling Brothers — Barnum and Bailey Circus for many years. "Nowadays people are so uptight, so tense, that it is difficult even to make children laugh," he complains.

In this complex age there is no way to be whole and happy except, "The God of hope fill you with all joy and peace in believing, so that by the power of the Holy Spirit you may abound in hope" (Romans 15:13).

There is no lack of orthodoxy. But we lack radiance, the contagious quality of joy.

In his *Explanatory Notes upon the New Testament*, John Wesley wrote, "Sour godliness is the devil's religion." Luther said that sadness is for the devil and not a legitimate fruit of the gospel. Strange that anyone should think he serves Christ better by being sad than by being glad. It's like saying a cloudy day is better than a day filled with sunshine, a poor photograph is better than a clear one, a garden of weeds is better than a clean garden of beautiful flowers. Certainly religion should be the source of goodness. But it should also be the source of gladness.

Dietrich Bonhoeffer in *Life Together* wrote,"God cannot endure that unfestive, mirthless attitude of ours in which we eat the bread of sorrow, with pretentious busy haste, or even with shame. Through our daily meals He is calling us to rejoice, to keep holiday in the midst of our working day."

Perhaps if we would weep more in confession, we could rejoice more after pardon. We should be like the lady who found her valuable coin after she had looked and looked for it. Then she held a party to celebrate her joy. Our joy should be as the shepherd who found his lost sheep and told his friends and they rejoiced together. Our happiness should be like the father's whose lost son came home. He killed the fatted calf and had a great party to celebrate forgiveness and reunion. No joy is like that of a person who just looks into the dark recesses of his soul, stands before God, says in honest and self-acknowledgment how things are, and then hears a gracious pardon.

Perhaps the reason we lack joy is that we take ourselves and our own efforts too seriously and we don't take the good news seriously enough. We are so preoccupied with the bad news we hardly hear the good news. We do not hear that "We won. It's okay! We are forgiven! Set free! Come celebrate, we have sinned much and have been forgiven much. Rejoice!"

R. W. Dale wrote, "We ask God to forgive us for our evil thoughts and evil temper, but rarely, if ever, ask Him to forgive us for our sadness."

Commanded to Rejoice

Good cheer, joy is not contrary to regulations. Joy is a command (1 Thessalonians 5:16; Philippians 4:4; Matthew 5:12). Jesus gave us three cheers. The cheer of forgiveness, "Be of good cheer, thy sins be forgiven thee" (Matthew 9:2,

KJV). The cheer of companionship, "Be of good cheer; it is I, be not afraid" (Mark 6:50, KJV). The cheer of victory, "Be of good cheer; I have overcome the world" (John 16:32).

In light of the good news in Christ it is strange that anyone would think that there is something sacred about a long face. H. L. Mencken defined Puritanism as "the haunting fear that someone, somewhere may be happy." Christians are, or ought to be, the most cheerful and happy people. Helmut Thielicke, the great German preacher, went so far as to say that the Christian who has lost his sense of humor has denied his Lord.

One of the promises Jesus gave is that we will experience joy in coming to Him. "Your hearts will rejoice, and no one will take your joy from you" (John 16:22). Jesus warned His people of trouble in the sense of hardship, danger, persecution, and misunderstanding.

Joy is the note we need today. The skeptical Nietzsche said to some Christians of his day, "You are going to have to look more redeemed than you do if we are to believe the message of redemption."

When we think about it, nothing in Christianity is conducive to melancholy. Paul, the great suffering servant of Christ, tells us to "Rejoice in the Lord alway." Although the New Testament centers in a cross, is bathed in blood of martyrs, and is filled with the fires of persecution, a note of triumphant joy rings throughout.

In Pierre Van Paassen's novel, *Earth Could Be Fair,* an organist became increasingly disgusted with the gloomy themes used by his preacher Sunday after Sunday. After a particularly sad sermon he spontaneously threw aside the planned music and pulling all stops bellowed out the Hallelujah Chorus from *The Messiah* with such volume that the congregation got the point. Perhaps we need more organists like that.

Dr. Paul Tillich says, "Is our lack of joy due to the fact

99

that we are Christians, or to the fact that we are not suffi-
ciently Christian? . . . The suppression of joy, and guilt about
joy in Christian groups, almost drove me to a break with
Christianity. What passes for joy in these groups is an emaciated, intentionally childish, unexcited, unecstatic thing,
without color and danger, without heights and depths." One
of the great leaders of Christian thought in our time almost
lost his faith because of cheerless Christians.

Dr. Charles W. Eliot, president of Harvard University,
was once in church in London. He wrote home to his son,
"Yesterday we attended M . . .'s church, heard an excellent
sermon, badly delivered. The whole service lacked cheerfulness. The tones of M . . .'s voice and his inflections were
all depressing. It is almost the worst of faults in a preacher.
Faith, hope, and love are all cheerful and ought to be
made to appear so by those who preach them. Life is not
always bright, but religion should be."

18. The Source of Joy

Kaufmann Kohler states in the *Jewish Encyclopedia* that no language has as many words for joy and rejoicing as does Hebrew. In the Old Testament thirteen Hebrew roots, found in twenty-seven different words, are used primarily for some aspect of joy or joyful participation in religious worship.

Hebrew religious ritual demonstrates God as the source of joy. In contrast to the rituals of other faiths of the East, Israelite worship was essentially a joyous proclamation and celebration. The good Israelite regarded the act of thanking God as the supreme joy of his life. Pure joy is joy in God as both its source and object. The psalmist says, "Thou dost show me the path of life; in thy presence there is fulness of joy, in thy right hand are pleasures for evermore" (Psalm 16:11).

Joy Not Earthly

Joy is not found in worldly attainment. Abd-er-Rahman I, the famed monarch of Cordoba, is quoted by Gibbon in his *Decline and Fall of the Roman Empire:* "I have now reigned about fifty years in victory or peace; beloved by my subjects, dreaded by my enemies, and respected by my allies. Riches and honors, power and pleasure, have waited on my call; nor does any earthly blessing appear to have

101

been wanting to my felicity. In this situation I diligently numbered the days of pure and genuine happiness which have fallen to my lot; they amount to fourteen. O man, place not thy confidence in this present world!"

Augustine said, "There is a joy which is not given to the ungodly, but to those who love Thee for Thine own sake, whose joy Thou Thyself art. And this is the happy life, to rejoice in Thee, of Thee, for Thee; this is it, and there is no other."

If God is the source of joy, then Jesus is the perfect picture of joy as we view the New Testament. His whole life and work reveals divine joy. Wherever He went gladness graced the people.

We find joy in the life and work of Christ often where we least expect it. The Bible portrays Christ's suffering on the cross in an atmosphere of joy. "Looking to Jesus the pioneer and perfecter of our faith, who for the joy that was set before him endured the cross, despising the shame, and is seated at the right hand of the throne of God" (Hebrews 12:2). The kind of joy which faces suffering rather than ignoring it is unique to the Christian faith.

Alexander Maclaren wrote, "The highest joy of the Christian always comes through suffering. No flower can bloom in Paradise which is not transplanted from Gethsemane. No one can taste of the fruit of the tree of life, that has not tasted of the fruits of the tree of Calvary. The crown is after the cross."

This understanding of joy also caught on with the early Christians. Luke writes of them, "When they had called in the apostles, they beat them and charged them not to speak in the name of Jesus, and let them go. Then they left the presence of the council, rejoicing that they were counted worthy to suffer dishonor for the name" (Acts 5:40, 41). Peter pointed out the same in 1 Peter 4:12-14. The joy of the Lord was their strength. Nehemiah 8:10.

102

Holy Spirit Brings Joy

If God is the source of joy and Jesus Christ is the perfect picture of joy, then the Holy Spirit is the bringer of joy. It is the fruit of the Spirit. The fruit of joy comes from the life-giving source, the Holy Spirit. The witness is clear that whoever lives under the rule of the Holy Spirit will live in joy through the work of the Holy Spirit. Romans 14:17. Joy is not an appendage. It is a fruit never tacked onto a tree. Fruit is a by-product of life that grows from within. The indwelling Spirit produces this joy.

Joy is as natural and spontaneous to the Spirit-filled Christian as song is to a bird, play to a child, and beauty to a rose.

Joy comes in doing Christ's will. We find it on the path of obedience. Meister Eckhart wrote in the 14th century, "Perfectly to will what God wills, to want what He wants, is to have joy." In John 15 Christ speaks of abiding in Him and obeying Him. Here He speaks of joy. Joy is not having our way but Christ having His way in us.

The secret of joy is to know you are doing what God wants you to do. Your place of service may not be easy or even the kind of job you might have chosen. No matter how good your present job may be, if it is not God's work for you, it can be terribly miserable, no matter how high the financial pay.

Spurgeon said, "If two angels were sent to represent the Lord, one to the court of St. James, the other to sweep the street crossings of London, each would feel equally honored, and each would be equally diligent and faithful in performance of his task."

A man came to the pastor one time and said, "I don't know what's wrong with my life, but that first Christian joy I knew has passed by. I still live a moral life. I go to church. But how can I recover the lost radiance of my

103

faith?" His pastor said, "This is what you should do: go to the store and buy a big basketful of groceries and go to an address of a poor family I will give you. Then when you have given your gift, you sit down to find what they need. Let them know that you are interested in them and that you are their friend. Then lead them in the Lord's Prayer before you leave, and the radiance will come back."

As long as our life is only a matter of contemplation the radiance cannot be recovered. Joy comes in the venture of faith. It comes in desiring to do Christ's will. Joy in the kingdom depends on obedience to God and service to men.

Joy Not in Pleasure or Things

Percy C. Ainsworth tells of a picture hanging in London. It is one of the most tragic pictures ever painted. It portrays the last rough slope of a mountain leading to the edge of a precipice at the foot of which one catches a misty glimpse of a graveyard. A crowd of men and women, some in evening dress, some of the garb of toil, some in rags pack the slope, all struggling for a foothold on the highest point and tearing at and treading upon one another. They are gazing upward where the filmy, beckoning, mocking figure of pleasure floats out of reach. The picture is called *The Pursuit of Pleasure.* On that grim, ghostly sunless canvas the artist had not painted one happy face; not a smile, not a flicker of gladness; nothing but fear, hatred, selfishness, and pain is seen.

That picture tells the story of the world's pursuit of joy. Jesus tells us joy is not found there.

Joy does not depend on circumstances. It does not depend on moods or on our physical or emotional makeup. It is not a matter of temperament or outward happenings, nor of material props. Joy is faith in Jesus Christ and a response to the Holy Spirit.

Happiness is expressed when "everything goes my way." Happiness is an outside feeling due to outside circumstances, what happens. Joy does not depend on right happenings. Paul opened his letter of joy from a Roman prison. Paul and Silas could sing for joy with their backs bleeding, their feet in stocks, and under the threat of death because of their relationship to Christ.

When the world grows darker, a Christian learns that the light shines brighter. The darker the night, the brighter the stars. So a Christian does not despair even when despised. He rejoices in Christ even though persecuted. He can have inner calm even though condemned by man. He has a spiritual eye that sees realities the natural eye cannot see. He has a joy no man can take away.

We cannot fake this kind of joy. It flows from within and from the satisfaction that God through His Spirit lives within us and walks by our side. In the center of suffering and difficulty it remains because it is not the by-product of good happenings but the fruit of the Holy Spirit. It remains because of the abiding relationship with Christ.

Principal Rainy, of whom a child once remarked that she believed he went to heaven every night because he was so happy every day, once used a fine metaphor about a Christian's joy. "Joy," he said, "is the flag which is flown from the castle of the heart when the King is in residence there."

Joy proves to be genuine as we relate to other people and to adversities of life. Real joy is the overflowing jubilance in the middle of suffering. Until one can rejoice in adversity one cannot claim this fruit of the Spirit.

19. Aglow with the Spirit

The face is the index of the person and expresses our inner selves. It reflects the presence of the Holy Spirit in our life. The more fully the Holy Spirit controls our life, the more marked is the spiritual radiance. One of the statements made of Stephen in the early church was that he was "full . . . of the Holy Spirit, . . . all who sat in the council saw that his face was like the face of an angel" (Acts 6: 5, 15). Similar statements are shared concerning numerous Christians who suffered for their faith.

Charles H. Spurgeon in training young ministers said to his students, "When you talk about heaven let your face light up with a heavenly glory. When you tell about hell, your everyday face will do."

Edward Latch, who tells the story, adds, "The everyday face of all too many of us is precisely like that. We have enough to make us miserable but not enough to make us magnificent, to make it a delight; enough to make it pessimistic but not enough to make it optimistic."

J. C. Macaulay in *Life in the Spirit* writes, "Before I left Scotland I had my only opportunity of hearing Dr. F. B. Meyer. At that time he was so enfeebled that he sat in a high chair to preach. The large church was crowded to capacity, and I had a seat far back. Although I well remember the theme and text of other notable preachers whom I heard about that time, I have no recollection of Dr. Meyer's sermon. But this I remember, as clearly as if I were looking at him now, that the radiance of heaven seemed to sit on his brow. His very appearance was the sermon for me that day.

"It was not always so. When F. B. Meyer was a young man, he caught a glimpse of himself in a mirror, and said aloud to himself, 'The face will not do!' It was a lifetime of walking with God, a lifetime of the indwelling and fashioning of the Holy Spirit, that made him the man whose face not only shone, but spoke."

Results in Radiant Living

We will not make it to heaven any sooner by being long-faced and sober. If our sad disposition comes from a lack of faith in what Christ has already done for us, we might not make it at all.

This work of the Holy Spirit is stated simply by the Apostle Paul. "And we all, with unveiled face, beholding the glory of the Lord, are being changed into his likeness from one degree of glory to another; for this comes from the Lord who is the Spirit" (2 Corinthians 3:18). We look to the Lord and the Holy Spirit transforms us into His likeness. When the goodness and glory of the Lord floods our inner life it must stream out in radiant living. The psalmist said, "Let the beauty of the Lord our God be upon us" (Psalm 90:17, KJV).

Macaulay writes, "This radiance is quite unconscious. Moses 'wist not that the skin of his face shone.' I am sure that Stephen was just as unaware of an angelic expression on his countenance. And I am equally certain that Dr. F. B. Meyer had no knowledge that the saintly light of his face was speaking to a youth sitting far back in his audience that night in Glasgow. The men who are most like Christ are least sensible to it."

We must remember that the Holy Spirit's work in our lives draws attention to Jesus. He can't work in the life that seeks to draw attention to self. Paul, who witnessed the death of Stephen, saw the radiance on the face of Stephen. He couldn't forget it. He realized that his own dedication and zeal could not equal Stephen's. Saul could see a new life on the countenance of Stephen. That radiant face condemned Saul. No wonder he finally yielded to Christ who through His Holy Spirit not only changes the inside but covers the outside with His glorious and radiant presence.

A Reflection of the Inner Life

Ralph Waldo Emerson wrote, "There is no beautifier of complexion, or form, or behavior, like the wish to scatter joy and not pain around us. In scattering joy we lift our own spirits and fill our hearts with joy. Joyful spirits and hearts cannot be hidden. What is more beautiful than a sincere smile which surfaces because of radiant joy within. Nothing attracts one to the face of another more than joy.

In the early days of America, tradesmen of all kinds went from door to door by horse and buggy, selling services and offering wares. Itinerant portrait painters often carried an assortment of picture frames with scenic backgrounds and even sketches of human figures, ready to have faces added "to order."

In life each of us still does his own portrait painting. Our countenance becomes the reflection of our inner self. One's face may reflect generosity or greed, confidence or suspicion, joy or defeat.

Joy mirrors our inner spiritual life. Two babies are in a bed. One is bright and laughing; the other is crying and sad. One is well; the other is ill. We see two persons. One is happy, ready to help others with cheerfulness. The other is unhappy, unhelpful, marked by self-centeredness. One is

108

spiritually well; the other is spiritually ill. Joy indicates good spiritual health. So it is not surprising when the story of those early followers of Christ, recorded in Acts, says the disciples were filled with joy and the Holy Spirit.

People who desire to appear righteous generally are joyless people. They are like the Pharisees of Jesus' day, long-faced, fasting, frowning, and complaining. They look on the gloomy side of life.

Best Witness for Christ

People filled with the Spirit radiate the fullness of joy to all they meet. This joy becomes something others desire. As the color of an apple makes us desire it, so the joy of the Christian life attracts others to Christ. Creed never satisfies. Handing a person something to read is not enough. Spiritual desire begins only when a person sees a living example.

The best witnesses for Christ are lighthearted Christians. The oil of joy is God's lubricant to keep the machinery of life from clanking. The Spirit of God brings faith to the heart of man, causes a plant of joy to sprout and spring forth. The Spirit of God causes cheeks to glow and eyes to sparkle with joy.

Joy and laughter are not out of place in a world where the prodigal son can come home to be met by the smile of his father, where the crippled in mind or spirit find healing, where the fearful are given hope, and the guilty are forgiven — all through Christ, the Savior of all men.

20. Again I Say, Rejoice!

John Chrysostom centuries ago observed it is harder to rejoice with those who rejoice than to weep with those who weep. Yet neither fits easily into our stoic age in which we control our emotions so well. Neither fits into the natural man. But the Scripture says in Romans 12:15, "Rejoice with those who rejoice, weep with those who weep."

We probably use the phrases, "I'm sorry for you," and "You have my sympathy," more than the phrase, "I'm happy for you," and "I'm happy it happened to you." Many times here the Spirit tests our lives. Is it easy to rejoice in the success of others? Do we love to rejoice when it goes well with others, particularly those who are doing the same things we are or who are in equal positions?

It is easier to rejoice with those who are above or below us or who have jobs different from ours. The real test of whether the Holy Spirit is producing the fruit of joy in our lives is in our ability to sincerely rejoice in another's success.

Enriched by Sharing

Joy is made richer and sorrow and suffering made easier when others share them with us. We love to share the joyful events, successes, and moments of pleasure with others. To hear the congratulations of a friend, to receive a

110

letter or card, to hear one say, "I'm glad for you, I rejoice with you," adds in a wonderful way to our moment of joy.

To feel that others share your joy without envy is most refreshing! Such sharing of joy is blessed to receive and more blessed to give. This fellowship of joy is possible only to those in Christ and filled with His Spirit.

Sharing achievement and blessing may also appear to be bragging or to satisfy personal pride. This attitude makes it difficult to rejoice with another. The test of Christian love and unselfishness still rests largely with the person who is challenged to rejoice with another in his success.

A mature Christian leader and his wife prayed for years for a work of God to happen in their community. They had a deep desire that people might be renewed and the witness of Christ might be strong. God answered their prayers. A man without great sermons was used of God to start the fires of revival. Confession of sin lasted late into the night. Restitution was made by many. Those who were cold and critical came to repentance and in the days following became some of the clearest and boldest witnesses to God's saving grace.

This test was a difficult one. Their leader became conscious that within him a spirit of criticism had built up. He found he was not rejoicing in the thing he had asked God for so many times. He found small flaws with the methods used and the message preached. He found it hard to appreciate the sharing time, and he did not rejoice with those who were rejoicing.

Then the Spirit spoke clearly to his own life. Why was he critical? Why was he not entering into the experience with others who came in confession of sin and of Christ? Was there a lack of evidence that it was God at work? Certainly not! When he searched his heart, he recognized a spirit of envy. He could not rejoice because God was doing His work through someone else and he was not at the center.

Joy Replaces Envy

That is the test. Envy becomes the great hindrance to real rejoicing with others in their experience of joy and acceptance. Only the Holy Spirit can remove that spirit of envy and replace it with a spirit of rejoicing. But we must respond to the Holy Spirit.

Heathen can weep with those who weep. Only by the Spirit can we rejoice with those who rejoice and find sincere joy in the good which happens to someone else. T. W. Robertson wrote, "To recognize with delight all high and generous and beautiful actions; to find a joy even in seeing the good qualities of your bitterest opponents, and to admire those qualities even in those with whom you have least sympathy, this is the very spirit which can heal the love of slander and of calumny [a malicious charge]."

The fruit of the Spirit produces the ability to see good in others. Even more it makes us able to see and encourage their possibilities. God does this through His Spirit in our own experience. He sees us as we are and as we can become in Christ.

A mother of four was talking about her neighbor who had eight children. "She's amazing! Her house is always neat as a pin; she's a wonderful cook and does her own sewing. Her children are polite and well-behaved. She is active in P.T.A., helps with the Brownies, and is a den-mother for the Cub scouts. She is pretty and has loads of personality. She makes me sick!"

C. S. Lewis observed, "We dislike the big noise at the party because we want to be the big noise." Bacon wrote, "Those are more subject to envy which carry their fortune in an insolent and proud manner."

Pride is basically a competitive thing. Because pride will not permit a person to be in the second spot it lashes out at the person at the peak.

Sympathy makes us "rejoice with those who rejoice, weep with those who weep." Envy reverses the practice, making us rejoice when others weep, and weep when others rejoice. Even when we do not sympathize with friends in their sorrows, envy makes it difficult to exult with them over their successes. Envy withers at another's joy. It becomes silent when another is complimented. The envious person feels others' fortunes are his misfortunes; their profit his loss; their blessing his bane; their promotion his demotion. Phineas Fletcher said of envy, "Sick of a strange disease, another's health."

Are We Like Crabs?

Charles L. Allen in *The Miracle of Love* writes of a fisherman friend who told him that one never needs a top for his crab basket. If one of the crabs starts to climb up the sides of the basket, the other crabs will reach up and pull it back down. Some people are a lot like crabs.

Leslie B. Flynn wrote, "But because it is not a gross fleshly sin, but rather slinky and subtle, envy can conceal itself under the guise of friendship, visiting in people's houses, dining with them, chumming with them, and all the time envying them. Or it can worm its way into church with little trouble. If someone suffers a temper tantrum in church, everyone around gets the benefit. If you envy, your closest neighbor need not know." No wonder the Scripture says, "A sound heart is the life of the flesh; but envy the rottenness of the bones" (Prov. 14:30, KJV).

"Rejoice with those who rejoice." It is the natural thing to complain when another wins or gets a prominent position. Paul could have complained more than any of us because while he was imprisoned, others were preaching in his place. Some criticized him for his preaching. They inferred that had he done things right he would be free. It

113

was his own fault. They spoke against him and added hurt to hurt. But the apostle rejoiced that Christ was preached. He said, "In that I rejoice. Yes, and I shall rejoice" (Philippians 1:18, 19). Paul was filled with the Spirit and demonstrated that the fruit of the Spirit was in his life.

Might it be that the answer to an inferiority complex is to rejoice in our neighbor's progress, or as Jesus said, to "love your neighbor as yourself"? When we turn from being a status seeker to a lover of others, we lose our inferiority complex.

Sydney Smith suggests, "Try to make at least one other person happy every day, and then in ten years you may have made three thousand, six hundred and fifty persons happy, or brightened a small town by your contribution to the fund of general enjoyment."

21. Praise — Joy's Twin

An English preacher by the name of Pulsford wrote years ago, "There is no heaven, either in this world, or in the world to come, for people who do not praise God. If you do not enter into the spirit and worship of heaven how should the spirit and joy of heaven enter into you? Selfishness makes long prayers, but love makes short prayers, that it may continue longer in praise."

There is an imaginative story about a conversation with Lucifer after he was cast out of heaven. He was asked what he missed most since he was cast out of heaven. "The trumpets," said Lucifer, "the trumpets in the morning." He no longer heard the note of praise.

Praise is the identical twin of joy. Joy is more inward; praise is more outward. Joy is pressure in the system while praise is the safety valve letting go. In our attempt to preserve Christianity from emotionalism and fanaticism we reject the expression of love, joy, and peace — *praise*. The frosty years of dry, drab religion can be conquered only by a fresh awareness of the precious joy the Spirit gives us in response to our praise. We have stressed discipleship, duty, and obedience in such a way that we have neglected the note of joy and praise.

Let's Limber Up

Leonard Evans tells how he was trying to undo his "stuffy training." He was a great minister at a church in Harlem and stood meeting members one by one. They came down the aisle singing and clapping on their way to meet him. Suddenly a great big, tall lady stood in front of him. "Sir, do you mind if I make a suggestion?" Evans encouraged her. She took both his hands and lifted them high above his head and said, "Man, limber up, man, limber up." From then on he began to realize how controlled his life was.

William Law, in his *Serious Call to a Devout and Holy Life* writes, "Would you know who is the greatest saint in the world? It is not he who prays most or fasts most; it is not he who gives most alms, or is most eminent for temperance, chastity, or justice, but it is he who is always thankful to God, who wills everything that God willeth, who receives everything as an instance of God's goodness, and has a heart always ready to praise God for it."

Praise is faith at work. Praise lifts our thoughts from that which distracts and drags us down. Praise opens our eyes and lifts them to the Lord of all, the Victor over all. It puts the enemy to flight. Praise pulls back the clouds Satan puts over our eyes and gives us clear sight so we can see our Lord who has every need of ours under His control. Praise magnifies our Father and multiplies our faith.

Praise lifts our eyes from the circumstances to the Creator, the One who rules over all. Allen Bowman said, "It was a glad day in my life when I broke through the last barrier of doubt into the glorious freedom of continuous praise to the Lord. Only when we 'continually offer up a sacrifice of praise to God' (Hebrews 13:15) can joy flow like a river.

"I must confess that for many years I praised God only when pleasant people and pleasant circumstances came my way. When adversity and disappointment struck, the praise died down. . . .

"But what about the thoughtless acts of friends and relatives? What about those traits of wife and children that irritated me day after day? And difficult colleagues? And sermons that bored me? . . .

"Needless to say my experience of grace during those years was a checkered one. Joy alternated with gloom, and triumph with defeat. The statement that 'the joy of the Lord is your strength' (Nehemiah 8:10) was not very meaningful to me.

"What I failed to see clearly was that folks who troubled and thwarted me, hardships that caused me headache — yes, even the frustrating mistakes I made -- were all part and parcel of God's loving care and love for me; that through trials as well as through enjoyments He was seeking to teach me the lessons I needed to learn. He wanted to burn out the dross and to make me 'a vessel for noble use, consecrated and useful to the master of the house, ready for any good work' (2 Timothy 2:21)."

In lines he called "God's Handwriting," John Oxenham said:

He wrote in characters too grand
For our short sight to understand;
We catch but broken strokes, and try
To fathom all the mystery
Of withered hopes, of death, of life,
The endless war, the useless strife —
But there, with larger, clearer sight,
We shall see this — His way was right. [1]

---

1. Reprinted by permission of the American Tract Society, Oradell, New Jersey.

117

Praise, the Language of Heaven

Praise hallows and puts happiness in all it touches. It kindles new faith and fans the sparks of smoldering love into a flaming love for God. The Apostle Paul said, "Be not drunk with wine, wherein is excess; but be filled with the Spirit; speaking to yourselves in psalms and hymns and spiritual songs, singing and making melody in your heart to the Lord" (Ephesians 5:18, 19, KJV). J. B. Phillips paraphrases it, "Don't get your stimulus from wine (for there is always the danger of excessive drinking) but let the Spirit stimulate your souls. Express your joy in singing among yourselves psalms and hymns and spiritual songs, making music in your hearts for the ears of God!"

Praise not only honors God but is also for our good. In Dostoevski's book, *The Brothers Karamazov*, Ivan imagines he sees Satan and a conversation follows. Satan says, "If I could praise God, I would cease to be a devil." His character would have to change.

Sorrow and sadness for sin are necessary. Many do not sense the full freedom and joy of forgiveness because they do not praise God for His cleansing in Christ. As someone suggested, "Praise is the melodious affirmation of God's person and power."

"Without praise," says W. Glyn Evans, "we automatically resort to complaining, a disease which destroyed the Israelites in the wilderness. A careful reading of Psalm 95 shows the admonition 'Harden not your hearts,' was given against refusing to praise, not against refusing to believe. On second thought, a murmuring, complaining, whining Christian is an unbelieving Christian. So 'harden not your hearts' when asked to praise God in adversity." Billy Bray named one foot "Glory" and the other "Hallelujah." Then whether he walked through the valley of trials or in the garden of blessing, his feet said, "Glory, Hallelujah."

118

Clothed with Praise

The Bible is full of praise and joy. "Be glad in the Lord, and rejoice, ye righteous; and shout for joy, all ye that are upright in heart!" "Make a joyful noise unto God, all ye lands; sing forth the honour of his name, make his praise glorious." There is the promise that God will give, even to those who mourn, "beauty for ashes, the oil of joy for mourning, the garment of praise for the spirit of heaviness" (Isaiah 61:3, KJV). Our part is to put on the garment of praise, God's part is to supply the comfort and oil of joy.

J. H. Jowett years ago referred to the words of the Christian Apollinaries in Ibses's *The Emperor Julian* as he looked at the great army of the emperor massed against the soldiers of the cross: "Verily I say unto you, so long as song rings out above our sorrows, Satan shall never conquer!" Dr. Jowett added, "I too will say that our praise is an invincible armor — we sing our way to the triumph we seek."

The day before John Wesley died in 1791 he asked for his clothes. He wanted to rise from bed. He began to sing Isaac Watts' great hymn in such spirit his family was amazed:

I'll praise my Maker while I've breath,
And when my voice is lost in death,
Praise shall employ my nobler powers.

So it is. Those who know the privilege and power of praise in the present look forward to singing the great songs of the redeemed in glory. Then shall there be perfect praise and fullness of joy forever.

George Herbert, a seventeenth century British minister-poet, left the church a rich legacy of devotional verse. In a short stanza he titled "Our Prayer," Herbert wrote:

Thou hast given so much to me,
Give one thing more — a grateful heart;
Not thankful when it pleaseth me,
As if Thy blessing had spare days;
But such a heart, whose pulse may be
Thy praise.

22. The Joy of Sharing

An early historian remarked that he could tell a pagan by the ugly pleasures he indulges in, an atheist by his sourness, and a Christian by his joy.

Roy Koch says, "Joy is the seasoning that tickles the taste buds of the unsaved. Theology, creed, or efficiency of organization cannot compare with joy in making Christ appealing to others."

Christianity loses its power to evangelize when it loses its joy, and a preacher is a heretic when he stands in the pulpit pretending to preach the gospel and speak these great truths without joy. Lack of joy may be the result of spiritual immaturity. Unripe fruit is sour. Only when the sun has ripened and mellowed the fruit does it become sweet and luscious. Green and sour souls are crabbed and full of acid as someone described them. They need to grow sweet and mellow under the smiling sun of God's grace.

An unhappy Christian is an unspiritual person. He has not yet learned that Christ's kingdom is characterized by joy in the Holy Spirit. The witness of Christianity has always been carried on the waves of song.

Christianity Sings Its Way

William Jones once said, "It is thrilling to recall that Christianity began with a song. It has been through this medium that it spread throughout the world, and it has been one of its most unique expressions of faith in this way. In considering the methods that other religions use in proclaiming their message to our civilization, it is revealing to discover that there is no other religion that sings its way into the hearts of the people as does Christianity. Our religion has been most successfully expressed through music and poetry and in so doing has produced a high note of joy in the worship of God that no other religion has captured."

Down through the ages many saints demonstrated the same deep abiding joy that Paul and Silas did when they sang praises unto God at midnight.

"A happy man or woman is a better thing to find than a five-pound note . . . and their entrance into a room is as though another candle had been lighted," said Robert Louis Stevenson. A saint of the past wrote, "The joy of the Holy Spirit must be engraved on our countenance for the glory of God so that we may draw souls to His service."

Samuel Shoemaker one time told the story of a person he describes as "one of the greatest saints" he ever knew. She was an old woman in New York who was struck when a tire flew off a passing truck and broke her hip. She was in the hospital in great pain yet said with a smile, "Well, I wonder what God has for me to do here!" On her back she could not read her Bible so she asked the nurse to read it to her. The nurse was a skeptic at first but not when she left. The radiance she saw reflected from this lady's face changed her.

That radiance is the love of God shed abroad in the heart. This radiance of inward joy flows forth as a powerful witness of complete confidence that God knows what He is doing and is interested in the best for us. It is the joy the world can neither know, give, or take away.

Our Crown of Rejoicing

Greatest of all joys is the joy we experience when we lead another person to Jesus. This was Paul's crown of rejoicing. Philippians 4:1. A story is told concerning John A. Broadus, the scholar and homiletical professor. The day following his conversion he went to one of his schoolmates, Sandy Jones, a red-haired, awkward chap, and asked him to become a Christian. And Sandy said, "Well, I don't know. Perhaps I will." Sure enough, soon after that, in a little church Sandy accepted Christ. Immediately Sandy walked across that little meetinghouse, held out his hand, and said, "I thank you, John; I thank you, John."

Dr. Broadus left the little town and became a great scholar, exegete, and seminary president. Every summer when he returned home, Sandy, the awkward, red-haired farmer, came up to him, stretched out his great bony hand, and said, "Howdy, John, I never forget you, John."

When Dr. Broadus was on his deathbed, he said: "I rather think the sound sweetest to my ears in heaven next to the welcome of Him whom not having seen, I have tried to love and serve, will be the welcome of Sandy Jones, as he will thrust out his great hand and say, 'Howdy, John! Thank you, John; thank you, John.'"

The Hebrew writer tells the leadership of the church to be faithful so that they will be able to give a final report to God with joy rather than with grief. Hebrews 13:17. William Barclay wrote, "When Samuel Rutherford was lying in jail for his faith, his mind went back to the little parish Anwoth where he had lived, ministered, and worked. He was thinking of the people he had taught and loved there and he was thinking of the end which he could not now escape. Mrs. Cousins puts his thoughts at that moment into words:

Fair Anwoth on the Solway
   To me thou still art dear,
Ev'n from the verge of heaven
   I drop for thee a tear.
Oh, if one soul from Anwoth
   Shall meet me at God's right hand,
My heaven will be two heavens
   In Emmanuel's land. [1]

---

1. William Barclay, *op. cit.*, p. 83.

Peace Fruit

23 Just Say, Shalom!

Before a recent trip to Israel, my good friend, Ken Wilson, editor of *Christian Herald,* told me, "If ever you do not know what to say in Israel, just say Shalom. It covers many things." This Hebrew greeting of peace, which means everything from "hello," and absence of ill will to health and heaven is particularly striking with all the signs of war in our world.

Peace, a most common word today, is on the lips of every news reporter, on the pages of every publication. We hear politicians speak of a "just and durable" or a "just and honorable" peace. Peace is part of the conversation of the average person as well as every ruler. Yet peace is a strange word for the twentieth century. Our world is rampant with nationalism, imperialism, racism, militarism, militant communism, and division.

People everywhere speak of peace because all desire peace. Thomas a Kempis wrote, "All men desire peace, but very few desire those things that make for peace." Out of the desire for peace a rabbi pens a plea for *"peace of mind."* A priest drives home his thoughts in his book *Peace of Soul.* And an evangelist preaches peace in his book *Peace with God.* Religious and political leaders have risen to make a plea for peace.

But What Is Peace?

Many times we give a false meaning to peace. On the personal level peace comes with old age, settling down in a country home in the quiet of nature. Or peace is a lad fishing for suckers on a lazy afternoon. In the family peace exists when no quarrels or verbal battles occur. In the church peace happens when the preacher doesn't say anything upsetting or when members are satisfied with the status quo. On the national level people think peace is the absence of war and when the oppressed do not cause any opposition or commotion.

The search for peace is not new. All the philosophers of all ages wistfully longed for peace and to find the meaning and way of peace. Some philosophers proposed that peace is the removal of desire and others said peace is the death of emotion. Still others said peace is the ability to maintain absolute indifference or is self-sufficiency which does not allow itself to become dependent on anyone or anything, defended by the determination not to care. One might say that all the philosophers saw peace as the absence of pain either in mind or body.

But what really is the peace of which the Bible speaks? In particular what is the peace which Paul says is the result of the Holy Spirit's indwelling? Is it the peace of detachment, self-isolation, and insulation?

Like the other fruit of the Spirit, peace is not merely or primarily a personal relationship between God and us. It is not detachment from the cares and concerns of life. Peace, in the Bible sense, is a right relationship in every sphere of life, with God and men.

Shalom

First, look at the Old Testament word for peace, Shalom. The New Testament concept of peace arises more out of

Shalom than out of the common concept which was current in New Testament times or before. It is not a negative word. Shalom was the familiar, friendly Jewish greeting, used in asking about the health and welfare of anyone. It refers to everything that makes for a person's highest good.

Shalom is not simply the absence of having war or trouble. It is prayer and hope that all is well. It not merely refrains from speaking evil but speaks good. Shalom reflects a relationship of concern and care between two persons, two nations, between God and His people.

We find the New Testament a book of peace. It mentions peace eighty-eight times and occurs in each New Testament book. The New Testament word has much the same meaning as Shalom in the Old Testament. Many of the letters of the New Testament bring together the pagan greeting "grace" and the Jewish greeting "peace" in "grace to you and peace." In Christ persons are brought together.

William Barclay points out that in the New Testament peace has certain sources from which it comes. First, peace comes from believing. Romans 15:13. It is "peace with God through our Lord Jesus Christ" (Romans 5:1). Peace comes when we stake our lives on what God says concerning Jesus. Second, peace comes from belief which has turned to action. Peace is not merely passive but it flows forth from active obedience in what God wills.

Jesus exhorted His disciples, "Have salt in yourselves, and be at peace one with another" (Mark 9:50). Paul says, "Live in peace, and the God of love and peace will be with you" (2 Corinthians 13:11). "Strive for peace with all men" (Hebrews 12:14). Third, peace is from God and so passes all human understanding (Philippians 4:7) or power to create. God is therefore called the "God of peace." Peace is at the center of ourselves if God is at the center of our thoughts. "You will guard him and keep him in perfect and constant peace whose mind is stayed on You, because he commits himself to You, leans on You and hopes confidently in You" (Isaiah 26:3, Amplified).

Peace from Within

A reporter asked the late President Herbert Hoover, "Mr. President, how do you handle criticism? Do you ever get agitated or tense?"

"No," President Hoover said, seemingly surprised at the question, "of course not."

"But," the reporter went on, "when I was a boy you were one of the most popular men in the world. Then, for a while you became one of the most unpopular, with nearly everyone against you. Didn't any of this meanness and criticism ever get under your skin?"

"No, I knew when I went into politics what I might expect, so when it came I wasn't disappointed or upset," he said. He lowered his familiar bushy eyebrows and looked directly into the reporter's eyes. "Besides, I have 'peace at the center,' you know," he added.

Inner peace comes from looking to God, our source. Fourth, peace is the gift of Jesus Christ. Jesus, before leaving His disciples, said, "Peace I leave with you; my peace I give to you" (John 14:27).

Finally, peace within is possible as the Spirit of Christ reigns within. The fruit of the Spirit is peace.

24. The Prince of Peace

Of all the prophecies which foretold the coming of Christ, none is more familiar or more loved than the first seven verses of Isaiah 9. The great darkness that settled over Judah and Israel at this time was typical of the night of sin which would be over the same land at the time of the coming of the Messiah. Out of this gloom the prophet foresaw the coming of One who would bring both light and victory over the "land of the shadow of death." The prophet pictures one of the most beautiful scenes of the person and work of Christ that we have in the Scriptures 700 years before Christ's birth.

Nowhere is the person and work of Christ more apparent than in the array of names which Isaiah uses to describe Christ. "Wonderful" suggests the many wonderful things concerning His birth, ministry, death, resurrection, and ascension. "Counselor" brings to mind the matchless instruction which He uttered, preserved in the Gospels. "The Mighty God" reveals His duty as the Son of God and equal with God. That He had the might of God was demonstrated by His power over demons, nature, disease, and death. "The Everlasting Father" tells us He was from everlasting to everlasting.

Then follows the name we especially notice now, "The Prince of Peace." It forecasts the message of the angels at Christ's birth, "On earth peace, good will toward men." This title tells the peaceable nature of Christ and His kingdom. His gospel is that of peace, requiring His disciples to be at peace. The Prince of Peace has come.

Christ Still a Stranger

To most of the world Jesus is still a stranger as the Prince of Peace. Although foretold concerning Him so many years before, expressed so clearly at His birth, taught so pointedly during His life, and demonstrated so dramatically in His death, Christ, as the Prince of Peace seems vague.

At Christ's birth all heaven let earth know that Christ came and His coming was to bring peace — peace in the heart and peace between persons and nations. "Peace on earth" was the angels' refrain. Zacharias, filled with the Holy Spirit, prophesied concerning Christ's coming that Christ is sent "to give light to them that sit in darkness and in the shadow of death, to guide our feet into the way of peace" (Luke 1:79, KJV).

During Christ's life He taught peace and called His disciples to this way. The Sermon on the Mount refers to the essence of Jesus' teachings. The truths taught here are nearly all repeated later in other portions of the New Testament. We know the spirit and truth which pervades the Beatitudes. "Blessed are the poor in spirit [not the proud]." "Blessed are the meek [not the arrogant]." "Blessed are the peacemakers. . . ."

Do these teachings find expression in our lives? Are they not the laughingstock of many Christians today when it comes to practicing them? Robert E. Goodrich, Jr., in *Dear God, Where Are You?* writes, "Furthermore, we are persuaded that if we practiced them in our personal lives we would be called 'crackpots' and probably suffer all kinds of ridicule and persecution. And we may be right! A cartoon pictured a young man, beard and all, standing on a street corner holding a sign which had only one word on it: 'peace.' And across the street two women were yelling at him, 'Troublemaker.' Something like that would probably happen to us if we were to put almost any one of the

Beatitudes on a sign and walk down Main Street.

"But we cherish the Beatitudes as poetry; we love the sound of the words. It is just that we cannot be expected to make fools of ourselves living them out day by day." [1]

Everything we know of Christ points us to the way of peace — His birth, His teachings, and His death. The Apostle Peter points out Christ's path is to be ours. 1 Peter 2:21-24.

The Great Betrayal

Paul says Christ brought "peace through the cross." Without a doubt the betrayal of the centuries is that the church which claims the benefits of the cross for salvation usually refuses the way of the cross in daily relationships. The temptation is to use Christ's name and call upon Him as our leader while we use methods He never allowed or blessed.

Robert Eyton wrote in 1895, "Nothing seems to show the absolute departure of the spirit of the church from the Spirit of Christ in so glowing a light as the history of Christianity in reference to wars. When one takes war to bits and thinks what it is and what it involves — the fierce and brutal passions that it stimulates, the hatreds which it inspires, the deadly ingenuity about the means of killing and maiming which it produces, the helpless crowd of men it sweeps off in the prime of their lives, the odious ambition of which it is too often the expression — when one takes it all to bits and looks at each piece without the false glamor which success so often casts over the general idea; when one strips off the fine phrases about dying for one's country, and honestly looks the facts in the face that so often men have been butchered like sheep — their homes made

---

1. Robert E. Goodrich, Jr., *Dear God, Where Are You?* (Waco: Word Books, 1969), pp. 30, 31.

desolate for some tyrant's whim or some noble's envy, it is hard to see how the whole history of the Christian attitude on the subject of war has been anything better than a great evasion."

Robert Saed suggested that had the heads of the church sat at the heads of nations there probably would have been no less wars. What a betrayal of the real head of the church — the Prince of Peace!

Since the first three centuries never have the clergy as a body exerted themselves to prevent or abridge any great war. Sad that ecclesiastical influence was very strangely at work promoting great wars, stimulating fanaticism of the crusader, or stirring up the hideous massacre.

Individuals spoke and worked against war but not the church as a whole.

Puritans praised God after burning an Indian village and destroying everyone inside, young and old. Is this the kind of religion for which Christ died? It is precisely because He substituted life for murder, truth for lies, love for hate that He has won the admiration of the ages. The iniquity of trying to use Him to sanctify war is that it makes Him into the exact opposite of all He was and stood for.

No one has ever dared paint a picture of Christ with a sword in His hand. All that the sword stands for is diametrically opposed to everything Jesus taught, lived, and died for. He, the Prince of Peace, has come to fill His followers with divine love, and love does not kill.

In all ways Christ calls us to preach peace. He comes to us as the Prince of Peace.

25. Peace, Perfect Peace

More then six hundred years ago the great poet Dante stood before the doors of a monastery. Three times the nobles asked him what he sought. At last the weary man said, "I seek peace."

So the search for peace is as old as man. In John 14: 27, KJV, Jesus said to His sad disciples, "Peace I leave with you, my peace I give unto you: not as the world giveth, give I unto you. Let not your heart be troubled, neither let it be afraid."

Peace results from a right relation to God. We cannot have peace with a wrong relationship to God. Our relation to others determines our relationship to God. God promises us a threefold peace — with Himself, with ourselves, and with others. True peace follows in that order. When at peace with God, we can be at peace with ourselves. Only then can we be at peace with others. If we fight against God we cannot experience peace.

Bunyan in *Grace Abounding* tells how he found peace, "I remember that one day as I was musing on the wickedness and blasphemy of my heart, and considering the enmity that was in me to God, that the Scripture came into my mind, He hath made 'peace through the blood of his cross' — by which I was made to see again and again that God and my soul were friends by His blood — yea, I saw that the justice of God and my sinful soul could embrace and kiss each other through His blood. This was a good day to me; I hope I shall never forget it."

Is Peace Possible?

"Peace, perfect peace, in this dark world of sin?" Sometimes in singing this song we do not catch the question that Edward Bickersteth asks. "Is it possible to have peace in a dark world of sin?"

Apart from the dark world of sin, of war, and of unrest, is it possible to experience peace with inner fears, frustrations, and failures? Yes, the writer says it is possible.

Yes, the Scripture also says. But not the kind of peace man provides; not the peace pursued at peace tables. It is not a negotiated peace. This peace is God's own peace, shed abroad in our hearts by the Holy Spirit.

This peace of God must, first of all, be peace with God. Unless our relationship with God is right, no peace is possible. Second, the peace of God is peace with ourselves. As long as we are torn by conflicting or contending loyalties there can be no peace. Only as we settle the supreme loyalty can we have peace within. Then it is peace with others. We cannot claim to have peace with God and be at odds with others.

God provides peace with Him through Christ, who took the penalty of our sin; peace with ourselves because He cleanses us from a guilty conscience; and peace with others, for God in Christ breaks down the walls which separate.

God did not wait for a peaceful world to send the Christmas angels with their song of peace and good will. Roman aggression and violence caused a nameless dread to settle into a sense of frustration. At such a time God sent peace through His Son.

Flows from Forgiveness

Peace flows from forgiveness in Christ. "Therefore being justified by faith, we have peace with God through our Lord Jesus Christ" (Rom. 5:1, KJV).

Peace results from undeviating devotion to God's will. "Thou dost keep him in perfect peace, whose mind is stayed on thee" (Isaiah 26:3). We lack peace when we let our minds center on ourselves. The fitful, frustrated, fearful mind centers on self. As selfishness can never bring satisfaction, so putting our own concern first never produces peace. The psalmist says the secret of peace is to center our minds on God — who He is, what His will is, and the fulfillment of His will. Joy comes not in doing our own will but in doing the divine will.

This peace remains in spite of circumstances. As shock absorbers in a car do not remove the stones from the rough highways, neither does Christ remove the difficulties and the disappointments from our lives. But Christ and His peace within enable us to travel life's hard roads with inner peace, assurance, and joy. The sorrows of the saints are no less severe than the sorrows of sinners. But the saints are kept in perfect peace because they have Christ within.

We lack peace when we let our minds center on circumstances. Circumstances distract, and double our doubts. We doubt God's care when we fix our minds on the adverse, the unexpected, the ill-happening rather than on the God who knows the end from the beginning. Temptation and trial tell us to turn our minds on God. God promises perfect peace not to the fearful and doubting heart but to the heart which puts all its confidence in Him.

"The hour is coming, indeed it has come, when you will be scattered, every man to his home, and will leave me alone; yet I am not alone, for the Father is with me. I have said this to you, that in me you may have peace. In the world you have tribulation; but be of good cheer, I have overcome the world" (John 16:32, 33).

Confidence in God

Peace comes from confidence in God's keeping power. The psalmist says, "In peace I will both lie down and sleep; for thou alone, O Lord, makest me dwell in safety" (Psalm 4:8).

One evening when Luther saw a little bird perched on a tree to roost for the night he said, "This little bird has had its supper, and now it is getting ready to go to sleep here, quite secure and content, never troubling itself what its food will be, or where its lodging on the morrow. Like David, it 'abides in the shadow of the Almighty.' It sits on its little twig content and lets God take care."

What peace can exceed that which rests in the will of God? To know that we are in the will of God means that we are safe regardless of what happens. It means that we abide under the shadow of the Almighty. We yield ourselves to His providence.

Trusting ourselves to God's providence does not always mean protection from danger or even death. It does mean that we have such confidence in Him that we trust ourselves to His care whatever may happen. Doing this we can rest, for there is no safer place than dwelling in God's will. This is peace.

That great missionary to China, Hudson Taylor, passed through trials which tested his faith almost beyond endurance. On one such occasion a letter from a friend restored him to trust and peace.

Taylor said, "When my agony of soul was at its height, a letter was used to reveal to me the truth of our oneness with Jesus." The letter declared that faith is

138

strengthened, not by striving after more faith, but by resting in the faithfulness of God. As he read the letter, the text came to his mind, "If we believe not, yet he abideth faithful." So he looked to Jesus and said to himself, "I'll strive no more, for has He not promised never to fail me? And He never will!"

When a boy, I was asked to go alone to the house of a certain man with whom I was totally unacquainted. I knew he was an important person. I had inner fears. I was hesitant at every step. I finally mustered extra nerve to knock at his door and deliver my message.

From the first few moments in this great man's presence my heart was at peace. He put me at ease with his gracious welcome into the house. He made me feel accepted by the way he introduced me to his family. I knew he trusted me and I could trust him by what he asked of me. Becoming acquainted with him put me at peace.

Today, as I read the words of Job, this experience takes on added meaning. "Acquaint now thyself with him, and be at peace" (Job 22:21, KJV). My heart is at peace because I have an acquaintance with God through Jesus Christ. His loving welcome to come to Him, His full acceptance of me just as I am, and His giving me work to do in His kingdom all give me peace.

As I learn to know Him better, I see Him as one who is over all. He is in control. The world is in His hand. The small world of persons and work which I know, He knows even better than I. He will not allow me to be tempted above that which I am able to bear. He provides a way of escape as I turn to Him. The more I acquaint myself with Him, the more at peace I am. Those times when I grow fearful and restless are the times I forget who He is and whose I am.

An unknown poet wrote:

Thou shalt know Him when He comes,
Not by any din of drums,
Nor by anything He wears,
Neither by His crown,
Nor by His gown,
But His presence known shall be,
By the holy harmony
Which His coming makes in thee.

26. Our Common Cause

From the beginning of time people have tried to reconcile differences of opinion. Christ came to reconcile persons. Difference of opinion will always exist in one degree or another. Large souls are not separated by these. Challenged, yes; but divided, no. When people are brought together in Christ, Christian grace and love prevail in spite of differences.

Communism teaches that all must think alike, live alike, and hate alike. Unwittingly Christians try to demand the same thing. This way is unknown in the New Testament. Paul in Romans 14 tells us not to despise another who differs.

When the apostle describes the new relationship which must exist in the church, he says the unity of the Spirit should be maintained in the bond of peace. Ephesians 4:31. In Colossians he says we are to let the peace of God rule in our hearts. Colossians 3:15. This means to let God's Word rule in our decisions. Decisions in the church should not be ruled by personal ambition, pride, position, or any other spirit but by the peace God makes possible in all our relationships.

Scripture Used for Division

Christ said, "I have not come to bring peace, but a sword" (Matthew 10:34). Did you ever hear this verse used as a reason for division among Christians? Or 2 Corinthians 6:17, "Come out from them, and be separate from them." Ever hear this quoted as a call to separate from fellow Christians? Other Scriptures are also twisted at times or lifted out of context in order to contend that Scripture sanctions Christians being at odds or for churches to divide over one issue or another.

Of course, with the use of such statements, it is assumed that the wrong is always on the opposite side and we are called to draw a sword and say it's time to separate. Things have gone far enough! Many justify church splits on the basis of these Scriptures.

Perhaps we should look sincerely at such Scriptures. For instance, the first Scripture above is a statement by Jesus given in the context of hostile and devilish forces working against Christ and His followers. The sword is drawn between the followers of Christ and the opposers or enemies of Christ. The sword is not between fellow Christian believers. Even where there is a sword dividing the enemies of Christ and the followers of Christ, the enemies or unbelievers do the sword drawing.

Look at the context. The enemies of Christ call Him and His followers Beelzebul. The enemies of Christ hate, persecute, and seek to divide the followers of Christ. The sword is between those who deny Christ and those who follow Him.

In the second Scripture above, those from whom we are to separate ourselves are unbelievers, the unrighteous, those still in darkness, and those who are idolaters.

What a misuse of Scripture to apply such statements of Christ so that we can justify division! It is completely out of keeping both with the tenor of Scripture and with the teachings of Christ. We are to expect that the world will not adopt us as its friends. Further, we are to separate from the world in our calling, commitment, and conduct. But as saints we are called to be united. Scripture teaches clearly that we are to build each other up, to pray for all saints, and when in error to restore each other in the spirit of meekness. The attitude too often is when another is in error, one must separate himself to remain pure. The concern to restore is absent.

If at any time we are tempted to quote Scripture to sanction division or separation between fellow Christians or to suggest that any division is divinely directed or predicted we had better look more carefully at the context. We will find that the division or cleavage spoken of is not between one Christian and another but between the believer and the unbeliever, the Christ follower and the Christ denier, and between God and the devil.

We need to search more sincerely to seek to follow those Scriptures which speak about love, forbearance, long-suffering, and mercy which we should demonstrate to each other. These are abundant and speak of the relation of Christians. God never calls true believers to divide but rather to demonstrate all the graces of the Spirit even as God for Christ's sake demonstrates these toward us continually.

Live by What We Love

Some persons become fast friends by having the same enemies. In Jesus' day opponents like the Pharisees and Herodians banded together to trap Jesus. The opposing groups of Pharisees and Sadducees also united against the Apostle Paul.

Times and persons change little. Some churches find a unity in what and whom they are against. Anyone can build

143

a quick following by taking a stand against something or someone. Most persons know better why they stay away from other churches than why they attend their own. They are long on what they hate and short on what they love.

Ilion T. Jones in *God's Everlasting Yes* says, "That person is already spiritually dying who tries to live by his disgusts instead of his admirations, by the things he is angry at or hates instead of the things he loves."

A person proves his opposition to unrighteousness and untruth more by dedication to Jesus Christ and the declaration of truth than by denunciation of wrong.

Some take seriously only the things they don't believe. These things really excited them. Pity the husband and wife who try to hold their marriage together by stressing what they oppose. Pity the church which seeks its unity around its disagreements with other churches. Shared divisiveness as well as shared doubts and disbeliefs will destroy.

Remember, souls live on what is believed and not on what is denied, doubted, or damned. The church and society live by banding together in a common cause rather than around a common enemy.

Repeating Mistakes Not Necessary

Francis Schaeffer, in his booklet, *The Mark of the Christian*, raises a question which strikes at the core of many spiritual problems: "How can we exhibit the oneness Christ commands without sharing in the other man's mistakes?" The author then lists a few ways by which we can practice and show this oneness even where we most differ.

First, he says, "We should never come to such differences with true Christians without regret and without tears." Rather than taking this approach we have often experienced satisfaction in finding others' sins. "We build ourselves up by tearing other men down." Our spirit of disagreement displays more the love of blood than the love of God. Paul's admonition in Galatians 6 to go "in the spirit of meekness" considering that we too may fall, is still good advice.

Second, Schaeffer says, "In proportion to the gravity of what is wrong between true Christians, it is important consciously to exhibit a seeable love to the world." The more serious the differences the more necessary it is that we not only speak for God's holiness but also demonstrate to the world and each other our love for one another. The reverse is usually the case. The greater the difference the more we hate. Yet the more serious the difference the more we need time for prayer and Holy Spirit guidance. We often think that the more serious the difference the quicker we can cut each other off.

A third point is that "we must show a practical demonstration of love in the midst of the dilemma even when it is costly. . . . In other words, we must do whatever must be done, at whatever cost, to show this love." We must declare what is wrong but according to 1 Corinthians 6:1-7 we must be ready to suffer loss in a practical way rather than destroy the observable oneness of Christians.

"A fourth way we can show and exhibit love without sharing in our brother's mistake is to approach the problem with a desire to solve it, rather than with a desire to win." The author points out that nobody loves to win more than a theologian. What is our desire when we discuss differences? Too often we must confess our desire to come out on top regardless. We make progress when we, in love, desire a solution rather than a victory.

Finally we can show a practical, observable love to the world without sharing in our brother's mistake by realizing it is easy to compromise wrong. We usually stress this one. But it is just as necessary that we do not forget to exhibit the love of Christ. We've had a lot of church conferences, says Schaeffer, to point out "the principle of the practice

145

of purity" of the church in relation to doctrine. But have we ever had a conference to point out "the principle of the practice of an observable love and oneness among all true Christians?"

So we spend much time over the point of doctrine and forget about the pattern of peace and unity by which the world knows we are Christ's or not. One cannot expect the world to understand our doctrines or differences. One thing they can see, however, is the oneness and love of those who love Christ and each other in the face of differences.

In fact the world is better able to see our love and believe in Christ when love is present in the midst of differences than when we get in little cliques where we all think and practice alike.

Years ago a beautiful little girl wandered out one cold day into the countryside of Canada. The family finally realized she was lost and started a search. Then they called the people of the community together. Each went his own way. It became dark and the cold of the Canadian winter settled down. After some time someone suggested the searchers join hands and cover the grass fields. But it was too late. They found the girl curled up, frozen in the cold. Then the shout went up, "If only we had joined hands before!" The spiritual meaning of this story is clear.

27. Broken Barriers

G. G. Parker of Manhasset, New York, writes in the *Pulpit Digest*, "We can't tell the story of the tragedy of today's world without talking about walls." The Apostle Paul says Jesus is our peace for He has made us both one, and has broken down the dividing wall of hostility. He has created in Himself one new man in place of two, so making peace. Ephesians 2:14-17.

Barriers between people are broken down in Christ. Man, in his ungodly state, builds barriers of all kinds. Three great barriers are race, riches, and religion. Between the Jews and Gentiles even the temple illustrated walls or barriers. The outer court was the court of the Gentiles, then the court of women, then the court of the Israelites, then the court of the priests, and finally the holy place. Today we speak of the iron curtain, the bamboo curtain, the purple curtain. All are walls between people.

So wall building goes on. The natural man says, "He is not like I am. He thinks differently than I do. He looks different. I can't fellowship with him."

The spiritual man, on the other hand, knows that such considerations are not the important ones. He asks, "How can I fulfill my ministry of reconciliation? What can I do to bring peace? How can I bring people together? How can I build love?"

The Apostle Paul wrote that in Christ there is neither

Jew nor Greek, slave nor free, male nor female. Galatians 3:
28. In Christ barriers are broken down. Paul in Ephesians
2 makes some striking statements telling us how this is possible. We are made near by the blood of Christ. Christ is our
peace. In Christ we are new persons. We have been reconciled to God. Christ came preaching peace to those near and
those afar off. We now have common access to God. We are
made fellow citizens with all other saints. We have a common
spiritual foundation no matter what our former background.

We are brought together and have peace between ourselves because of our love for Christ. As one person says,
"The problem between many members of the church is that
they don't love Christ enough."

Not by Law

Paul goes on to say that we cannot experience peace
and oneness by any list of laws or commandments (v. 15).
That is, we are not brought together by a document, code
of conduct, a list of do's and don'ts, a creed, or the same
way of doing or not doing things. All these tend to divide
further.

The problem today is that we center our attention
around practices, customs, cultures rather than around
Christ. He is our center and our peace. We can usually tell
where our center is by what divides us. Only when our commitment and love is to Christ we love one another.

Before Paul found peace in Christ he was hard to get
along with. He had great knowledge and zeal. Paul was a
good preserver of the faith. But he could not get along with
anyone who differed with him. In fact he felt so strongly
against Christians that he set out to kill them.

But after his conversion and after he found peace in
Christ his attitude changed. He loved people and pleaded
with them to love one another even as Christ did. Now

he had the Spirit of Christ. Now he could call those carnal Corinthian Christians, with all their painful personal, political, and church problems, "brethren," "fellowlabourers," "saints in Christ Jesus."

Christ came to make one new man so making peace. He does not make us all alike when He makes us Christians. He does not make Jews into Gentiles or Gentiles into Jews. Black or white or whatever we are, we become Christlike. We now are at peace and that peace transcends our local and racial differences. We find and love each other because we find our center in Christ.

Another result is that now we are members of "the household of God.' In every home there are many differences in height, color, interests, and levels of maturity. Because of love we stick together. So in the household of God. Someone said, "You can tell the difference between real brothers and the neighbor's children, because when trouble or difference arises the neighbor children take their marbles and go home." When we are part of God's family we continue to live together in spite of differences and troubles.

Division Makers

Paul in his last loving appeal to the Romans tells them to mark those who cause divisions and to avoid them. He writes, "I appeal to you, brethren, to take note of those who create dissensions and difficulties, in oppositon to the doctrine which you have been taught; avoid them. For such persons do not serve our Lord Christ, but their own appetites, and by fair and flattering words they deceive the hearts of the simple-minded" (Romans 16:17, 18).

Paul picks out two characteristics of men who hurt the church and hinder Christian fellowship. First, these men cause divisions among brethren. Anyone who does anything which disturbs the peace and love of the church is certainly not doing the work of God or the Holy Spirit. The Holy Spirit brings brethren together. Those who divide must answer before God. Always! No Scripture sanctions division between brethren.

Second, such men, Paul says, puts hindrances in the way of others. They make it harder for others to be Christians. They make rules which the Scripture says nothing about and without consultation with the body of believers. The man who dilutes or emasculates the Christian faith he professes to promote, will bear his own punishment. Jesus points out that punishment will be severe for the one who causes one of His little ones to stumble.

Two different kinds of persons promote divisions. The one we are quick to think about is the kind who pretends to serve Christ but is actually destroying faith by preaching wrong doctrine.

A second kind of divisive person, in spite of all his pious words, outspoken orthodoxy, and fighting for the faith, sows discord and division wherever he moves. He pretends to stand for the doctrine by his attitude and opposition to others. Under the facade of great swelling speeches and pious words on the faith, he deceives the hearts of the simple while all the time seeking, as Paul says, to serve his "own appetite." That is, he seeks his own ego and a following.

So Paul says quite simply, "Take note of those who create dissensions." The Christian is one whose utter sincerity must be beyond all question and all doubt. When we see those who cause divisiveness in the flock we are called to take special heed because such persons do not serve our Lord Christ, but "their own appetites."

28. Portrait of a Peacemaker

Peter Miller lived near Ephrata, Pennsylvania, during the days of the American Revolutionary War. He and his brothers were conscientiously opposed to participation in war. For this they suffered the ridicule and persecution of their neighbors. One superpatriot in particular, Michael Wideman, stirred up community hatred against these pacifist brethren and accused them of being disloyal citizens. A riotous mob, led by Michael Wideman, burned the barn of Peter Miller and destroyed other property of his and his nonresistant brethren.

As the war dragged slowly on, the situation changed. Michael Wideman was accused of being a British spy. He was arrested and held for military trial. Peter Miller knew George Washington personally. Peter walked the 73 miles from Ephrata to Valley Forge to make a personal plea for the life of Michael Wideman. He walked because his horse had been killed by the rioting patriots.

Seeing Peter Miller coming, Wideman shouted, "There comes Peter Miller to get even by seeing me put to death." Peter, however, went to General Washington and put in a plea for the exoneration of Wideman. Washington replied, "I would like to dismiss the charge against your friend and neighbor, Michael Wideman, but we have evidence that must be examined further before I do so." Said Miller, "My friend! This man is my bitterest enemy. He hates me because I cannot support the war you are fighting. I plead for him because I believe the charges are false and not because he is my friend."

As Christians we must strive to have a right relationship with all men. 2 Peter 3:14. A mark of evil men is that they do not know the way of peace. Romans 3:17. Jesus said, "Blessed are the peacemakers" (Matthew 5:9). In fact He says when people are at the work of peacemaking and reconciliation between other people they are so much in keeping with the character of God that "they shall be called the sons of God." Where are the children of God in our churches? Why is it that the churches have been poor supporters of peace except in their creeds? A few small denominations are known as "peace churches." Should not all churches be known as such? Does this mean all other churches are "war churches"?

Reo M. Christenson writes, "It still seems reasonable to me that the church should condemn such public evils as racial discrimination, cruelty, oppression, hypocrisy, deceit, corruption, and war — especially war, which I find wholly incompatible with the Sermon on the Mount and all that Jesus stood for. And I think the church should encourage its members to oppose these things by every peaceful and ethical means. All of these are evils that Jesus opposed by word, or example, implicitly or explicitly." [1]

Seeks to Follow Christ

First of all a peacemaker is one who seeks to follow Jesus. Not only has he experienced peace within, which means the war between himself and God is over, but he seeks to live in the Spirit of Jesus and the power of the Spirit. He seeks to obey the commands of Christ, who says,

---

1. *Christianity Today,* Jan. 5, 1973, p. 12.

"Love your enemies." In his book, *The Bible Speaks to You*, Robert McAfee Brown says, "Nothing in Jesus' life or teachings can be 'twisted' in support of killing or warfare."

Seemingly the New Testament is unconcerned about the basic concern of the traditional militant. Self-defense wasn't given emphasis by Jesus. Rather Jesus says expressly the opposite. Matthew 5:44; Luke 6:27, 28. Paul tells Christians to overcome evil with good. Romans 12:17-21. On the cross Jesus demonstrated that the weakness of God is stronger than the might of men and that God's way of working is the way of forgiving love. 1 Corinthians 1.

History says that for nearly three centuries Jesus' followers did not participate in military activity. They took seriously Christ's command to Peter to put up his sword. The Son of man didn't come to destroy but to save.

Further, one of the clearest concerns of the Scripture is to present Christ as the cosmic Christ. He is come to be the Savior of the world. He died for all and He cares for each person. Herein is a chief difficulty of the church. We love to localize Christ. We think He is a respecter of persons. We demand He become a national, denominational, or personal God only.

Especially during wartime, in spite of confessions of faith, we many times do not put into practice the truth that Christ's love knows no bonds. It seems difficult to believe that He came to save our enemies as much as us. So we try to confine Christ in the small container of one country, one denomination, or one church. We label Him with little slogans and speak of Him as being on our side. We make long speeches about His love for us and longer speeches against those whom we do not love, thinking that He always agrees with us.

But Christ cannot be so confined. He calls people to be His followers from every tribe, tongue, and nation. To assume God has favorites is foreign to the heart of God.

153

A friend of mine attended a businessmen's banquet. He told of a man speaking about his wish that the United States president would be granted the courage to drop the big bomb on Vietnam before China would get too powerful. Moments later he turned to an Asian student whom he sponsored to the banquet and urged him to give his life to Christ. This man, as many others, applied Jesus only to the personal dimension of peace with God, but overlooked Jesus' teaching about being peacemakers.

A Global Gospel

A peacemaker also believes the message of Christ is for the whole world. The gospel of peace is to be preached to every creature. The reconciling work of Christ cannot be restricted to one community or one continent.

A peacemaker belongs to the universal church. He sees the church as those redeemed from every land and nation. Regardless from what land, the person who finds new life in Christ is a part of that one body. According to Scripture the church is a fellowship of believers in Christ called out from all nations, an international community of Christians.

Isn't it strange, in the great cry for church unity today, that not much is said even now about the great division and destruction of Christ's body that war brings?

In war Methodists kill Methodists, Baptists battle Baptists, Lutherans take the lives of Lutherans and Presbyterians put to death Presbyterians. The words of Charles Clayton Morrison are true. "Nothing more antithetical to Christianity can be imagined than war. It is the denial in the boldest possible form of the very life principle of the religion of Jesus. It is anti-Christian in the rawest, nakednest form."

The Frenchman Jean Lasserre, in *War and the Gospel*, says, "It would seem impossible for a French believer, on the grounds that his government was in conflict with the German government, to resign himself to taking part in the slaughter of Germans, when there are believers among them who like him form part of Christ's body."

Peacemaking Is Positive

A peacemaker is not negative. He works for peace. He prays for peace. He becomes God's instrument for peace. He sacrifices for peace and serves in the middle of the wreckage wrought by war. He overcomes evil with good, prays for the enemy, and seeks to reconcile at every opportunity. He, as his Lord, believes in the power of love over hate. Instead of believing in the power of the fist, the bayonet, and the bomb he has implicit faith in the power of God, the helping hand, the reconciling word, the listening ear. So, in the Spirit of Christ, his peace is not a sentimental affection but a positive force for justice and righteousness. Jesus said the desire to call down destruction on enemies is a different spirit from His.

Historian John A. Lapp points out that on the frontier of France and Germany are two large military cemeteries: one French and one German. On all the countless tombstones in both cemeteries is the inscription that they died "for God and Fatherland." Claiming the same Father's blessing warriors killed and dismembered each other.

To all the statutes of Jesus on love and peace the church many times has added an "except." "Love your enemies" except in wartime; "resist not him that is evil" except in wartime; "put up thy sword into its place, for all they that take the sword shall perish with the sword" except in wartime; "avenge not yourself" except in war; "do not be overcome by evil, but overcome evil with good" unless your country is at war; "the weap-

155

ons of our warfare are not carnal" except when the government tells you to fight; "if a man say, I love God, and hateth his brother, he is a liar" except when he fights in war.

Christopher Butler, in *The Catholic Worker*, October 1965 wrote: "Let us take the opportunity of saying clearly that the church, the people of God, does not seek protection from its enemies — whoever they may be — in war, and especially not in war of modern type. We are the mystical body, and Christ is our Head. He refused to defend Himself and His mission by the swords of His disciples or even by legions of angels, the ministers of God's justice and love. The weapons of the gospel are not nuclear but spiritual; it wins its victories not by war but by suffering. Let us indeed show all sympathy for statesmen in their immense difficulties; let us gratefully acknowledge their good intentions. But let us add a word of reminder that good ends do not justify immoral means; nor do they justify even a conditional intention of meeting immoral attack with immoral defense. Our help is in the name of the Lord who made heaven and earth."

A Peacemaker Is a Realist

The peacemaker is a realist because he knows the power of sin, how bad the world is. He does not define peace as the absence of conflict. He knows the danger to his own life, for the way of peace means death many times in the present as in the past. He is not blind to the cost of peacemaking. He does not ask, What will happen to me if I prove faithful to Christ? His primary concern is to be faithful regardless of the cost. He knows what it cost Christ. He knows the way of Christ who committed the end to God, who is the final Judge. 1 Peter 2:23.

Someone said Teddy Roosevelt was always in favor

of peace, provided it didn't interfere with the fighting. Everyone wants peace. It is the price of peace we're not prepared to pay. The price of peace is the cross. Men will carry guns until they learn to carry the cross. Lecomte Du Noury in *Human Destiny* wrote, "The world will believe in peace only when the church will demonstrate that it can exist."

A peacemaker must be prepared to give his life for others. The divine peacemaker was crucified. He said, "a servant is not greater than his master." The peacemaker does not hold his life of more value than any other. Rather than take life he chooses to give his own life. Does it all sound silly, impossible, irresponsible? Yes, so it was also thought of Jesus and of all true peacemakers, children of God who follow Him.

157

29. Mandate for Peacemakers

His young daughter was working so diligently at her homework when her father became curious and asked her what she was doing.

"I'm writing a report on the condition of the world and how to bring peace," she replied.

"Isn't that a pretty big order for a young girl?" her father asked.

"Oh, no," she answered, "and don't worry. There are three of us in the class working on it!"

Christ's mandate to be peacemakers is a large one. In fact it seems the church has almost completely failed to follow this mandate down through the centuries. Peacemaking is the most active of all the virtues Christ puts before us in the manifesto of His kingdom. Peacemaking is a daring thing because it wishes the best for both sides; it sees the good points of both parties; it speaks its mind firmly but gently; it must rebuke without a touch of bitterness; and it must many times defend the right when it is most unpopular. Peacemaking implies the absence of all ill will.

There is, of course, a spurious peacemaking. It lets things alone. It refuses to ruffle the causes of unrighteousness or to rock the boat. A spurious peacemaker lets vice run unchecked, ungodliness grow rampant without a word, and would rather let secret grudges fester within people's hearts than to deal with the difficult problems.

Today's talk about war and peace has again popularized some labels. The hawks think that military strength makes peace. The doves oppose war as the way of peace. *Time* magazine suggested that in addition to these two, there are the "dawks." These do not know if they are hawks or doves and try to be both.

In one sense it is always difficult to be a dove, to be for peace, especially when the country is at war. Peace, a nice word between wars, becomes a dangerous word for discussion during wartime. So those who refuse to fight and have the audacity to speak of peace during wartime are called names like peacenik, are cursed, are cruelly treated, and sometimes killed as traitors. To such doves are dangerous birds. Thus, as Jesus stated, those who take His words seriously should not expect easy sailing.

God probably isn't concerned about all the talk of war and peace and the dove and hawk issue. However, He is interested in His followers helping where people are hurting. There He is desirous of peace. The real question is not, Are we doves or hawks? but Are we in the right place and are we a reconciling, saving force for Christ where we are?

Word and Ministry of Peace

As Christians we receive the word of reconciliation and also the ministry of reconciliation. 2 Corinthians 5:16-21. We preach the gospel of peace. Ephesians 6:15.

We can become so caught up with the currents around us that we lose our sense of balance. The prevailing attitudes become ours. In a subtle way we sometimes unwittingly imbibe the same spirit we criticize in others. Particularly is this true in our position on peace. We may try to call people to peace and love in most unpeaceful and unloving ways.

If our peace witness is to count and remain biblical, certain things must characterize such a witness.

First, we must maintain a sincere spirit of humility. A peacemaker is not arrogant or proud. The test of peacemaking is whether we are really peacemakers among those close to us.

So we may preach loud and long about the warmongers of the state yet be all the time creating havoc and hatred within our own fellowship and family. Such a spirit negates what we try to say or do.

In any area of life we begin to make progress when we first admit our own failures and inadequacy and then in humility seek to witness to something better.

Understandably no one is much influenced for peace by the belligerent, brash, proud person who calls himself a peacemaker merely because he develops an excellence in denouncing the warmongers. Peacemaking always starts with a sense of humility and repentance on the part of the peacemaker. In this sense many peace movements today are unchristian.

Second, if our peace witness is to be biblical and lasting we must seek in every situation to be redemptive. This applies to both friend and foe. Sometimes there seems to be almost a sense of glee when those whom we dislike are put to shame or suffer loss. We may claim to be greatly concerned about the redemption of the enemy but build up hate toward persons in our congress or neighborhood. This is wrong. All killing is wrong whether it be the killing of a communist or the assassination of the president's character.

So the Christian cannot feel satisfaction or joy when even enemies suffer or are defamed. Christian love reaches all. In much of the talk about peace today, the spirit of the Anabaptist, Dirk Willems, who returned over the ice to save his enemy from drowning, even though it meant his own death, is completely missing.

If we love only those who love us we are no better than the heathen. If we are inclined to feel good when harm of any kind comes to our enemy we had better check again if we are really the peacemakers we claim to be. Many present peace movements speak more of hatred than redemption when their methods result in destruction, name-calling, and building of alienation.

Third, we must maintain more of a spirit of prayer than of criticism. We can easily develop expertise in speaking against national leadership. We need, of course, to bear witness against wrong. The fact that we believe in separation of church and state means a responsibility for evaluation and witness. Yet the Scripture calls us to "Honor all men. Love the brotherhood. Fear God. Honor the emperor" (1 Peter 2:17).

Call to Prayer

We are told to pray for leadership. "First of all, then, I urge that supplications, prayers, intercessions, and thanksgivings be made for all men, for kings and all who are in high positions, that we may lead a quiet and peaceable life, godly and respectful in every way. This is good, and it is acceptable in the sight of God our Savior, who desires all men to be saved and to come to the knowledge of the truth" (1 Timothy 2:1-4).

In our feelings toward those in authority this passage is a guide. This must be our basic approach rather than caustic, disrespectful, and derogatory remarks. Our condemnation of leaders can become greater than our concern. Our denunciation of wrong can become greater than our declaration of right. Our placards can so easily outnumber our prayers. When this happens we are wrong.

Finally, we need to keep the perspective Peter presents in 1 Peter 2:21-23. "For to this you have been called, because Christ also suffered for you, leaving you an example, that you should follow in his steps. He committed no sin: no guile was found on his lips. When he was reviled, he did not revile in return; when he suffered, he did not threaten; but he trusted to him who judges justly." Today we say little about this method of submission.

Toyohiko Kagawa wrote: "The principle of absolute nonresistance started with the idea that it is better to mobilize God than to exert oneself; that is to say, it made God's intervention the basis of morality. Just for this reason I advocate nonresisting love. The principle of nonresistance cannot be supported with human power alone." Tolstoy says that God will surely avenge, and without that faith everybody will resist. Since God's power is greater than ours, we leave the issue to God. Those who observe this technique of love, of righteousness, and of submission are assured of a victory. The history of the past 2,000 years validates this truth. The fall of the Roman Empire and the triumph of Christ are examples.

"God saves even sinners. If there were no salvation, nonresistance would be a folly. In the interest of salvation, therefore, we deny violence. This sentiment is expressed in Jesus' Sermon on the Mount."

30. The Gospel of Peace

"How beautiful are the feet of them that preach the gospel of peace, and bring glad tidings of good things" (Romans 10:15, KJV).

"To sum up, you should all be of one mind living like brothers with true love and sympathy for one another, generous and courteous at all times. Never pay back a bad turn with a bad turn or an insult with another insult, but on the contrary pay back with good. For this is your calling — to do good and one day to inherit all the goodness of God. For

He that would love life,
And see good days,
Let him refrain his tongue from evil,
And his lips that they speak no guile;
And let him turn away from evil, and do good;
Let him seek peace and pursue it" (1 Peter 3:8-11, Phillips).

One of the main reasons young people today see so little use for the church and feel it has betrayed them is that it refuses to face many of the basic issues and sins of life — a primary one being the question of war.

When the church waxes bold, honest, and New Testament enough to declare unequivocally its opposition to Christians engaging in killing and destruction and when it is clear in its call to reconciliation and peace, then the church will experience again the power and persecution of the apostolic church.

When the church today declares with the early church its primary creed that "Jesus Christ is Lord," rather than Caesar, it will again know what it means when the Lord says "All . . . [authority] is given unto me," therefore "Go ye into all the world, and preach the gospel."

The feet of the church have been soiled in the stampede of death it has so often sanctioned and marched on. It has walked in bloody valleys and helped slay instead of save. Too long the best Christian has been the best patriot of Caesar. Too long the church has blessed killing the enemy rather than praying for the enemy. Too long the church has encouraged its faithful to fight rather than to pray for the foe. Too long the church has tried to both "praise the Lord and pass the ammunition." William Blake said many years ago, "They said this mystery never shall cease, the priest promises war and the soldier peace."

Glad Tidings of Peace

Only as the church walks again the paths of peace will its feet be beautiful. Then too it will bring glad tidings of the gospel of peace. In fact, when Jesus gave His manifesto of the kingdom, "Blessed are the peacemakers," He was saying that for His followers war has ceased. Theologian and historian John Howard Yoder says, "The gospel does not only imply an ethic of peacemaking or being set at peace. It does not merely lead to a nonviolent life-style, it proclaims a reconciled view of the world."

Phillips' version of Ephesians translates Paul this way, "For he reconciled both [Jew and Greek, insider and outsider] to God by the sacrifice of one body on the cross, and by this act made utterly irrelevant the antagonism between them. Then he came and told both you who were far from

164

God [the outsider, the Gentile] and us who were near [the insiders, the Jews] that the war was over."

Yoder continues, "That is the gospel: not that war is sin. That also is true, but alone it would not be the gospel. The gospel is that the war is over. Not merely that if you have had a 'born-again experience' some of your hate feelings will go away. Not merely that if you deal with your enemies lovingly enough, some of them will become friendly. All of that is true, but it is not the gospel. The gospel is that all men being loved by God are my beloved too, even if they consider me their enemy, even if their interests clash with mine."

"How beautiful upon the mountains are the feet of him who brings good tidings, who publishes peace, who brings good tidings of good, who publishes salvation, who says to Zion, 'Your God reigns' " (Isaiah 52:7).

Would Revival Bring Peace?

Sometimes the implication is that if real spiritual renewal came, everything would be fine — riots would run out of steam, campuses would be calm, and all of us would live in peace and quiet.

While real spiritual renewal always brings new life, it never makes the world all sweetness and light. In fact it seems throughout history when a true work of God took place, the hosts of hell, the principalities and powers, the rulers of the darkness of this world, suddenly became openly active. Real revival is a disruptive force in society and more often than not it carries in its wake terrible persecution. Some who thought themselves "in the faith" turn aside from the consequences of commitment at such times.

American society has been so safe the past half century or so that it is difficult to understand the Scripture, "All that will live godly in Christ Jesus shall suffer persecution."

Those are strong words! Are we ready to read the word "all" in this Scripture?

Many of the prayers for peace can easily be made for our own safety and the protection of our own prosperity. It's good to ask sometimes why we want peace and what kind of peace we want. Those who are poor, oppressed, and suffering injustices do not pray for peace. Such pray for change. Those who have plenty pray for peace so that all will be preserved.

Of course it is proper to pray for all in authority out of a desire for peace so that the gospel may go forth freely. The message of the church is muzzled under hostile rule. Yet the Christian who says his first loyalty is always to Christ as Lord (and that is really what revival is) is headed for persecution. The sword of which Jesus spoke and which divides between the professor and the possessor is drawn.

Christ says this loyalty will divide even the closest companions. This loyalty will bring the severest persecution. This loyalty will drive a wedge between a nation and its Christian citizens, between husband and wife, parent and child. The Christian will hear the same cries as made against Christ that He was a traitor, a destroyer of past practices, and one who cast aside all which was considered safe. These same words, in one form or another, will again be screamed against Christians who put the claims of Christ first.

So renewal is not a return to places of peace and safety. Real spiritual renewal could well mean intense persecution, ostracism, and suffering for those who declare unequivocally that Christ is Lord and only Savior. But even though the result may be different from what we think or like, it may be that our land may yet be saved.

God is the only one who can change things. Let us never assume that in His bringing change He will be a respecter of persons, blessing our sins while punishing other persons. His work of renewal means that there will be a drastic change in our lives. Peace within, yes, but also persecution from without.

31. Peace — Our Divine Calling

"In the past fifty years we have arrested tens of thousands who advocated peace. Many hundreds of them were tried, fined, and imprisoned. But we have in the past hundred years never arrested, tried, or convicted even one advocate of war." These revealing words by Sam Darcy show how sick society is at the very center.

As stated in an earlier chapter, peace begins in the individual's relation to God. Peace is more than a particular position in wartime or during military conflict. Like the other fruit of the Spirit, peace given by the Holy Spirit relates to our attitudes and actions toward others. Peace is the result of love shed abroad in our hearts. Peace is our divine calling in that when we become Christ's followers we enlist in the service of reconciliation. We are entrusted with the ministry of reconciliation. The peace witness must be the essence of our lives. We must do the things that make for peace.

Therefore the Scripture says, "Let us therefore follow after the things which make for peace, and things wherewith one may edify another" (Romans 14:19, KJV). "For God is not the author of confusion, but of peace, as in all churches of the saints" (1 Corinthians 14:33, KJV). "Follow peace with all men, and holiness, without which no man shall see the Lord" (Hebrews 12:14, KJV). "Follow righteousness, faith, charity, peace, with them that call on the Lord out of a pure heart" (2 Timothy 2:22, KJV). "Eager to maintain the unity of the Spirit in the bond of peace" (Ephesians 4:3). Literally this means we are to spare no efforts to make fast with bonds of peace the unity which the Spirit gives. We must "seek peace and pursue it" (1 Peter 3:11). We must "be zealous to be found by him" in peace (2 Pet. 3:14). The word "seek" means to make it the object of all endeavor. The word "pursue" means to hunt peace as a hunter looks for a deer. The word for "zealous" means to seek for something with a burning enthusiasm.

Peace Requires Sacrifice

What does all this say? It says peace does not come easily. We have a responsibility to seek out and do the things which build peace and to refrain from those attitudes and actions which break peace. It means peace is not a passive, inactive, withdrawn position. Rather it is actively engaged in. John Foster Dulles said, "Our world will never have lasting peace so long as men reserve for war the finest human qualities. Peace, no less than war, requires idealism and self-sacrifice and a righteous and dynamic faith."

Christian love never despises another or works ill against his neighbor. The fact is that true love deepens for the other when difficulties appear. How often our lack of love is worse than our brother's fault!

How long will Christians think that the crowning evidence of spirituality and devotion to the Lord is expressed in a bitter, vehement defense of what is called "the faith"? Although we yield to no one on "the faith . . . once delivered unto the saints," an unlovely defense is more the result of a distorted self-complex or a false front for wounded pride than the result of Holy Spirit urgings. Some who charge others with using a penknife on Scripture have them-

169

selves cut out 1 Corinthians 13. Remember, love is the perfect tense of life. It has been the mistake of every age to make faith rather than love the test of Christianity. But "he that loveth not . . . abideth in death."

Someone has given a good guide: "No man is trained to use Paul's rod until he knows how to anoint it with Paul's tears." It's better not to speak about a brother's fault unless we can do it to him personally after fervent prayer for him.

The redemptive approach to life will need not only to be taught but also to be seen in the home, in the congregation and at all levels of life.

Most of our differences and difficulties arise because we do not know persons. How often have we heard or said, "When I learned to know him, it looked altogether different and I understood better what he was saying."

As Christians we ought to be specialists in reconciliation. The church ought to be made up of persons who have learned to bring people together, to bring peace between persons. We ought to be so expert in bringing peace that the world would wonder and stand in amazement. We ought to be theologically and psychologically prepared to stand in the center of tension with the word and ministry of reconciliation and love.

Now it is easy to love mankind. It is not easy to love particular persons. It is easy to love humanity in mass, to be moved with compassion for the crowd, and to love a flock of sheep. This presents a pretty picture.

But Christ takes the one sheep — the silliest, stupidest, straying sheep, the one that causes most concern and bother — and risks His life to find it. He shoulders the burden, carrying it miles to safety. There's nothing poetic about carrying mutton over the mountains, but it is the test of our love and of our desire to reconcile.

Tested by the Unlovely

Love and peace are not tested by rhetorical phrases from the pulpit or platform. They are tested by the way we behave toward others who continually go astray and are at odds. The test of our love and peace for another is in our behavior toward particular persons with whom we talk, walk, and work. To be concerned for these is the test of our love.

At the heart of that which makes for peace is a tender, forgiving love as Christ forgave and loved.

Forgiveness is one of the strongest expressions of Christ-like love. Sir Thomas Brown, in *Christian Morals* says forgiveness is to "draw the curtain of night upon injuries, and shut them up in the tower of oblivion, and let them be as though they had not been. To forgive our enemies, yet hope that God will punish them, is not to forgive enough. To forgive them ourselves, and not to pray God to forgive them, is a partial piece of charity. Forgive thine enemies totally, without any reserve."

Ian Maclaren in *Beside the Bonnie Briar Bush* tells of Lachean Campbell, a strict Presbyterian of the old school, a man of iron principle. When his young, motherless girl ran off to London he disowned her and struck her name off the old family Bible. In the months that followed, as his highland neighbors watched the old man go about his farm chores they knew that behind the grim exterior was a broken heart. As Margaret Howe put it, "It was waesome tae the auld man gatherin' his bit things wi' shakin' hand, and speakin' tae me aboot the weather, an' a' the time his eyes were sayin', 'Flora, Flora!' "

At Margaret's pleading the poor girl was persuaded to come back to the Glen. In fear the trembling she reached Drumtochty. It was nighttime, and the Glen was bathed in the light of the harvest moon.

"A turn of the path brought her within sight of the cottage, and her heart came into her mouth, for the kitchen window was a blaze of light. . . . But when she reached the door her strength had departed, and she was not able to knock. But there was no need, for the dogs, who never forget nor cast off, were bidding her welcome with short joyous yelps of delight, and she could hear her father feeling for the latch, which for once could not be found, and saying nothing but 'Flora, Flora!'

"She had made up some kind of speech, but the only word she ever said was 'Father,' for Lachean, who had never kissed her all the days of her youth, clasped her in his arms and sobbed out blessings over her head, while the dogs licked her hands with their soft kindly tongues.

" 'It is a pity you have not the Gaelic,' Flora said to Margaret afterwards; 'It is the best of all languages for loving. There are fifty words for darling, and my father could be calling me every one that night I came home.' "

Patience Fruit

32. Patience — Love Under Pressure

H. W. Beecher suggested, "There is no such thing as preaching patience unto people unless the sermon is so long that they have to practice it while they hear. No man can learn patience except by going out into the hurly-burly world and taking life just as it blows. Patience is but lying to and riding out the gale."

Ours is an impatient age in which we do not like to wait. We want instant gratification. Our "now generation" of youth is only characteristic of society at large. The "instant" pre-mixed, freeze-dried food in the supermarket is dedicated to save time and preparation. Toothpaste takes away bad breath instantly. Instant cereals, instant coffee, instant shaving cream, instant relief for colds and headaches, and instant starting in cold weather are a must. In every area the necessity of instant results and instant gratification is stressed. Time payments relieve us of the need for patience before a purchase. The more materialistic the more impatient.

An Attitude Toward People

Long-suffering or patience is love under pressure. It expresses an attitude toward people. It suffers long with people no matter how unreasonable they are or how unloving and unteachable they appear. Patience does not retaliate. Chrysostom defined this fruit of the Spirit as "the

Spirit which could take revenge if it liked, but utterly refuses to do so."

We are not born with patience. We need only to hear a baby cry or see a child's restlessness to realize this. Greeks of the New Testament times considered long-suffering or patience as weakness and not virtue. They believed, as many today, in the strong stick. Only the fearful and weak refrain from retaliation. Richard Flecknoe called "patience, a virtue of the poor" and George Granville in the play "Heroic Love" says

"Patience is the virtue of an ass,

That trots beneath his burdens and is quiet."

However, it doesn't take much wisdom to see it is harder and more mature to keep from getting ruffled by insult and injury than to get angry and hit the offender. The weak are quick to return evil and the insecure are quick in taking offense. Wisdom teaches it takes courage and strength not to return injury and insult. La Fontaine wrote, "By patience and time we sever what strength and rage could never." An Eastern proverb says "Patience is power. With time and patience the mulberry leaf becomes satin." Patience is the power to see things through.

So the scriptural word for long-suffering or patience suggests forbearance, a willingness to wait, an endurance and continuance in spite of difficulties. It means the deferment of judgment in hope of repentance of wrong just as the purpose of God in His patience is to lead to repentance and joy.

Patience is a fruit of the Spirit lived out in relation to our fellowmen. Love suffers long. 1 Corinthians 13:4. We are called to be patient and forbearing of one another. Colossians 3:12. Patience means we do not lose hope in others. Love hopes all things.

Patience is not passive. It is concentrated, active strength. The picture of patience is not folded hands, the

176

acceptance of everything without surprise, the waiting for the inevitable or sitting still with a smiling face. The Hebrew writer tells us to "run with patience." Patience keeps doing God's will regardless of the difficulties or the discouragements. The New Testament word means "to abide under." It does not suggest compromise or complacency but pulses with persistence and a dogged faithfulness which refuses to yield to voices or values other than God's. Patience is keeping the course in spite of everything.

Francis de Sales shares a story Cassian told, "Cassian relates how a certain devout maiden once besought St. Athanasius to help her in cultivating the grace of patience, and he gave her a poor widow as a companion who was cross, irritable, altogether intolerable, and whose perpetual fretfulness gave the pious lady abundant opportunity for practicing gentleness and patience."

Patience Is Redemptive

Paul refers to patience as a partial proof of his apostleship. 2 Corinthians 6:6. A person who is not patient should not have authority. Impatience pushes people out rather than practicing a redemptive spirit and letting patience do her perfect work. Impatience is a result of blindness to what the Holy Spirit is doing. Paul sees patience as an essential for every Christian. It is included in the fruit of the Spirit because it its true sense, it is produced only by Christ's Spirit within us.

Patience is necessary if we are to walk worthy of our calling. Ephesians 4:2. As one of the great characteristics of love (1 Corinthians 13:4) it is to be exercised toward all persons. Christian fellowship is not possible without patience for each other. Paul contrasts the patient love of the Christian teacher with the folly of the false teachers. 2 Timothy 3:10.

No one can preach, teach, or help others without patience. Gerald Kennedy says, "As one grows older, one comes to the conclusion that more lives are destroyed by impatience than any other sin." Jesus said, "By your endurance you will gain your lives" (Luke 21:19).

An old legend says that one day Abraham was standing by his tent door when he saw an old man coming along the way, weary with his journey, and with bleeding feet. With true hospitality he invited the old man to share his meal and be lodged with him for the night. Abraham noticed that he asked no blessing on the meal, and inquired why he did not pray to the God of heaven. The old man said, "I am a fire worshiper and acknowledge no other god." At this Abraham grew angry and sent him from his tent.

Then God called Abraham, "Where is the old man who came to you?" And Abraham answered, "I thrust him out because he did not worship You." Then said God, "I have suffered him these hundreds of years, though he dishonored me, and could you not endure him one night?"

An Attitude Toward Events

Long-suffering describes the response of the Christian to events and situations. In spite of difficulties or persecution we are called to patience. The Old Testament saints illustrate patience. They did not see the end but because of their patient faith they received the reward. Again and again the New Testament writers summon us to patience and point to the Old Testament saints as our example. "Take, my brethren, the prophets, who have spoken in the name of the Lord, for an example of suffering affliction, and of patience. Behold, we count them happy which endure. Ye have heard of the patience of Job, and have seen the end of the Lord, that the Lord is very pitiful, and of tender mercy" (James 5:10, 11, KJV).

much spirit

William Barclay says, "In some ways *makrothumia* (long-suffering) is the greatest virtue of all. It is not clad with romance and glamour; it has not the excitement of sudden adventurous action; but it is the very virtue of God Himself. God in His *makrothumia* bears with the sins, the refusals and the rebellions of men. God in His *makrothumia* refuses to abandon hope of the world which He created and which so often turns its back on its Creator. And man in his life on earth must reproduce God's undefeatable patience with people and God's undiscourageable patience with events." [1]

Patience has a calm anticipation and hope. The New Testament speaks of the patience of hope. Hope produces patience. When we love and have hope in God or in others we are inclined to be more patient. Paul says, "To those who by patience in well-doing seek for glory and honor and immortality, he will give eternal life" (Romans 2:7). The Hebrews writer says, "Ye have need of patience, that, after ye have done the will of God, ye might receive the promise" (Hebrews 10:36, KJV). James writes "Be patient, therefore, brethren, until the coming of the Lord. Behold, the farmer waits for the precious fruit of the earth, being patient over it until it receives the early and the late rain" (James 5:7).

If we believe in the promises of God, we can patiently wait for them. The hope of the gospel quiets and calms the spirit and fills us with patience. Pessimism is often due to lack of patience. We look around and see the awful condition and think God is too slow. We lose hope. True faith can wait. Pride cannot.

---

1. William Barclay, *op. cit.*, 97.

33. Our Pattern for Patience

Years ago a book was published in England, *The Discipline and Culture of the Spiritual Life*. It is a compilation from the writings of A. E. Whitham. One of the chapters is a beautiful meditation on the patience and humility of God. Whitham imagines if he were God he would advertise himself, put a brass plate on the door, and let people know who he is and compel them to conform to his will.

"Yet," says Whitham, "God does not drive. He is very patient, sending rain on just and unjust, making His sun to shine on the evil and the good, pouring forth His gifts without reserve, without resentment or grudge. He does not deny His gifts even when we deny the Giver. . . .

"If He comes through the laughter of a little child, and you spurn Him, He will go quietly away, and return when your mood is less bitter and sullen. If, when He comes through the beseeching hands that plead for help, through the hungry that want food, and the poor that want shelter, you snap up your purse strings and slam the door, He will go and come around another way. If you ignore Him through an enemy who seeks your care, He will go, and come through a friend who offers you sympathy."

Paul, the apostle, prays an impressive prayer in 2 Thessalonians 3:5, "The Lord," he prays, "direct your hearts into . . . the patience of Christ" (AS). This points to Christ as the perfect pattern of patience. This fruit, like all the other fruit, finds its culmination in Christ. We are to keep on looking to Him as our example, our Savior, our Lord. We are to walk in His steps. We are to be imitators of Him. This is possible only by our open response to His Spirit who indwells us.

Patience with His Disciples

Notice Christ's patience in dealing with His own disciples. They were so diverse in personality. They were at times distressingly selfish. Yet Christ was patient through it all.

Think how difficult it was to love, accept, and be patient with the twelve disciples day after day. Here was Simon the Zealot. And there was Matthew the tax collector. Previous to Christ's call to them they were bitter enemies. Zealots swore that, if the chance ever arose, they would cut the throat of any Roman sympathizer. Clarence Jordan was probably correct when he said, "Unless I miss my guess, Jesus had to sleep between those two fellows more than one night."

Think of the patience of Jesus when His disciples learned His teaching so slowly. One day Philip said to Him, after years of instruction, "Lord, show us the Father, and we shall be satisfied." Jesus made that patient reply, "Have I been with you so long, and yet you do not know me, Philip? He who has seen me has seen the Father: and can you say, 'Show us the Father'?"

Think of Jesus' patience that day when a pair of His disciples insisted that they be allowed to sit one on the right hand and the other on the left hand in His kingdom. How slow they were to comprehend the nature of His kingdom, and yet how patient Christ was with His dull and selfish disciples.

All the way through life and to the time of His ascension Christ was a picture of patience. When Judas joined the opposing forces to betray Him, He still was very patient and pleaded, even at the last supper together, for his repentance. When Peter denied Him three times when the going got rough, Jesus came to him and patiently restored him in all love and full acceptance.

Think of Christ's patience with the people who pressed upon Him from every quarter for help. They followed Him and found Him wherever He went. They must have tried His patience. The disciples decided numerous times to send the crowd away, to push the small, crying children aside and to protect Jesus from all the jostling tumult. Jesus, however, demonstrated perfect patience.

Patience with Enemies

His patience toward His enemies is still more wonderful. No one in all history had persons who were more persistent in attempting to circumvent His plans and frustrate His work. Wherever He went there were those who tried to destroy Him. His knowledge of it all was complete. Yet His patience was undimmed and undiminished through it all.

Nor was His patience that of weakness. He reminded His opposers that at any time He could call down more than twelve legions of angels to come to His aid. But that would not have been in keeping with His Spirit or plans. Never, before or since, has anyone shown such strength in gentle and enduring patience. With all power in His hands He prayed for His murderers, and returned only kind words in answer to their cruel ones. Finally He climbed Calvary's hill and died on the cross for all.

No wonder the Apostle Peter writes years later, "The Lord is . . . longsuffering . . . not willing that any should perish, but that all should come to repentance" (2 Peter 3:9, KJV). How merciful, how patient, how tenderhearted He always was. How patient and long-suffering we need to be to others.

Paul prayed for the Colossian Christians that they "might walk worthy of the Lord unto all pleasing, being fruitful in every good work, and increasing in the knowledge of God; strengthened with all might, according to his glorious power, unto all patience and longsuffering with joyfulness" (Colossians 1:10, 11, KJV).

In His work our Lord demonstrated His patience. While here He saw few visible results of His work. At first great multitudes followed but in the final hours many walked no more with Him. One day He turned to His disciples and asked, "Will you also go away?" Still He did not falter. Nor was He discouraged. He fulfilled the prophecy of Isaiah, "He will not fail or be discouraged."

Patience in Doing God's Will

See the strength of Christ's patience in His persistence in doing God's will. He learned the abiding peace in the unreserved acceptance of God's will. "My meat," He said, "is to do the will of him that sent me, and to finish his work." He accepted God's will in Gethsemane, as well as when all life seemed cloudless and filled with music. Finally on the cross, physically tortured and mentally tormented, never once did He stoop to a gesture of defense. With patient, enduring, unending love He met the worst His enemies could do. Out of this patience came our salvation. Of Him it is said, "Who for the joy that was set before him endured the cross." He saw ahead to our salvation.

We are the beneficiaries of that patience. So quick-tempered, so easily provoked, so cocky about our little positions of prominence, we jump at anyone who trespasses on our territory. We shout at those dearest to us when our lines are crossed, and we face the world with clenched fists and breathe fire when we are wronged. We can't bear the thought of coming out second best. We can hardly imagine patient love in the face of injury. Why? Because we do not see, as Christ did, that patience is a virtue, a fruit of the Spirit, the character of God Himself.

"Love is patient." This is a revolutionary doctrine.

Badger Clark inspires us to be more patient in his words from *The Job*. After he reflects on his own failures he thinks of how men are a disappointment to God in spite of all His efforts. He concludes:

Why don't You quit?
Crumble it all, and dream again! But no;
Flaw after flaw, You work it out, revise, refine —
Bondage, brutality, and war and woe,
The sot, the fool, the tyrant and the mob —
Dear God, How You must love Your job!
Help me, as I love mine.

"Now the God of patience and consolation grant you to be likeminded one toward another according to Christ Jesus" (Romans 15:5, KJV). Paul wrote to the Galatian believers over whom he was deeply concerned, "My little children, with whom I am again in travail until Christ be formed in you" (Galatians 4:19)! "The Lord direct your hearts into the love of God, and into the patience of Christ" (2 Thessalonians 3:5, ASV).

34. Patience — Love's First Test

A cultured woman found herself among people of a strange language and race. While there she became a close friend of a devoted missionary. "One day," she said, "I was troubled by an experience with those quarreling people. I related my grievances to my missionary friend. 'They are so self-interested,' I complained, 'so self-absorbed, so soft on themselves, so violent with others, so unreasoning.' When I had finished rehearsing their faults as I saw them, my friend smiled a little and said something I have never forgotten; 'That's why they need us.'"

"Love is patient and kind." In the list of fifteen characteristics of love in 1 Corinthians 13:4-7, this one comes first, "Love is patient." All the relations in life call for the fruit of patience. We need patience with ourselves. Otherwise we lose the battle over temptation and trial.

Not only do we need patience with ourselves but we need it for proper relations with others. It is needed in that most important circle of all — the home. As parents we need this grace in abundant measure. In the home is the place where it is easiest to lose patience. Impatient parents pave the way for all kinds of problems in their children. Perhaps nothing inclines children against parental guidance or spiritual truth as much as impatience on the part of parents.

How often what we teach in the home is nullified by

impatience. One thing the Spirit does is that He makes us easier to live with. He makes it easier to absorb hostility and avoid touchiness.

Henry Drummond in "Pax Vobiscum" says, "There is a disease called 'touchiness' — a disease which, in spite of its innocent name, is one of the gravest sources of restlessness in the world. Touchiness, when it becomes chronic, is a morbid condition of an inner disposition. It is self-love inflamed to an acute point."

Impatience and Unhappiness

Most of our unhappy experiences in the family flow from impatient words and acts. We lack the ability to wait without irritation or ill feeling. It is natural for those whose patience is short to feel that others need the grace of discipline.

Unless we practice patience we will often misunderstand and misjudge others. If we knew all the background in other people's lives, our attitude and judgment would be different.

A story told by the famed evangelist, Sam Jones, stresses the same point. The train was filled with tired persons, most of whom spent the day traveling through the hot plains. At last evening came and all tried to settle down to a sound sleep. However, at one end of the car a man was holding a tiny baby and as night came on the baby became restless and cried more and more.

Unable to take it any longer, a big, brawny man spoke for the rest of the group. "Why don't you take that baby to its mother?" There was a moment's pause and then came the reply. "I'm sorry. I'm doing my best. The baby's mother is in her casket in the baggage car ahead."

Again there was an awful silence for a moment. Then the big man who asked the cruel question was out of his seat and moved toward the man with the motherless child. He apologized for his impatience and unkind remark. He took the tiny baby in his own arms and told the tired father to get some sleep. In loving patience he cared for the little child all through the night.

How we need to magnify wise and worthy patience. The Holy Spirit places that patient love so that we can see beneath the surface and care. In 1 Corinthians 13 patience is characterized by four things: it suffers long; it bears all things; it continues to hope; and it endures uncomplaining.

"Intaking" Christ's Patience

F. B. Meyer tells of an incident that revolutionized his whole life. In a meeting of ministers they were talking about giving up all for Christ. One minister remarked that his life was one of "intaking from Christ." He told of being with some children who were very unattentive and restless, but when he was tempted to be impatient he looked up into the face of the Lord and said, "Thy patience, Lord!" Instantly the Lord dropped into his heart some patience. He testified, "I have always dared to believe that God put me into difficult situations to reveal the things in Christ which I was to claim. In a moment when I am tempted to irritability I say, 'Thy sweetness, Lord,' In a moment of weakness, 'Thy strength, Lord.' " Meyer had learned the secret of intaking; a lesson he never forgot.

W. S. Plumer wrote, "Be patient in little things. Learn to bear the everyday trials and annoyances of life quietly and calmly, and then, when unforeseen trouble or calamity comes, your strength will not forsake you.

"There is as much difference between genuine patience and sullen endurance, as between the smile of love and the malicious gnashing of the teeth."

Finally, we need patience with God. Phillips Brooks was

187

one day pacing his study so furiously a friend asked him his trouble. "I'm in a hurry," said Brooks, "but God isn't."

Sometimes God's providential dealings with us try us to our depths. Sometimes our cherished plans are broken. Sometimes doors are closed and we are compelled to give up deep desires. Such times and situations try our faith so that patience can perfect her work in us.

When all doors to Bithynia were closed, to the deep disappointment of Paul, God opened to him the continent of Europe. Because he went to Europe, blessings immeasurably vast came to the world. God's plans for us are larger and better than our plans for ourselves. But we need patience which God by His Spirit will supply.

There is a subtle truth in the verse by Jane Merchant:

Let me be patient, Lord, forever
In every large and little woe,
And grant me grace that I may never
Let my patience show.

35. Triumph over Trouble

An old legend says that at creation the birds felt cheated and hurt because they received wings. Wings appeared to be burdens which none of the other animals were asked to carry. All was changed, however, when the birds learned that wings were not burdens but blessings that bore them to the sky. Because they were given wings they could rise above the earth and see sights which no other animal could see. What seemed like burdens were really blessings. A little patience teaches us the same thing many times.

What at times seems to hamper our progress or hurt our possibilities becomes in the end the thing which helps us rise higher. Suffering enables us to understand and help the sufferer. Financial failure teaches us to put our trust higher. Disappointment drives us to see things from a divine point of view. Betrayal on the part of another teaches us better to understand the cross. The apostle wrote, "We rejoice in our sufferings, knowing that suffering produces endurance, and endurance produces character, and character produces hope" (Romans 5:3, 4). Patience is not a gloomy thing. It does not wear a long face. It continues to hope in every situation.

So we need a spiritual life to rejoice in suffering, to see that patience comes only when we are stopped in our tracks and we find the only thing to do is to suffer it out. We see that character is produced only as we exercise patience in the trying experiences of life. We see that hope is always ahead for the one whose character is built on a solid rock rather than on sand.

Burdens or Blessings

We can look on the experiences of life as burdens or blessings. As long as they are burdens we are under them. But when we receive them as blessings they bear us above so that we see sights others cannot see.

In this life alone we can learn lessons of patience and self-denial, for there are no sickbeds to watch by, no sufferers to soothe, no mourners to comfort in the mansions of the Father's house.

All of us suffer adversity, persecution, and trial. It is possible to take such in a Christian or non-Christian way. Patience says, "Do not rebel, God has something in this for your good." Patience asks, "Lord, what shall I learn from this?" It is not that we say nothing can be done or that we take a stoical submission to the inevitable, "What will be, will be." It is not the pride of not revealing feelings or a denial of burdens or wounds. The patience God gives is not the patience that sits down but that which rises up and goes on, which wills to follow step after step in the Savior's footprints; accepting all His terms and discipline.

Patience goes beyond what a person without the Holy Spirit can demonstrate. Patience is possible when we recognize God's will and when we believe that "all things work together for good to them that love God." Patience is possible when we know that nothing happens outside the permissive will of God. "Knowing this, that the trying of your faith worketh patience. But let patience have her perfect work, that ye may be perfect, and entire, wanting nothing" (James 1:3, 4, KJV). Sometimes it is only through sorrow or

190

suffering that God is able to teach us the vanity of worldly desire and to bring us close to Himself.

Bearing Inglorious Trouble

Francis de Sales writes, "Do not limit your patience to this or that kind of trial, but extend it universally to whatever God may send, or allow to befall you. . . . A really patient servant of God is as ready to bear inglorious troubles as those which are honorable. A brave man can easily bear with contempt, slander, and false accusation from an evil world; but to bear such injustice at the hands of good men, of friends and relations, is a great test of patience."

Thomas a Kempis says, "When you hear someone saying unworthy and hard words of you it is then given you to drink medicine for your soul out of the cup of the Lord."

And Basil the Great speaks of the trials of the saints. "Therefore, brothers, first of all be patient under every trial, and what are the trials by which the faithful are tested? Loss of worldly goods, accusations, falsehoods, disobedience, slanders, persecutions. By these and similar tests are the faithful tested."

A telephone operator one day turned to another and said, "That's a patient man: I gave him the wrong number four times and he kindly said, 'Try again.' I wonder who he is." The other girl replied, "I know him; he's my minister." Then said the first girl, "I'm going to hear him preach."

Patience is love on the anvil bearing blow after blow of suffering. Patience is moral strength. It is that virtue which enables us to remain calm and quiet no matter what the circumstances may be. It is that virtue which helps us to bear the everyday trials and annoyances of life quietly and with a composure which is past human understanding.

As I began, let me close with an old legend. A woman prayed to God for patience. In answer she received nothing but trouble. She then said to the Lord, "I did not pray for trouble. I prayed for patience." The Lord answered her, "How else will you learn patience, or even know you have it?"

36. Hang in There

A young woman dreamed she died and went to heaven. As one of the angels was showing her around the room of the glorious city, she saw a stack of boxes in one corner. Finding her name on them she asked the angel what it meant, for, she said, "I remember praying for these things when I was on earth."

The angel replied, "Yes, when any of God's children make requests to Him preparations are made to give the answer. But the angels are told that if the petitioner is not waiting for the answer, they are to return with it and store it in the room."

An old prayer proverb says, "When you come to the end of your rope, tie a prayer knot, and hang on." But we want immediate results. It is a sign of our lack of faith and hope in what God will do. "But if we hope for what we do not see, we wait for it with patience" (Romans 8:25). "Commit your way to the Lord; trust in him, and he will act. Be still before the Lord, and wait patiently for him; fret not yourself" (Psalm 37:5, 7).

One of the difficult things to learn in life is that God's delays are not His denials. Oftentimes the greatest blessings come in continued fellowship and prayer when we do not see an immediate answer to prayer. It does much for our spiritual equilibrium to rest assured God is at work and will accomplish His purposes though His time schedule may be different from ours.

Someone said, "God gives one of three answers to prayer. Sometimes He says 'No.' Sometimes He says 'Yes.' And sometimes 'Wait.' " George Mueller prayed nearly sixty years for the salvation of a certain man. The man was saved at Mueller's funeral.

Patience Is Commitment

We may not pray in a demanding way. Rather than commit our way to God we plot it out ourselves and ask God to follow our plans. True prayer is first of all a complete commitment to God's will. Not our desire but His desire must be foremost. Be assured when we come with such commitment He will act.

But He may not always act in the way or time we feel He should. His desire is to "do exceeding abundantly above all that we ask or think" (Ephesians 3:20, KJV). We are not ready for His best while we hurry around trying to do a spiritual work ourselves.

I heard of a missionary who did not receive her monthly check. She was seriously ill and because of no money had to live on oatmeal and canned milk. She received the check thirty days later. After mentioning this incident while on furlough a doctor asked the nature of her illness. She described the digestive trouble she had. The doctor said, "If your check had arrived on time, you would now be dead. The best treatment for your illness was a thirty-day oatmeal diet."

No wonder the Scripture says, "Be still," "wait patiently," and "fret not." Our call is to commit our way to Him, trust fully in Him, and He will act.

Virgil in the *Aeneid* said, "Every misfortune is subdued by patience."

Ulysses' crew stopping their ears with wax against the

194

siren's song is an example of self-command or self-control; the same Ulysses battling against the tempest is an example of what Scripture means by patience.

Sometimes we find it difficult to believe God's promises when He does not fulfill His Word as soon as we think He ought to. Moses had the same difficulty. When God promised him to free the Israelites from Egyptian bondage, Moses supposed it would happen immediately. He asked Pharaoh for their release, but the Egyptian ruler made the Hebrews' task in the fields harder than ever. Right away Moses complained to God that He had not kept His word. God, of course, later brought to pass all He had promised.

Our problem is that we do not wait upon God. We forget that it is "through faith and patience" that we obtain God's promises.

The great poet Milton was totally blind at forty-four. In the poem "On His Blindness" Milton speaks of the patience needed in effective service:

When I consider how my light is spent,
  Ere half my days, in this dark world and wide,
  And that one talent which is death to hide,
  Lodged with me useless, though my soul more bent
To serve therewith my Maker, and present
  My true account, lest he returning chide,
  Doth God exact day-labor, light denied,
  I fondly ask; but patience, to prevent
That murmur, soon replies, God doth not need
  Either man's work or his own gifts. Who best
Bear his mild yoke, they serve him best. His state
  Is kingly; thousands at his bidding speed,
And post o'er land and ocean without rest;
  They also serve who only stand and wait.

37. The Witness of Patience

In Tennessee Williams' play, *Cat on a Hot Tin Roof*, the redemptive power of patient love wins. In the play, "Brock," the son, tries to escape all his problems with himself, his wife, his father, and his work with alcohol. The Father, Big Daddy, in his rough, profane way, is deeply concerned for his son.

Big Daddy pursues his son through every kind of evasion and rationalization, trying to break through to him. Nothing the son says is sufficient to turn the father away. He could easily have avoided the pain by abandoning his sick son. "Instead he hammers at the door of Brock's life with a love that is willing to accept every rejection that his son can offer." Finally his love and patience breaks through to his son and Brock is restored to life with his family and his work. Such is the resourcefulness of Godlike patience.

Sam Shoemaker writes concerning patience, "If we have ever seen a real Christian (and all of us have), we know that what impressed us most was not that he was loving. Somehow he had more patience with exasperating people, more hope about wicked people, more time for tedious people, and — most particularly — more forgiveness toward opponents, than the rest of us have. Sometimes we write him off as having a more equable and easy disposition than we have or say he doesn't have to do with as vexing people as we do, but we just can't get away from the fact that there is a little register within us, even the most pagan of us, that proves when a person is being a Christian in his life, and when he is not. And our gauge and standard is largely what is best called by the name of love." [1]

A Mark of Leadership

The further we go in the development of the life in the Spirit, the greater is our need of patience. The apostle says that a mark of mature spiritual leadership is patience. "But in all things approving ourselves as the ministers of God, in much patience, in afflictions, in necessities, in distresses, in stripes, in imprisonments, in tumults, in labours, in watchings, in fastings; by pureness, by knowledge, by longsuffering, by kindness " (2 Corinthians 6:4-6, KJV). "The signs of a true apostle were performed among you in all patience, with signs and wonders and mighty works" (2 Corinthians 12:12).

Paul further says (1 Timothy 3:3; 2 Timothy 2:10, 24) that if a spiritual leader or teacher does not stand the test of patience he should not have spiritual responsibility. Impatient leaders only produce unruly and unfruitful followers.

British Prime Minister, William Pitt, was once asked what he would name as the first qualification for the British Prime Minister and he answered, "Patience." The questioner asked, "What would you name as the second qualification that he should have?" And the answer came quickly, "Patience." The questioner asked for the third qualification. And again the quick reply was, "Patience." How much more important is patience in the spiritual realm. So important is patience, that it is no wonder Jesus said, "In your patience possess ye your souls."

---

1. Samuel Shoemaker, ed. by Cecile C. Offill, *And Thy Neighbor* (Waco: Word Books, 1967), pp. 87, 88.

Someone said it is often the finest natures which are sorely tempted to exhibitions of impatience, just as the fairest lakes of Scotland are often swept by unexpected storms. Think of Moses, the meekest of men, so losing his patience that he shattered the tables of the law. Think of Simon Peter who allowed himself such impatience that cut a man's ear off. Jesus needed to remind him, "Put up again thy sword into his place; for all they that take the sword shall perish with the sword." James and John, some of the closest companions of Christ, were called the "Sons of thunder" because they became impatient so easily.

Jesus had a big job to teach those early disciples patience. Today He still has a big job to teach us, His disciples, patience. Patience is the result of our response to the Holy Spirit in the midst of trying, difficult, and impossible situations. By patience we preach a powerful message of the miraculous work of the Holy Spirit in our lives.

When Stanley went out in 1871 and found Livingstone, he spent some months in his company, but Livingstone never spoke to Stanley about spiritual things. Throughout those months Stanley watched the old man. Livingstone's habits were beyond his comprehension, particularly his patience. He could not understand Livingstone's sympathy and patience for the Africans. For the sake of Christ and His gospel, the missionary doctor was patient, untiring, eager, spending himself and being spent for his Master.

Stanley wrote, "When I saw that unwearied patience, that unflagging zeal, those enlightened sons of Africa, I became a Christian at his side, though he never spoke a word to me about it."

Kindness Fruit

38. Kindness — Love in Little Acts

Beth Robertson, in her beautiful verse says:

When I think of the charming people I know,
It's surprising how often I find
The chief of the qualities that make them so
Is just that they are kind.

Hidden behind the stately but now sometimes misunderstood speech of the King James Version is our next fruit of the Spirit. The word means what we now define as "kindness." In connection with not grieving the Holy Spirit the Scripture says, "And be kind to one another, tenderhearted, forgiving one another, as God in Christ forgave you" (Ephesians 4:32).

Kindness is awareness of how the other feels, consideration of these feelings, and adaptation of one's attitudes, words, and behavior accordingly. Some want to pull out of the fabric this thread of love because it too often seems sentimental, indulgent, or even hypocritical. But love is kind. 1 Corinthians 13:4.

Kindness understands the other person even when he does wrong. Tenderheartedness seems to remove the case for misunderstanding and the reason for doing wrong. Forgiveness restores the wrongdoer in a right relationship so that love removes the wrong.

Plummer on 2 Corinthians 6:6 says that kindness in men is "the sympathetic kindliness or sweetness of temper which puts others at their ease, and shrinks forgiving pains." The English word "gentleness" partly covers the meaning, but does not go far enough, as the Greek word means a kindly disposition shown in active service.

Loving-kindness in the Scripture refers to kindness growing out of love. Although this word is dropped by most modern translations it is still beautiful and corresponds to 1 Corinthians 13:4 where Paul says, "Love is kind." Epictetus centuries ago said that he knows a man belongs to God when he has on him the spirit of gentleness, generosity, patience, and affection.

The psalmist was continually amazed at the kindness of God. This was his only claim to God's gifts for him. This was the only claim to God's forgiveness. God's kindness is that which draws us to Him with the cords of love.

Not Mere Sentiment

Kindness is not an artificial, shallow niceness or unreal feeling or weakness. Kindness is that spiritual grace which flows from spiritual strength and stature. David in 2 Samuel 22:36, KJV, in speaking of God says, "Thy gentleness hath made me great." Only the strong can be gentle. God is great enough to be gentle. The insecure and the weak must be burly and boasting. Such must advertise their ability to punch other people's noses. The strong do not need to retaliate, defend themselves, or boast.

A weak Christian deals in harsh criticism, makes verbal attack on others, and cannot stand those who may differ or those who do not treat him as he thinks he should be treated. The strong Christian is the most gentle Christian. The Spirit of Christ makes one kind, friendly, generous, and gentle. Kindness takes us off the judgment seat and puts us on the mercy seat.

So it is that the Holy Spirit makes our ways gentle. To walk in the Spirit means we walk in the way of kindness, in speech and action. We are strong enough to admit that we do not have all the answers and the Spirit gives us a yieldedness out of kind concern for others.

A church usher was instructing a young successor in the details of his office. "And remember, my boy," he concluded. "that we have nothing but good, kind Christians in this church until you try to seat someone else in their pew."

The Test of Kindness

Kindness, like the other Christian graces, is only tested when we are rubbed the wrong way. The test of a person's kindness is not when all is going well. It comes when something or someone goes wrong.

So we grow in the Christian grace of kindness when something difficult or rude comes into our lives and we remain kind. Kindness is tested and demonstrated in the home, not when everything goes smoothly but when the milk is spilled, when the window gets broken, when a member of the household gets hurt, when one is impatient or says hasty and cutting words. These are the opportunities in which the Spirit helps us to remain kind.

Francis de Sales wrote, "Bear in mind that the bee which makes the honey lives upon a bitter food; and in like manner we can never make acts of gentleness and patience, or gather the honey of the truest virtues, better than while eating the bread of bitterness and enduring hardness. And just as the best honey is that made from thyme, a small and bitter herb, so that virtue which is practiced amid bitterness and lowly sorrow is the best of all virtues."

The same is true in the shop or office. The test as to whether we have kindness, this fruit of the Spirit, is when

203

things go wrong, when another is disagreeable, and when we have every reason to react in rage. "The fruit of the Spirit is . . . kindness."

In the church also a little kindness is needed. Just a little goes a long way. "Love is kind," says the Apostle Paul. In the church our love is shown when, under adverse circumstances, we can remain kind. We are kind when through the power of the Holy Spirit we respond in kindness, when angry words are said, when things are done against us, and when things go wrong.

Remember, kindness is only tested and can only mature when it faces unkindness.

Love in Action

What then is kindness? Kindness is love in little things. It is respect for the feelings and personhood of another. It is thoughtfulness put in action. It is the kind of spirit which builds togetherness and love in situations which could be explosive. Kindness brings blessing and good feeling in the places where bitterness and ill will would flourish.

What is kindness? Kindness is helping another in need. It is consideration of the relationships between persons. Kindness is conversation which centers on the good qualities of others. Kindness avoids speaking evil. Kindness reaches out to others in trouble or suffering. Kindness supports others. Kindness gives a helping hand or healing touch in time of trouble. Kindness refrains from words which will hurt another or cast doubt on character. Instead it will speak kindly and hope for the best.

Kindness is more than humility;
It bears a load the second mile,
It gives to the man who begs

Before he speaks his need —
And it is given
Not grudgingly,
But with a smile!

Kindness is not fearful meekness;
No! It is the extended hand,
The overflowing cup,
The extra measure, pressed down and flowing o'er the
    brim.
It is the unexpected grace,
It is compassion — a feeling with
A fellowman clutched by a fate
He did not seek.
It is weeping with the sorrowful
And sharing the joy
Of those whom life has blest.

Kindness is kinship.
It is hailing every man as brother!
It is yielding to him the honor;
Recognizing him
As a son of God.

Roy O. McClain says, "When I look back on my own
paltry life the things that stand out are few. Not the publicity, the degrees, not the facts memorized. The only
things that stand out are the few things in which I have
tried to be kind."

What is kindness? Kindness is a word or act that will
not be forgotten. "Put on then, as God's chosen ones, holy
and beloved, . . . kindness . . ." (Colossians 3:12).

205

39. One Letter Different

While attending the Berlin World Congress on Evangelism in 1966, I heard evangelist Martin Higgenbottom describe his mother as being "love personified." One day he found her sitting at the table with an old tramp. Apparently she had gone shopping, met the tramp along the way, and invited him home for a warm meal.

During the conversation the tramp said, "I wish there were more people like you in the world." Whereupon his mother replied. "Oh, there are! But you must just look for them." The old man simply shook his head, saying, "But lady, I didn't need to look for you. You looked for me!"

When that mother reflected her Christian kindness toward the tramp she did something more than simply offer him welfare. It was a compassion that went out of its way to love the unlovely. That is the story of our Savior's life, death, and resurrection. He came looking for us in the sin-sick, the maimed and lame, the bruised and broken-hearted, the wretched wanderer, the poor and forgotten, the prisoner and the lonely rich.

Wherever Jesus went people felt toward Him exactly as the tramp felt about that mother. They could only lament that so few demonstrated by their daily acts of kindness the saving power of divine love. Hearts of compassion were so completely absent in the climate even among the religious.

Kindness is no lavender and old-lace virtue. It is a most virile, workable relationship when put to practice. The word "kindness" in the original Greek is spelled *Chrestos*, while the word for Christ is spelled *Christos*. Just one letter difference. Little wonder then that the early pagans got the Christians confused with kindness as they should then and as people should today. God's kindness was exemplified, demonstrated, and incarnated in Jesus Christ. It is also to be the same in us.

Jesus Looked for People

Read the Gospels again. Jesus spent His time showing kindness to all kinds of people. He moved among people adding new dimension to their lives. Kindness shone from His eyes, for little children loved to be near Him. Children have a cunning ability to detect the unkind heart and mind.

One day Jesus passed by a certain pool of water. A man lay there who was sick for a long time. No one else was kind enough to lift him into the water at the proper time. Jesus turned aside and made him well.

Jesus, tired from travel and the pressures of people, sat one day on the edge of a well. While His disciples were gone, a woman who longed so much for love that she gave herself time and again to lust, came to draw water. She came at noon because she was ostracized by other people. Jesus saw her thirst for love and spoke kindly with her. In a few moments she knew such words could come only from the Messiah Himself.

Another day Jesus was eating at the house of Simon the Pharisee. When a sinful woman interrupted the dinner, Jesus did not ignore or deny her the opportunity of demonstrating her devotion to Him. Aware of her deep gratitude for His forgiveness, He allowed her to do what any other religious teacher of His day would have considered inappropriate and improper. He cared for her. Because He cared, His kindness was considerate. While others sought to demonstrate their purity by pointing out the impurity in her, Jesus demonstrated His purity by His kindness to one in need.

A Multitude of Love

The entire Bible speaks of this same kindness concerning the God we love and serve. A kind and loving God stood in sharp contrast to the gods of the heathen.

Isaiah said, "I will mention the lovingkindnesses of the Lord, and the praises of the Lord, according to all that the Lord hath bestowed on us, . . . according to the multitude of his lovingkindnesses" (Isaiah 63:7, KJV).

Last night I was tired and just about asleep when my son, just turned four, came to my bedside with a book.

"Daddy," he said, "would you be kind enough to read this book to me?"

Asking it that way, what father could refuse? If there is one thing I want to be more of, it is to be more kind. Here was an opportunity to prove kindness at a hard time.

Today his question remains with me. I wonder why he phrased his question the way he did. In fact, last night I laughingly asked him, "Where did you learn to ask a question like that?" He simply smiled and sat down beside me.

It was an eloquent and persuasive way of asking me to fulfill his desire. Today as I thought about it I was reminded of the description of our heavenly Father. He is characterized by "loving-kindness." When we come to Him, the question is not, "Would You be kind enough?" We know He is kind. Even when our askings are not for our good; when they are selfish, He is kind enough to withhold that which will hurt. He waits to give us anything in His treasury that will help us.

How easy it is to forget the kindness of God! Because

of His kindness we are not consumed. In spite of our selfishness He remains kind, because all His acts toward us are
motivated by love.

Though num'rous hosts of mighty foes,
Though earth and hell my way oppose,
He safely leads my soul along,
His loving-kindness, oh, how strong!

When trouble, like a gloomy cloud,
Has gathered thick, and thundered loud,
He near my soul has always stood,
His loving-kindness, oh, how good!
— Samuel Medley

40. Kindness Is Kinship

A mother developed the habit of being cross and complaining at home. Away from home she was all sweetness and light. One night after she was especially irritable she heard her child pray, "Dear God, make Mommy be kind to us like she is to people we visit."

At first she felt the prayer was funny. She told it to her husband. He looked at her with a serious expression. Then he said, "You do not treat us with the courtesy you show to the business people and our friends." It was a turning point for the mother.

One of the marks of the Christian life, a fruit of the Spirit, is kindness. An old Scottish proverb says, "Remember if you are not very kind, you are not very spiritual." As family members it is all too easy to develop an unkind disposition. So the ones we love most often bear the brunt of discourtesy and irritability.

Kindness carries a note of kinship. It is an act between creatures of the same kind. Dr. William Bede McGrath, Fellow of the American Psychiatric Association, says, "Ninety percent of all mental illness that comes before me could have been prevented, or could yet be cured, by simple kindness." If but a simple act of kindness goes so far in its therapeutic ministry, it should be no insurmountable burden for Christian people to be kind.

Kindness is love in little things. In little things we fail most often. While we wait for something big to happen in which we might show our character, the truth is that character comes forth the clearest in how faithful we are in little things. Wordsworth wrote: "The best portion of a good man's life is his little, nameless, unremembered acts of kindness and love." Every happy home or church is made loving by little acts and words of kindness. Amy R. Raabe says:

Scatter seeds of kindness
Everywhere you go;
Scatter bits of courtesy —
Watch them grow and grow.
Gather buds of friendship;
Keep them till full-blown.
You will find more happiness
Than you have ever known.
Gather every bit of love,
All that you can find;
With it bind the broken hearts,
For love heals all mankind.

Kindness Is Greatness

Two plain farmers walked out of a railroad station where they had received rude treatment at the ticket window. Said one to the other, "The smaller the station, the bigger the agent." That holds for many other positions as well. It is good, however, to remember that great persons whether in high positions or low, grace their position with kindness.

Kindness is a grace needed everywhere and it can be practiced anywhere. Anyone can complain and be rude. Only great souls are really kind.

Now it is possible to do many great things yet never learn the grace of kindness. It is, however, a mark of love. "Love . . . is kind." It should be the mark of the Christian. Yet at times a waitress in a restaurant manages to show more kindness than a renowned church leader. In this the waitress is more Christian and the church leader lacks in Christian grace.

The lack of Christian kindness is no small thing. How often have persons turned in disgust or dismay from Christians because of rudeness?

A lack of kindness or tenderness leads to self-righteousness. In *The Mill on the Floss* by George Eliot, Maggie Tulliver speaks to her brother Tom, "You have always enjoyed punishing me. You have always been hard and cruel to me. Even when I was a little girl, and always loved you better than anyone else in the world, you would let me go crying to bed without forgiving me. You have no pity; you have no sense of your own imperfection and your own sins. It is a sin to be hard; it is not fitting for a mortal — for a Christian. You are nothing but a Pharisee. You thank God for nothing but your own virtues — you think they are great enough to win you everything else. You have not even a vision of feelings by the side of which your shining virtues are mere darkness!"

Kindness Enlarges Life

On the other hand kindness, tenderness, love for others, expressed in daily life enlarges the soul. An impressive story was told several years ago by R. Lee Sharpe in the *Alabama Baptist.*

"I was just a child," related Sharpe. "One spring day, Father called me to go with him to old man Trussell's blacksmith shop. He had left a rake and a hoe to be repaired. And they were ready, fixed like new. Father handed over a silver dollar for repairing. But Mr. Trussell refused to take it. 'No,' he said, 'there's no charge for that little job.' But Father insisted.

"If I live a thousand years," said Mr. Sharpe, "I'll never forget that great blacksmith's reply. 'Sid,' he said to my father, 'can't you let a man do something — just to stretch his soul?' "

Isaac Watts penned the following lines about kindness:

Kind words toward those you daily meet.
  Kind words and actions right,
Will make this life of ours most sweet,
  Turn darkness into light.

Kindness, it has been observed, is a language which the blind can see and the deaf can hear.

Forgiveness is also an element of the kindness, "Forgiving one another, as God in Christ forgave you." Forgiveness means that we show kindness, arising out of a tender heart, even to those who injure others, us, and themselves. Kindness does not harbor the thought of who is guilty. It seeks only that joy of right relationship. Then only can the Spirit produce in the life the image of Christ.

When Leonardo da Vinci was working on his painting *The Last Supper*, he became angry with a certain man. Losing his temper he lashed the other fellow with bitter words and threats. Returning to his canvas he attempted to work on the face of Jesus, but he was unable to do so. He was so upset he could not compose himself for the painstaking work. Finally, he put down his tools and sought out the man and asked his forgiveness. The man accepted his apologies and Leonardo was able to return to his workshop and finish painting the face of Jesus.

A minister serving a church in Brooklyn in the days of Henry Ward Beecher told of a man who hated Beecher so much that he would have nothing to do with him. Later, however, he came to be the famous man's devoted friend.

His explanation of the change was simple. Whenever a man did Beecher an ill turn, Beecher was not happy until he had done the offender a good turn. It came to be a whimsical proverb in Brooklyn, "If you want a favor from Beecher, kick him."

Never does the human soul appear so strong as when it foregoes revenge and dares to forgive an injury. Like his Lord, Beecher forgave as often as there was occasion to do so.

"And be kind to one another, tenderhearted, forgiving one another, as God in Christ forgave you" (Eph. 4:32).

41. The Kingdom of Kindness

Henry Penn, former president of the Society of American Florists, tells what he calls one of the memorable incidents of his life as a florist. One day two boys and a girl about ten years of age made a visit to his store. They wore ragged clothes, but had clean faces and hands. The boys took off their caps when they entered the shop. One of them stepped forward and said solemnly, "We're the committee, and we'd like some very nice yellow flowers."

Penn showed them some inexpensive spring flowers. But the boy said, "I think we'd like something better than that."

"Do they have to be yellow?" asked Penn.

"Yes, sir," was the reply. "Mickey would like even better if they were yellow. He had a yellow sweater."

"Are these for a funeral?" the florist quietly inquired.

The boy nodded. The girl turned to keep back the tears. "She's his sister," the boy explained. "He was a good kid. A truck — yesterday — he was playing in the street. We saw it happen."

Then the other boy added, "Us kids took up a collection. We got eighteen cents. Would — would roses cost an awful lot, Mister? Yellow roses?"

Touched by the story of the tragedy and the loyalty and love of these youngsters, Penn replied, "I have some nice yellow roses here that I'm selling for eighteen cents a dozen."

"Gee, those will be swell!" exclaimed one of the boys.

"Mickey'd like those," the other one confirmed.

"I'll make up a nice spray," promised the sympathic florist, "with ferns and a ribbon. Where shall I send them?"

"Would it be all right, Mister, if we took them now?" asked one of the boys. "We'd kinda like to — you know, take 'em over and — sort of give 'em to Mickey — ourselves. He'd like it better that way."

Penn accepted the eighteen cents. The "committee," carrying the "kind of flowers Mickey would like," walked out of the shop. Said Penn, "I felt uplifted for days. Unbeknown to them, I had a part in their tribute to their friend."

Known for Kindness

Kindness and love go together. Christians down through the centuries have had no greater compliment paid to them than that they have shown kindness toward others. Without kindness we are unworthy to be called Christians, unworthy of fellowship in God's kingdom of love. If we accept love as the heart of the Christian way of life, we must start building the kingdom of kindness. No devil can claim a person's soul when he is sincerely serving the needs of others.

In light of the centrality of love and concern which Christ calls for and in light of what Jesus said when He called us to love others as we love ourselves, isn't it strange that Christians, many times, are not known for kindness?

Jerome Davis years ago wrote, "If we study the history of the church, we find that the ethical and moral teachings of Jesus naturally follow from loving one's neighbor as one's self even when not written into a single one of the great creeds of Christendom. This has often made the church less effective than it might have been."

To be kind means we must beware of hardening of the

attitudes. It is so easy to become indifferent. The great danger facing all of us is that someday we will wake up and find that we were busy with everything else except helping others.

Step into Another's Shoes

Millicent Basore of Dallas, Texas, tells of an experience we can all identify with. "While I waited at the bus stop, I met a man who seemed to have the problems of the world on his shoulders. God presented this opportunity for me to witness. I witnessed, but how I did it bothered me.

"As the man talked to me about his problems, I quickly detected that he had been drinking. Rather than show compassion, I was infuriated by the smell of liquor on his breath. Rather than listen or try to help with a kind word, I turned my back.

"Who was I to judge him? Was I supposed to set myself apart from him? Could I not have taken a few minutes to listen to him? I could have witnessed to my faith in Christ and spoken to him of the way of salvation He offers to everyone.

"What must Christ have thought of me in that moment of failing?

"When I turned my back to the man, he sensed that I did not want to be bothered. He apologized. It left me disturbed. I am still disturbed." [1]

Gandhi one time said, "Three fourths of the miseries and misunderstandings of the world will disappear if we step into the shoes of our adversaries and understand their viewpoint." This is true not only of adversaries but of everyone we meet.

---

1. From *The Upper Room,* May 27, 1971, copyright by The Upper Room and used with permission.

Napoleon thought he could be great because he founded a kingdom on force. Perhaps it is worth listening to his words of warning at the end of his life. Napoleon said, "Alexander, Caesar, Charlemagne, and myself founded empires. But on what did we rest the creations of our genius? Upon force. Jesus Christ alone founded His empire upon love; and at this hour, millions of men would die for Him."

Helen Good Brenneman, well-known devotional writer, speaks of the need for kindness this way. "There was once a man who had a heart transplant. But the operation was a total failure. For the man was a mean man and the heart was a kind heart. His body simply rejected it.

"The Bible tells us, however, of a heart transplant which was successful;

'And I will give them a new heart,
and put a new spirit within them;
I will take the stony heart out of their flesh
and give them a heart of flesh, that they
may walk in my statutes and keep my ordinances
and obey them; and they shall be my people,
and I will be their God.'

"Someone has changed David's prayer to read, 'Create in me a kind heart, O God, and renew a right spirit within me. Amen.'"

God speaking through the Apostle Peter says, "Giving all diligence, add to your faith virtue; and to virtue knowledge; and to knowledge temperance; and to temperance patience; and to patience godliness; and to godliness *brotherly kindness*; and to brotherly kindness charity. For if these things be in you, and abound, they make you that ye shall neither be barren nor unfruitful in the knowledge of our Lord Jesus Christ" (2 Peter 1:5-8, KJV).

42. Kindness Transforms

A young lady went to work for an executive who had the reputation of being the most cantankerous and critical spirit in the firm. At best he kept a secretary several months. This young lady needed work and determined to do her best to keep the job. Working for the man was all she could bear until she decided on a strategy to pay the "old goat" a compliment every day.

On the first day of her new approach, all that she could think of nice to say to him was, "That's very fine material in your suit, Sir!" Each day she found some little thing to compliment him on. In a short time she saw that it wasn't so difficult to find something real to say and her employer was becoming a different person. In fact, her looking for ways of being constructive in what seemed like an unbearable situation transformed an unlovable boss into a lovable man, who later became her husband.

In that great novel *Les Miserables* it is the story of gentleness which makes it great. Jean Valjean, caught in crime and hardened by the rough treatment of years, is dragged back into the old priest's presence, having been caught with the silver candlesticks he stole from the kindhearted man who had taken him in for the night.

But the look of fear in his scared face changed to bewilderment as the kindly father beamed on him and in love

said, "My son, didn't you understand I gave them to you?"
That was the moment of Jean Valjean's regeneration.
Kindness is the transforming power of life.

Kindness Leads to Kindness

Last winter, on a bitter cold night a stranger stopped
at my neighbor's home. His car had broken down nearby.
Now he needed a way home. Since it was quite a distance
to drive and my neighbor and his family had an appoint-
ment elsewhere for several hours, he invited the stranger in,
told him to make himself at home. "After we get back
tonight I'll take you home."

My neighbor came home about 9:30 and he took the
man to his home. When he arrived at the house of the man
the stranger said, "I can't believe it. I never would have
taken a person such a distance myself. After this I will help
people when they need help."

Jesus made an amazing claim for simple kindness. He
said that when we give a person so little a thing as a drink
of cool water we are really giving it to Him. "Inasmuch
as ye have done it unto one of the least of these my brethren, ye have done it unto me" (Matthew 25:40, KJV). In
serving others we are really serving Him and this act of
kindness is the direct road to the presence of God Himself.
People know God is at work and that we have passed from
death to life when we are "kindly affectioned one to another"
and "in honour prefer one another."

"Kindness from a good friend may be more helpful to
persons than long sessions in a doctor's office," said the head
of the psychology department at the University of Oregon.
"A good talk with a close friend," said Dr. Joseph Mataroz-
zo, "can solve problems, or at least put them in perspective
before they become overpowering. One of the problems we
face today is a scarcity of friends."

Kindness Is Friendship

Being a friend does not take a special gift. It takes a special grace — the grace of kindness. A friend is one who is kind, patient, and loving enough to listen to what bothers us. A friend is one who does not look down upon us because we feel broken, discouraged, or mixed up. A friend listens and hears the need we ourselves have difficulty understanding. A friend is one who, simply by letting us share, helps us hear our own words so that we gain a proper perspective.

How often have we said to a friend who listened, "You have been such a real help. Thanks a lot." After reflecting we remind ourselves that our friend just listened, not only with the ears, but with the heart. He hardly said a word. Yet we were refreshed and encouraged. But there is a scarcity of friends.

F. W. Robertson wrote, "Let the weakest, but the humblest, remember, that in his daily course he can, if he will, shed around him almost a heaven. Kindly words, sympathizing attentions, watchfulness against wounding men's sensitiveness — these cost very little, but they are priceless in their value. Are they not almost the staple of our daily happiness? From hour to hour, from moment to moment, we are supported, blest, by small kindnesses."

Robertson suggests that love shows itself in small kindnesses and in our desire to do nothing which hurts another. We know "we should love one another." However, we sometimes forget this means in the small things of life which happen every moment of every day. The small things transform all of life.

Mary Beth Littlejohn tells of her experience when her kindness to another also transformed all of life. "A wise college teacher made a most unusual assignment to a group of us seniors. She said in effect, 'Select the person on campus whom you dislike the most. Daily during the coming month go out of your way to do some act of kindness for that person.'

"In the same building with me roomed a freshman girl who seemed to delight in disobeying all regulations and to take pleasure in being rude to everyone. She was my immediate choice. By the end of the month my dislike of her had been replaced by a growing compassion and understanding. I found myself glad for an opportunity to help her overcome the warping effects of an unhappy childhood.

"She helped me see things about myself — my unfriendliness, my lack of compassion, my judging without first trying to understand the causes of behavior I disliked."

Jesus always tried to help persons free themselves from attitudes and influences that kept them from becoming their best selves. He did it mainly by kindness.

In Baltimore over 25 years ago a class in sociology went into the most horrible slum in the city and selected the two hundred worst children, marked two hundred cards with their names and records, and labeled each card: "Headed for Jail."

Twenty-five years later another class took these cards and began to check to see how accurate the prediction was. What was their surprise to find that only two of the two hundred had ever gone to jail. What was the reason? The answer is just one teacher, Aunt Hannah. She was a schoolteacher in this slum section and she had loved and believed in the children. When one stole, she helped him "go straight" and she created positive recreation for all the children. She transformed the slum by kindness.

43. The Witness of Kindness

Andrew Blackwood, Jr., wrote, "Usually when God speaks He speaks through the human voice that is kind. Nothing stops the sound of His voice so quickly as criticism, carping, unkindness." "The greatest thing a man can do for a heavenly Father," said Henry Drummond, "is to be kind to some of His other children." And Frederick William Faber said, "Kindness has converted more sinners than zeal, eloquence, or learning."

In the Book of Proverbs the highest praise is placed upon a godly mother by the statement, "In her tongue is the law of kindness."

Kindness is shown by the words we speak and the tone in which we speak them.

Frederick William Faber wrote, "Kind words are the music of this world. They have a power which seems to be beyond natural causes, as if they were some angel's song which had lost its way and come on earth. It seems as if they could almost do what in reality God alone can do — soften the hard and angry hearts of men. No one was ever directed by a sarcasm — crushed, perhaps, if the sarcasm was clever enough, but drawn nearer to God, never."

Small words of love and understanding work wonders. A father was reading his evening paper. His small son came in from playing to show him a scratch on his finger. Finally the father turned from his paper with some annoyance and said, "Well I can't do anything about it, can I?" "Yes," said the boy. "You could have at least said oh."

So also the small words, "Please," "I'm sorry," "Excuse me," and "Let me help you," are words used in the ministry of kindness which may be achieved by all. While great brilliance and intellect are to be admired, they cannot dry one tear or mend a broken spirit. Only kindness can accomplish this.

Kindness is shown by the small acts we do. One's ability for kindness is proved at the points where others mistreat us.

Love and Kindness

In an article on China in *Eternity*, the writer records a story of Christian love and kindness. "A Chinese cook was put into prison one night. It was bitterly cold — about twenty-six degrees below zero. He had on his padded clothes and a big fur coat, but a heathen man who was later thrown in with him had no wraps at all. The Christian man began to pray that God would get him out of prison, but while he was praying it seemed God spoke to him. 'I won't hear your prayer until you've taken off your fur coat and given it to this man who's got none.'

" 'But if I do that, I'll be frozen to death by morning,' the man thought.

" 'Well, if you don't,' he seemed to hear God reply, 'this man will be dead before morning.'

"So he took off his fur coat, gave it to the man and his life was saved.

"Later on at a Christian gathering in communist China I was present when the heathen man who had received the coat got up and gave his testimony. 'I'm here today because a man shared his coat with me in prison,' he said simply.

"The winning of souls to Christ doesn't depend upon platform appearances; it doesn't depend upon having foreign missionaries around; to some extent it doesn't depend on our doctrine. It depends upon whether we are prepared to share our coat. People are in need. People are suffering. And the very fact that you show Christian love and kindness makes you stand out." [1]

Kindness is not always bearing witness but kindness is the first step one must take to witness. Kindness is communication. It needs no voice to speak or ears to hear. It is understood in every language.

If our hearts are full of the love and kindness Christ commanded and Paul described, it cannot be hidden. It will show on the highways, in the way we drive our cars. It will show in the shopping centers, in the buying process. It will show in our home relationships by the tone of voice and the words we use. It will even show on our faces.

Pushing up to a stranger a man said, "Thank you, Sir. Thank you very much."

"But I have said nothing or done nothing for you. Thanks? What do you mean?"

"Your face is so wondrously kind," he said as he disappeared in the crowd.

Marcus Aurelius said that "kindness is irresistible when it is sincere and no mock smile or a mask assumed."

Many years after the great Welsh revival which renewed the church and raised the moral tone of the entire land, visitors met an old man who lived through those remarkable times. They asked him if he could recall anything about the times that struck him as being most characteristic of the revival.

He thought a moment. Then he said, "Yes, I can tell

1. Reprinted by permission from the September 1971 issue of *Eternity*.

you the characteristic feature of that wonderful time. For months before and for months afterward, the atmosphere was one of brotherly kindness and love." It reminds us that our spiritual light is not greater than our Christian love.

Gordon M. Forgersen tells of meeting a Filipino Methodist bishop on a Europe-bound ship. The bishop told of his experience when he came to North America as a student years before. The first Sunday his roommate appeared in the doorway, an umbrella under each arm. He offered to show him the way to his place of worship and then planned to go on to his own church. As they started down the street he thought, "If this man has this kind of faith and interest in my spiritual life, surely I should find out what his faith is like." He asked his friend to take him to his church and he attended it all four years. As a result he attended Drew Theological Seminary and years later became a bishop in the church.

Forgersen concludes his story by saying, "There is such a thing as a direct call from God without intermediaries, but rarely. Usually there is a man with two umbrellas."

Goodness Fruit

44. Goodness — Love in Action

In a biographical note on Francis of Assisi, Paul Sabatier wrote a beautiful comment which corresponds so closely with the life of our Lord. It should describe the commitment of all Christians. "When he saw suffering, wretchedness, corruption, instead of fleeing he stopped to bind up, to heal, feeling in his heart the surging of waves of compassion. He not only preached love to others; he himself was ravished with it; he sang it, and what was of greater value, he lived it.

"He went, not to the whole, who need no physician, but to the sick, the forgotten, the disclaimed. He dispensed the treasures of his heart according to the need and reserved the best of himself for the poorest and the most lost, for lepers and thieves."

While patience refers to bearing injuries, and kindness returning good for evil, goodness deals primarily with the motives of our speech and conduct. It lies at the heart of our character, behind all we say and do. Goodness refers to the strong, the pure, the sincere, within which it springs forth in godlike action toward others. Anglo-Saxon god meant "good" and "God." They are related.

Goodness Is Godliness

Goodness is the sum total of godliness in every area of thought and action. A good person is defined as a person with a good heart. Matthew 12:35. W. H. Murray described such a person: "A good man! Who shall describe him, or with what language shall we depict him? In his heart is love. In his bosom is joy. The atmosphere of his nature is peace. Enthroned within him is a divinest patience. Gentleness spreads its mild light over his countenance, and falls in charming language from his lips. But in him, too, is courage; courage to do and die. Strength also braces him like a guide. Temperance orders his life with discretion. Purity keeps his records stainless. Faith steadies his footsteps as he walks the high levels of his aspirations. . . . The fruit of the Spirit, therefore — its object and aim — is to produce a good man. . . . The good man or the good men that are to be must be born, not after the will of the flesh, but after the birth of the Spirit."

Goodness takes us back to the hidden sources of speech and conduct. It must first manifest itself in the heart before it can give proper accent to speech and expressive conduct. When the spirit purifies our motives, the fruit is goodness — both being good and expressing goodness.

Moffatt translates goodness as "generosity" having to do with liberality in spirit and action and magnanimity. Weymouth translates it "benevolence," dealing with the disposition to do good, wishing goodwill to all races of men and desiring their happiness, a lover of humanity.

Goodness joyfully serves in spite of blindness and obstacles. It doesn't ask for appreciation from those it serves. Goodness serves whether appreciated or not. It only wants to be a channel of good to others.

Goodness is always open-eyed and sees the need. It doesn't just see people but sees need and the sorrow another carries. It shares the sorrow and lends a helping hand to the one struggling at a hard task. It encourages the person who is ready to give up. It stands by the side of the lonely. Goodness spends itself without calculation of the expenditures because Christian love is the willingness to be inconvenienced.

A good person is one whose talent and skill are actively directed toward "good" purposes. Synonyms of goodness are generosity and benevolence. It means more than gentleness in that it displays sterner qualities. It can also display a zeal for truth and right by rebuking, correcting, and chastening. A parent displays goodness when he shows love to an erring child and along with love corrects and gives clear guidance for the right.

Jesus said in Luke 6:43-45, "For no good tree bears bad fruit, nor again does a bad tree bear good fruit; for each tree is known by its own fruit. For figs are not gathered from thorns, nor are grapes picked from a bramble bush. The good man out of the good treasure of his heart produces good, and the evil man out of his evil treasure produces evil; for out of the abundance of the heart his mouth speaks." Paul wrote to Titus, "And let our people learn to apply themselves to good deeds, so as to help cases of urgent need, and not to be unfruitful " (Titus 3:14).

Goodness Is Twofold

Goodness is what we receive and what we do. God gives us righteousness and transforms character. But goodness is not abstract. Aristotle understood when he wrote, "People must become just by doing what is just and temperate by doing what is temperate. . . . But most people, instead of taking such action take refuge in theorizing; they imagine that they are philosophers and that philosophy will make them virtuous."

Goodness is not mere abstention from evil. It will never be satisfied to speak the right and good. A "good" professor, teacher, preacher, or Christian is never satisfied with simply stating what goodness is. He does what is good. His good deeds become his purest prayers. Milton praised "no fugitive and cloistered virtue." Jesus asked for a life which can be seen as good and His was described years later as one who "went about doing good."

James Hamilton says it well: "Goodness is love in action, love with its hand to the plow, love with the burden on its back. It is love carrying medicine to the sick, and food for the famished. It is love reading the Bible to the blind, and explaining the gospel to the felon in his cell. It is love at Sunday-school class, or in the school. It is love at the hovel door, or sailing far away in the missionary ship. But whatever task it undertakes, it is still the same — love following His footsteps, 'who went about continually doing good.'"

Good is possible only as the Holy Spirit has freedom to work it out through our lives. As the old nature is changed and we receive the new nature, goodness becomes the fruit of the Holy Spirit. Education does not make people good. Over half of Hitler's high command were highly educated. Most had their master's degrees and several their doctorates. These are the men who practiced genocide, devised mass murder methods, injected children with TB germs and watched them die, and had the furnaces built to burn millions of people.

Goodness is the result of the new life within and not the result of self-struggle, the notion that we are essentially good, the attempt to make a list of whether we do more good things than bad, or a matter of good intentions.

When we see that any goodness we do is through God at work in us through His Spirit we will not boast or pretend something we are not. We will only thank God that He has given us spiritual eyes and the desire to be His person, doing His work in the world.

45. Jesus Went About Doing Good

An English nobleman, Sir Bartle, was known for his kind and helpful spirit. A stranger in the city asked how he might identify Sir Bartle. "Look for the tall gentleman helping somebody," was the prompt reply.

No doubt when people of Jesus' day asked, "How do you identify this Jesus?" those who knew Him answered, "Look for the man who is helping someone." Years later when the disciples described Christ's ministry, they said that God had anointed Him with the Holy Spirit. "He went about doing good and healing all that were oppressed by the devil, for God was with him" (Acts 10:38).

People knew where to go for help. Jesus never put a sign outside His door announcing His availability to counsel, heal, or help them. Even when He tried to go to the desert to rest, the crowds followed Him. When He entered a ship to cross the sea, so that He might find relaxation, the people walked around the edge to meet Him on the other side. Jesus was always ready to help, to be inconvenienced, to be generous to those in need.

Goodness Sees Opportunities

Jesus was kind and good to all. The most beautiful portrait given Him in the New Testament is the five words: "He went about doing good." His constant attitude toward people was that of overflowing helpfulness. His actions magnified His words, "The Son of man came not to be ministered unto, but to minister, and to give his life a ransom for many." Graciousness, kindliness, active helpfulness toward others marked all the earthly steps of Jesus. He showed us what love means by promoting the well-being of others.

A friend told me recently that the great impression he came away with after prolonged fellowship with Frank Laubach, the great leader in literacy work throughout the world, was Laubach's great and constant desire to help people. He saw all kinds of opportunities to help. I remember riding on a plane beside Dr. Laubach one evening. His words to those who spoke with us and his actions to all who served us were gracious and helpful. Together we noticed a rainbow outside the window of the plane before takeoff. "There is our sign of God's blessing on our meeting together," he whispered to me.

In the tragedy recorded in John's Gospel, chapter five, concerning the sick man by the pool of Bethesda something is usually missed. The religious people who were pushing around saw a mattress and missed a miracle. They saw a man carrying his bed on the Sabbath day. This was a tragedy to their way of thinking. But the greatest tragedy was in the answer of the man to Jesus, when He asked, "Do you want to be made whole?" The poor man responded, "Sir, I have no man . . . to put me into the pool."

The man had remained by the pool for many years. While in his great need for help, he had likely heard plenty of prayers of religious people. He noticed all the religious observances. He saw them keep the Sabbath and other special services and festivities with great pomp and holy air. Who could judge him wrongly, if all this religiosity had made him bitter as he waited week after week for someone to care enough to help him?

The Scripture concerning Christ which ought to be the

text for every preacher's sermon at some time or other is, Jesus "went about doing good." What does that mean for Christians today? Perhaps people are tired of the repetition of our church sermons and activities, sermon after sermon, and program after program. Perhaps many people real close are still saying as the man in John 5 must have said many times, "There is no man to help me."

Goodness Helps and Loves People

Jesus tried continually to get through to people that "goodness" was something different from what they surmised. The people of His day, like us, assumed they were good if they kept certain rules, lived a clean life, and kept from doing certain evils. It was a negative notion of goodness. Jesus pointed to goodness being something much different.

I can imagine the ire which Jesus must have sometimes raised. Think of how hurt some were when He said adulteresses and adulterers will get into the kingdom before many of the pious religious leaders. I can hear His religious critics clamor for Him to repeal such a statement lest He imply that such sins were not serious.

Think how angry some were when He criticized persons for the manner in which they tithed every little thing. By doing this He was certainly a threat to their whole, good program of giving. Not only did He break man's rules regarding the Sabbath, but He said things which sounded to many as if He desired to do away with the commandments. I can hear someone say that He was a real heretic, and people should not listen to one who hinted that some of the sacred teachings should be looked at again. What was He trying to do after all — give people a false hope and a false freedom? Why did He need to use such outrageous illustrations of goodness and righteousness?

What Jesus really said was that the entire Old Testament taught that "goodness" or godlikeness consists in loving people. It consists in helping people to become better persons. How often He taught this idea!

Another illustration which must have caused pious people considerable consternation was the story Jesus told about a Samaritan. He implied that a despised Samaritan who showed "goodness" to another was nearer to God's will than they were. Of all people a Samaritan! A Samaritan was a dog, the scum of society in the eyes of those who heard Jesus. Think how they must have burned with anger when He spoke of a Samaritan being a better neighbor and one who kept God's will in contrast to their respected religious leaders. One can hear such cries as, "Now Jesus is even getting our young people to think that Samaritan unbelievers are good people to pattern their living after." They missed the whole point.

How might Jesus tell the Samaritan story today?

Now it came to pass that a certain man was traveling Lonesome Street, a lonely and dark road, from Tom's Tavern to Bill's Bar. And behold liquor got hold of him and stripped him of all his goods and left him destitute and dying on skid row.

There came that way a certain respected religious leader, a bishop in the church. He saw the drunk with the bleeding skull and vomit covering his clothes. Deciding he was too drunk to talk to about his soul, he felt society should do something to prohibit such drunkenness. He passed by on the right as far and fast as possible.

Soon a Christian social worker, whose training taught him how to care for persons with all kinds of social and personal problems, came that way. He saw the man stretched out on the sidewalk. He looked at him. But concluding that the man was beyond help or hope, he straightway continued on his way.

After some time an outcast of society, a hippie, came down Lonesome Street. Though hated by respectable people and watched with suspicion by the police, the hippie saw the dying drunk. And when he saw the man he came where he was. He called a fellow hippie to help him. While he spoke soothing words he lifted the man in his arms and took him to a place he knew the man would be cared for.

Now who was neighbor to him that fell through drink? Who demonstrated the clearest meaning of goodness?

46. The Basin Stops Here

Harry Truman, while president, had a motto on his desk which read, "The buck stops here." He could not leave decisions to someone else. The final decision was his.

I would like to suggest that an excellent service motto for us Christians is, "The basin stops here." As Christians we dare never avoid opportunities to do good and to serve others. Christ wants us to answer as best we can the call of need, be it large or small, spiritual or physical. We dare not pass by on the other side or hope someone else will help.

In spite of Christ's story of the good Samaritan, the example of Christ Himself, and the New Testament teaching of the Christian's obligation to help others in need, many Christians do not believe this truth. The Scripture says that if we see a person in need and turn away, the love of God does not indwell us.

Compassion Fatigue

"Compassion Fatigue" is a new term heard among some people of our affluent society today. It means, "I'm tired of repeated calls to do good." Why must our enjoyment of bountiful feasting be spoiled by reminders that over half the world is slowly starving, that many in our own neighborhoods are terribly poor. Our superhighways and our by-passes help keep these people out of sight.

The Apostle Paul writes in Galatians, "Let us never tire of doing good. . . . Let us work for the good of all, especially members of the household of the faith" (Galatians 6:9, 10, NEB).

A Servant Stance

Christ calls us as Christians to be servants. Concerning His own coming Christ said, "The Son of man came not to be served but to serve, and give his life as a ransom for many." Again He said, "Whoever would be great among you must be your servant, and whoever would be first among you must be your slave."

Of course this is a radical reversal of our age and every age. The world tries to get the highest position. To be great is to see how many persons will serve us. We love our lunch counters and our names in the paper noting our promotions. Jesus reverses it all when He points out we are not called to status but to servanthood. It is not the prominence of position but a certain posture — servanthood. This image of the servant appears in the New Testament at least fifty times in eighteen different writings.

Voltaire said in speaking of philosophers, "We never cared to enlighten cobblers and maidservants. This is the work of apostles."

"Thank God it is!" commented G. Campbell Morgan. "There is the supreme difference between all philosophy apart from Christ and the Christian evangel. Paul, just between midnight and the first flush of dawn upon the sky, took time to teach that brutalized jailer, the man who came in unworthy panic saying, 'What must I do to be saved?' The answer came quick and sharp and vibrant with the music that the listening men knew not of; 'Believe on the

Lord Jesus Christ.'

"It is a picture of all time. Philosophers do not care to enlighten cobblers and maidservants; but apostles never speak of cobblers and maidservants. They speak of men and women in the image and likeness of God and it is always worth while to spend time with them, to explain to them the mightiest things of the universe. That is the picture of Christianity." [1]

The call of Christ is to think of ourselves as Christ's servants wherever we go in whatever we do. To do good in the sense of the Scripture is to see no duty too small to do, and to see no task too meager to tackle, to see no person too insignificant to encourage and lift, and to see no brother too unimportant to help, to see no feet too unclean to stoop and wash.

After all, the church is what it is and what it does. We are what we do. When Jesus washed the disciples' feet they watched in shocked silence. Peter protested but the rest sat speechless and ashamed. Jesus was not trying to teach charity. All religions teach charity. Jesus was teaching a life of unconditional service to those in Christ and to those like Judas.

Measure of Life Realized in Service

What is the meaning of life? Is it in how long we live, how famous we become, or how rich we are at retirement? Jesus says the measure of life is in our service, the good we do for others. Out of this spirit has come every Christian college and school, and orphanage and beneficent work in the world.

George W. Truett, the great Baptist preacher, said, "It

---

1. G. Campbell Morgan, *The Acts of the Apostles* (Old Tappan, N.J.: Fleming H. Revell, 1924), pp. 393, 394.

is not the talents one has that make him great, however many and brilliant they may be; it is not the vast amount of study that gives mental enrichment to the mind and life; it is not in shining social qualities; it is not the large accumulation of wealth that secures peace and honor; in none of these, measured by God's standards, does greatness reside. But true greatness consists in the use of all the talents one has in unselfish ministry to others."

One of the greatest hindrances to goodness today is the passion for money and material things. It is unquestionably the black plague of our individual, social, and national life. Stealthily but surely it is corrupting our highest ideals in education, literature, statesmanship, and religion. We talk about heathen idolatry, but no heathen temple was more crowded with eager devotees than the temple of mammon. We sell our souls for dusty gold, status symbols, and refrigerators.

> Ill fares the land, to hastening ills a prey,
> Where wealth accumulates, and men decay.

The grace of goodness is a reversal of this spirit. While selfishness puts to death the beautiful, the useful, and the right, goodness gives life. While selfishness covers the face with coarseness and puts harshness and discord in the singer's voice, goodness gives gladness and glow wherever it goes. While selfishness takes away the intensity and conviction of the orator's lips and corrodes the soul, goodness imparts grace and cleanses all it touches.

Where Happiness Dwells

In seeking to find happiness search for the one who has scars on his hands, feet, and heart. We do not find happiness in the life of one with smooth hands, uncalloused feet, and a heart that has no pain. It is the one who suffers with others and moves among men to help and to share the best one possesses who knows true happiness. These are the radiant few, and you'll know them by their faces. These spend their time making themselves, not free and independent, but sympathetic and indispensable. Even the world knows to what doors it must build its roads.

Happiness is the inevitable result of a certain kind of life. If you don't believe it, someday take time to see how frustrated people spend their time. You will likely find their lives filled with desire for beaches, banquets, and belongings. Then search out the radiant few and you will find them sitting by sickbeds ministering to them of God's goodness. They will be carrying food to the hungry. You will find them around a family altar beseeching God on behalf of others. You will find them behind pulpits and teachers' lecterns giving themselves so that others might have. In fact you will find them in nearly every kind of occupation and place on the globe. But there will always be one thing true. They will not be searching for happiness; they will be sharing happiness. They will not be asking to be served but they will be asking to serve. From first to last, the men and women who were and will be the regnant forces of the world, are those who rejoice in the title of "servant."

So it isn't primarily a question of what you get out of life. It's not the dividend complex you need. It is rather the kind of investment you are making. The dividends have a way of taking care of themselves. Dorcas, with her needle, will be immortal when Napoleon is forgotten. Mary with her alabaster box will live on and on when Alexander's name shall be buried in oblivion. The cup of cold water lifted to lips of the thirsty child will count for eternity while the great act done for self dies at the doing.

Don't you wish that our billboards and magazines would quit advertising the things that don't matter, the stuff that stifles life? How would it be to advertise the contributions of men and women: a great electric sign showing a teacher in the classroom, a doctor devoted to his patient, a mother with her children — something that really matters?

They tell me that Dr. Chalmers was a marvelous man when he lectured to his divinity students. He was great when, in his matchless eloquence, he spoke to vast audiences throughout the length and breadth of Scotland. But he was greatest of all when, in his own city of Edinburgh, he might be seen daily going through the alleys and lanes with groups of ragged children clinging to his fingers and coat as he gathered them into training schools for their benefit.

47. Goodness Cares

While waiting in a college president's office some years ago I picked a book from his shelf and began reading. In one chapter three questions were asked: How much do you care? How much will you share? How much will you dare? Although I do not remember the comments around these questions they have remained with me. I have reflected on them many times.

Christianity is caring: God caring for us and we caring for others. The test of our orthodoxy is not so much how strongly we say we believe in a long list of dogma but in how much we will risk for Jesus Christ. Finally, the vitality of our faith is shown in how anxious we are to share it personally. The Holy Spirit comes into our lives to help us care, bear, and share.

Some think the Holy Spirit is given to make us feel good. Sermons are preached not to make people feel good but rather to help them to be good. The Holy Spirit is given to us so we do good, so we minister to others. The fruit of the Spirit is produced so that caring, sharing, and doing are a present reality. That's goodness.

Christianity is caring. The church is the caring body. Archbold Temple wrote, "The church is the only institution in history which exists not for its own members but for others." Some old pagan philosopher said, "Teach yourself not to care. You must not, on any account, allow yourself

244

to become personally or emotionally involved in the human situation."

On the opposite side, the Christian message says, "Teach yourself to care passionately and intensely for others. Teach yourself to enter into the human situation so that you see, think, and feel with the other person's eyes, mind, and heart in your deep identification with others." The Scripture says, "We know what love is — because He laid down His life for us; and we ought to lay down our lives for our brethren. But if any one has this world's goods and sees that his brother is in need, and yet closes his heart against him — how can love for God continue in him?" (1 John 3:16, 17, Weymouth).

Courage to Care

Usually it is not that we do not have the "know-how." It is that we do not have the "care how." Caring is pity that performs. It is mercy which moves. Caring is goodness grasping the hand of anyone in need and saying, "I'm here."

A student told about a famous lecturer who came to the college he attended. The lecturer spoke about feeding the people of India. He saw several good results. More men would be employed. Friendly relations with other countries would be established. In addition he would be in the continued good graces of the Indian people.

During the informal discussion the oldest and most revered professor asked, "Doctor, don't you think maybe we ought to feed them because they are hungry?" That is the question of goodness, the one the Christian asks. That is why the early Christians formed the first committee of concern.

C. Ray Dobbins, editor of *Cumberland Presbyterian* said his seatmate told him of riding a plane from Miami on which there were sixty-five psychiatrists traveling home from a convention. During the flight a woman became ill and mentally upset. Yet none of the doctors offered to help. The plane had to put down in Nashville so they could take the woman to a hospital. His companion's comment was that life is like that. There is a great deal of intelligence and expertise but often this is of no help in the face of human needs.

The response of most Christians is many times the same. We see great spiritual need. As Christians we have the answer to help. In fact we go to great lengths to say that we have what this world needs. But in the situation we continue unresponsive. We sit in another section and assume that we are guiltless.

We lack so often the courage to care. Why? Because caring is costly. It involves the giving of ourselves, our time, our effort. The implications of caring may last a long time. It may involve many days of giving ourselves. So we keep a secret store of indifference about us so that we need not get involved. Or we think it someone else's job.

We are often like the man who was telling his wife about passing a woman in the downpour of rain that afternoon. She had a flat tire and was standing helpless by the side of her car. "I thought to myself," he said, "how awful it is of people not to help such a poor woman. I would have stopped if I were not on my way to work."

It takes courage to care because to care usually means that it is inconvenient to do what needs to be done. It means doing more than what is demanded. It means going out of one's way, sacrificing one's time, and sticking with the situation or person until the problem is solved. That's costly. Because it's costly, we so often stay in our comfortable seats. In spite of our intelligence and expertise we are of no help in the face of human and spiritual need.

To claim to be Christ's followers means we can no longer pass by on the other side of any person in need. To be a

Christian means we have found the answer of life in Christ and we care enough to share that answer where needed.

Paul Tournier, well-known Swiss psychiatrist, says, "Love is not just some great abstract idea or feeling. There are some people with such a lofty conception of love that they never succeed in expressing it in the simple kindness of ordinary life. They dream of heroic devotion and self-sacrificing service. But waiting for the opportunity which never comes, they make themselves very unlikable to those near them, and never sense their neighbor's need.

To Care Is to Communicate

How often it happens. Here is one with all the psychological skills and theological and social information who seems helpless in solving a situation. What he tries hardest to communicate doesn't get through. One thing he lacks and this one thing makes all the difference. What is it? It is a sincere concern for the person as a person.

I saw it again the other day. "How is it," I asked, "that that girl can communicate so completely with those people with whom she has almost nothing in common? What makes them love her and respond so fully to her help?" My friend answered with wise words. "Ann cares about them and they sense it."

To care is to communicate in the pulpit, by a sickbed, in a refugee camp, in a youth camp, with our children in the home, and with the people who work beside us. How quickly we sense if someone really cares.

Most of the time we are too calloused to really care. And when we cease caring we cease communication no matter how correct our words or our actions.

But caring costs. That is why we do not care as we ought in many situations. We cannot care without giving something of ourselves or of the things we have. So we protect ourselves by refusing to care, by making ourselves indifferent.

In his book, *The Yoke of Christ,* Elton Trueblood quotes a letter from a schoolgirl who probes the depth of her soul. She writes, "I've been thinking much this year about the importance of caring, of the passion of life. I have often realized that it takes courage to care. Caring is dangerous; it leaves you open to hurt and to looking like a fool; and perhaps it is because they have been hurt so often that people are afraid to care. You can't die if you are not alive, and then who would rather be a stone? I have found many places in my own life where I keep a secret store of indifference as a sort of self-protection."

That's a penetrating insight, "a secret store of indifference." We've forgotten the story Jesus told about the Good Samaritan and how He said, "Go, and do thou likewise." God cares. We are to care even though it means a cross. Because God cared our lives have been transformed.

Some years ago after a man made a world trip, he moved from place to place showing his pictures. He had one picture, in particular, which attracted attention and constant comment. It was a photo of an emaciated, thin, little girl, whose face was pressed hard against a window. Inside was bread and meat and other food.

One night after he had shown his pictures, a man came to him and asked, "Did you give the little girl something to eat?"

"Suddenly it dawned on me," he said, "that I was simply taking pictures of the world need. I had not done anything to meet the need."

Goodness is interested in the picture so that it can meet the need. When the Holy Spirit puts the fruit of goodness within, it means we can no longer only see the scene of sorrow and suffering. Goodness compels us to help.

Harold E. Kohn in *Thoughts Afield* tells of a lad carrying eggs down the street who tripped on a curbstone and sprawled headlong on the pavement. The eggs were smashed. A crowd of sympathizers gathered around the sobbing youngster. One dear old lady cried, "Dear me, what a pity!" A man exclaimed, "Poor little fellow; I hope his dad doesn't give him a trimming." One matronly looking woman said tenderly, "There, there, don't cry." Then a man stepped out from the crowd and declared. "I care fifty cents' worth." Another announced, "I care a quarter's worth." In a few moments the boy had enough for another basket of eggs because some people translated sympathy into action.

A little fellow in the ghetto was teased by one who said, "If God loves you, why doesn't He take care of you? Why doesn't God tell someone to bring you shoes and a warm coat and better food?" The little lad thought for a moment, then with tears starting in his eyes, said, "I guess He does tell somebody, but somebody forgets."

God's plan is to care through His followers and that caring is the fruit of goodness.

48. Barnabas, a Good Man

Barnabas, in Acts 11:24, is described as "a good man, full of the Holy Spirit and of faith. And a large company was added to the Lord." Barnabas presents to us a portrait of goodness. His life led many others to Christ. Barnabas demonstrated goodness because his character was expressed in action.

Earlier in the Book of Acts we see the goodness of Barnabas in his generosity. He could not see another in want while he had something to give. Before his conversion to Christ he owned large properties in Cyprus. Now he sold his farm and laid the money at the disciples' feet. He did not even seek the glory of distributing it himself. That's goodness.

Then Barnabas was one of those loving persons who was always eager to see the best in others. With this kind of love goes the ability and insight to discern between the insincere and the genuine. When the young church was afraid of Saul, the persecutor, "Barnabas took him, and brought him to the apostles, and declared unto them how he had seen the Lord in the way." Barnabas was good in this that when he saw Saul was genuine he stuck by him and sponsored him when all was suspect in Acts 9. He pleaded later to give Mark a second chance. That's goodness.

Not Self-Seeking

When the church at Jerusalem wanted to get a correct report on the work beginning at Antioch, they sent Barnabas. Why? Because he was a kind, affectionate, loving person. He was free of jealousy and self-seeking, and they knew such a man could give good judgment. The church sent the good Barnabas, and it was the grace of God they did.

Sometimes persons are sent on spiritual work who are rigid and narrow, shackled by rules and regulations, and who put reins on the Holy Spirit. They have little or no yieldedness. Because they are self-centered, they make hasty judgments. If things are not done exactly as they decide, they divide and destroy rather than unite and build.

Many a leader, harsh and critical when things go contrary, is startled later in life when his followers jump at each other's throats. Why should they be surprised? It is possible to preach about God, the world, and other Christians, in such a way that rather than build a loving spirit a leader causes an atmosphere of antagonism and enmity. Rather than loving people as Christ did. We loathe the sinner, and the church is lost.

Gladdened by Goodness

Barnabas was always happy when good happened to others. He was never glad when others were in trouble. He had a largehearted tolerance for others' weaknesses and failures and loved them back to the right path. When he arrived at Antioch, the Scripture says three things — what he saw, what he felt, and what he said.

Barnabas saw the grace of God. We see grace the same way we see love. We see what it does. We prove the gospel, not by argument, but by what good it does. Here were licentious, lustful, unclean people who had become chaste, holy, and clean. When we see what the grace of God does, we don't need a lot of words. Only when goodness and love are weak do we need a lot of words to describe them.

An ancient poet told the painters of Greece, in a period of great decadence in art, to write under their paintings the names of the animals they had painted. He told them to write horse, ox, and cow underneath, implying that without the name it was impossible for viewers to tell one shape or color from another.

When faith is low and Christianity is not lived men talk of their goodness. Christianity is vital when it is seen. When Barnabas came to Antioch, the moment his eyes caught the canvas he could see the picture.

Barnabas saw the grace of God and was glad. That's a mark of goodness — to rejoice at the success of another. Barnabas "exhorted them all, that with purpose of heart they would cleave unto the Lord." He knew persecution would soon come to Antioch. He knew the lordship of Christ was their only safety and solution.

Goodness and Vision

Barnabas saw the people's need at Antioch and realized his own limitations. Then he thought of Paul. Paul, after his conversion, had received a rather formal and frigid reception from the other Christians at Jerusalem. The Christians didn't trust him and others tried to kill him. So Paul retired from public life and went back to Tarsus. The church seems to have lost sight of him and for perhaps nine years they heard nothing of Paul.

But Barnabas thought of his ability in teaching and found him. He knew Paul had ability he didn't have. He discovered his retreat. I can see Paul, sitting at home, perhaps discouraged, saying, "Guess the Lord can't use me.

People don't hear my message." Suddenly there is a knock at the door. His old standby Barnabas enters.

The conversation must have been interesting. It ended by Barnabas persuading Paul he was the man for the job. He brought him to Antioch and gave him the leadership. Barnabas would be worthy of grateful remembrance if for only this, that he started Paul as the apostle to the Gentiles.

When they came to Antioch. Barnabas encouraged the people, and Paul taught the people. They were grounded in love by Barnabas. Now they need to be grounded in knowledge.

To have the heart to discover a more talented person than yourself, and then to have the heart to go to Tarsus for him and to make way for him in Antioch, is far better than to have all Paul's talents. Luther says that we cannot help being jealous of the men who are in our own circle and are more talented than ourselves. Not so with Barnabas. Christlike conduct like his instantly reacts to character and manifests itself more and more in the spirit of goodness.

No wonder the Scripture says of Barnabas, "He was . . . full of the Holy Spirit and of faith. And a large company was added to the Lord." No wonder the apostles called him the son of encouragement. One could not be near this good man without being helped, renewed, and restored. He radiated encouragement, life, hope, and power because Christ lived in him by the Holy Spirit. Where Christ's Spirit is, we find *goodness*.

49. The Witness of Goodness

Think not the good,
The gentle deeds of mercy thou hast done,
Shall die forgotten all; the poor, the prisoner,
The fatherless, the friendless, and the widow,
Who daily owe the bounty of thy hand.
Shall cry to Heaven, and pull a blessing on thee.
Nicholas Rowe, *Jane Shore*, Act 1, Sec. 2

According to legend, the angels of heaven, observing the beauty of a noted bishop's life offered him the power to heal the sick or to convert sinners. The old bishop declined, saying, "The thing I most desire is that God would bestow upon me the gift of doing a great deal of good without even knowing it myself."

Consequently, as the bishop walked upon the earth, wherever his shadow fell, the hearts of men cheered, little children laughed, and tired men rested. That's the result of goodness.

Jesus wants our lives to be that way. We are to bear witness that God is at work to glorify God by the good we do. "Let your light so shine before men, that they may see your good works and give glory to your Father who is in heaven" (Matthew 5:16). "Maintain good conduct among the Gentiles, so that in case they speak against you as wrongdoers, they may see your good deeds and glorify God on the day of visitation" (1 Peter 2:12). A little boy when asked if he knew what saints are, answered, "Sure, they're the men the light shines through." How true!

Years ago a minister preached a sermon called "The Fine Art of Making Goodness Attractive." Goodness is attractive when good deeds are performed in the lives of people. Genuine goodness needs no other publicity than the performing of the good things of Christ. Nothing so wins the approval of the Christian faith as its ministry. Even the atheist is silenced by Christian tenderness to the sick, the sorrowing, and the sinful.

When Henry James was asked for a definition of spirituality he answered, "No, I'm afraid I can't give you a good definition of spirituality, but I can point you to a good example of a spiritually minded man, and that man is Phillips Brooks."

On the wall of Christ Church in Winnetka hangs a memorial bearing this inscription, "Thanking God for the dear memory of Frederick Greely, whose unfailing courage and kindly cheer enriched the life of this parish and made lighter the common burden." That's the witness of goodness.

To Christ Through Us

Christ can witness only through His people today. He has no other way. Centuries ago Teresa Avila wrote lines, simple yet as true today as ever:

Christ has no body now on earth but yours,
No hands but yours,
No feet but yours.
Yours are the eyes through which is to look
Out Christ's compassion to the world;
Yours are the feet with which He is to go about doing good;
And yours are the hands with which He is to bless us now.

Keith Miller in *A Second Touch* tells of a businessman who one night turned his life over to Jesus Christ, after struggling long in his own strength. The next morning he was late for his train. In his hurry he bumped into a small boy with a puzzle in his hand, scattering the puzzle across the sidewalk.

Instead of rushing on he stopped, stooped down, and helped pick up the puzzle while the train moved out of the station. After he had finished the little lad looked up into his face and asked, "Mister, are you Jesus?"

"Then," said the man, "I realized that at least in some ways I was." That witness of goodness gave the small boy a better understanding of Jesus.

So the witness of goodness goes on and on. Sometimes we recall the good deeds long after they are done and find them the prized possessions of our loved ones. Thackeray in *Henry Esmond* tells how kindness and goodness is often taken for granted and remembered too late; "It was Lady Castlewood's disposition to think kindness and devise silent bounties, and to scheme benevolences for those about her. We take such goodness for the most part as if it were our due; the Marys who bring ointment for our feet get little thanks. Some of us never feel their devotion at all; others recall it years after, when the days are past in which these sweet kindnesses were spent on us. The forgotten tones of love recur to us, and kind glances shine out of the past — oh, so bright and clear! — Oh, so longed after! — Because they are out of reach; as sunshine through bars — more prized because unattainable."

Robert L. Glover of Scotland wrote, "I have the privilege of studying under an internationally famous professor. He writes books and Bible study guides which are read the world over. Through television he has brought countless men to Christ.

"Yet what attracts some of us who see him daily is not the great scholarship for which he is renowned, but the warmth of his faith. After being in this man's presence the first time, I really felt as if I had been with the Lord Himself. Incredibly busy though he is, he is calm, unruffled, friendly, approachable, always ready to help in time of trouble." That is the witness of goodness.

Faithfulness Fruit

50. Faithfulness — Love's Loyalty

A small boy was standing by a horse tied to a post. A stranger asked him, "Can that horse run fast?"

"I don't know," said the lad, "but he can stand fast."

The seventh fruit of the Spirit is the word for standing fast, for steadfastness. It means not faith, but faithfulness. It is the quality of reliability, trustworthiness, which makes a person one on whom we can utterly rely and whose word will stand. Phillips translates this fruit "fidelity." Barclay translates it as "loyalty." Westcott wrote, "A person is said to be 'faithful' in the discharge of his duties where the trait is looked at from within outwards; and at the same time he is 'trustworthy' in virtue of that faithfulness in the judgment of those who are able to rely upon him."

Faithfulness speaks of endurance also, a firmness of purpose, especially amid danger and calamities. It describes the faithful discharge of duties and undying devotion to persons and principles. It is the love which endures all things — difficulties, dangers. and differences.

Faithfulness is not the shrugging of the shoulders or a passive posture. Nor is it a "grin and bear it" attitude. It is a positive, active attribute. It results from a love which keeps moving forward and comes out victorious. It remains steadfast and true in the midst of evil. The faithful person does not sidestep a situation or endeavor to escape to the easy path or flee when threats come. The faithful person stays at his station.

Moffatt also translates faithfulness as "fidelity" describing it as a careful regard for the discharge of obligations, unwavering adherence to veracity and honesty. The faithful person is dependable. We can put our full faith in him. Faithfulness is love performing its prowess, never growing weary. Faithfulness is steady, true, and trustworthy. It possesses a staying power in spite of feelings and difficulties, even after the first joys seem to have disappeared.

The Grace of Grit

Peter Ainslie III writes: "I shall never forget the first time I saw Poynter's great picture 'Faithful unto Death' in the Walker Art Gallery in Liverpool. There stood the Roman guard on duty while the palace was falling into ruins during the destruction of Herculaneum. The dead were lying in the background; others were falling to the pavement amid the red-hot eruptions of Vesuvius; everyone who could was fleeing for his life. The Roman guard might have made his escape, but there he stood like a marble statue, preferring to remain at his post faithful unto death. The picture clung to me like an individual — not simply the man standing at his post of duty but the expression of faithfulness that showed in his countenance. I have thought of it a hundred times since, and I have felt its influence as I have felt that of a living person." [1]

A person is pitiful and powerless if he is unfaithful and undependable. He is of no benefit or blessing to God or man. But "a faithful man will abound with blessings" (Proverbs 28:20).

Without faithfulness we cannot be called the children of God. No amount of ability can compensate for its lack. A

---

1. Peter Ainslie, *Cultivating the Fruit of the Spirit* (St. Louis, Bethany Press, 1968), p. 57.

little ability used faithfully is worth far more than much ability used unreliably.

Someone said it was prayer for the grace of grit.

In the Christian life we are especially tempted to be quitters. We run into the smallest snag or difficulty and we give up. Or we receive a little rebuff from someone and we make it clear if that's the way the church feels, okay, we'll quit. The important questions, of course, are: How does Christ feel? What is right? What ought we do? If we know answers to these, then God will give us the grace of grit to stick to it. Further, the cause of Christ will be strengthened.

Jesus said, "Happy are those who stand for the right and take joyously the results, whatever such might be." God grant us the grace of grit.

51. Jesus Is Faithful

We understand fully the meaning of faithfulness when it is used to describe Jesus Christ. He was faithful in fulfilling God's will and His loyalty was to death itself.

In Hebrews 2:17, KJV, we read that Jesus is "a merciful and faithful high priest in things pertaining to God." When we are in need we want help along with mercy. We do not want to be scolded. Christ is merciful. But He is also faithful in that we can depend upon Him. He came and opened the way to God for us. When He came in the flesh, He did not expect to escape the severe disciplines of men. He experienced without hesitation sorrows, afflictions, and temptations. Hunger, thirst, weariness, disappointment, misunderstanding, calamity, scorn, misrepresentation, persecution, loneliness — all entered the life of our Lord. But He proved faithful through it all.

J. C. Macaulay, in his devotional studies in the Epistle to the Hebrews, recalls the manner in which the king and queen of England shared the privations of their countrymen in World War II. When the windows of the king's private apartments in Buckingham Palace were shattered in an air raid, he waited his turn like any private citizen to have them repaired. The royal family received the same ration coupons as any other person. The queen, like other housewives, saved her meat coupons for a Sunday roast.

So also the blue line around the bathtubs which marked

the five-inch limit of water for other Londoners was also marked for the palace. The king's horses were sent to farm work. The queen personally drove around with a station wagon getting paper, bones, and scrap metal in the national drives. The king and queen walked among the rubble of bombed homes. One Londoner said to an American reporter: "They share the same dangers and privations I do. Their home was bombed just like mine."

No wonder they had such a large place in the hearts of the people. But even the king and queen's devotion pales beside Christ who came from heaven, the Lord of all who emptied Himself to bear all for us.

Christ with Us

As a priest representing us before God, Jesus went through all the struggle, temptations, bewilderment, and suffering that we have to understand and sympathize with us. Thus we can ask the question and know the answer as the poet does:

Is there anyone can help us, one who understands our
    hearts
  When the thorns of life have pierced them till they
    bleed:
One who sympathizes with us, and His wondrous love
    imparts
Just the very, very blessing we need?

Yes there's one, only one,
The blessed, blessed Jesus, He's the one.
  When afflictions crush the soul,
  And waves of trouble roll,
And you need a friend to help you, He's the one!

In Hebrews 3:2, 5 the Scripture says that Jesus was faithful to God who appointed Him to His task. Not only we, but God also can depend on Jesus to be faithful to His calling. Moses is the example of faithfulness in the Old Testament. Jesus became the great example of faithfulness in the New Testament.

Faithful fulfillment of the Father's will was the great desire of Jesus. In Revelation 1:5; 19:11, the Scripture says that Jesus was the faithful and true witness. We can stake our lives on what Jesus did, the way He taught, and what He told us concerning God and ourselves.

The Gospels picture Christ as one of absolute faithfulness to God regardless of the cost or consequences. At the age of twelve He reminded His mother that His first obligation was to God in fulfilling God's will. At His baptism He faithfully fulfilled the divine will. In His temptations the question was, Would He do His own will or would He take God's way? Would He be faithful? And He was faithful in every detail.

Time and again in the Gospels we have statements like, "I must be about my Father's business"; "I must go through Samaria"; "I must go to Jerusalem." In what sense did Jesus have to do these things? The answer is that He knew the Father's will and desired to fulfill it. Also we have Christ's statements such as His meat is to do the Father's will.

We see the climax of faithfulness in Gethsemane. Here, confronting the cross, Christ wrestled with the doing of the Father's will and being crucified or escaping the cross. The choice was clear, "Not my will but thine be done." Therefore the Hebrews writer tells us to look "to Jesus the pioneer and perfecter of our faith, who for the joy that was set before him endured the cross, despising the shame, and is seated at the right hand of the throne of God. Consider him who endured from sinners such hostility against himself, so that you may not grow weary or fainthearted" (Hebrews 12: 2, 3).

Out of His own faithfulness Christ comes to make in us a character like His own. Jesus called from Capernaum the man, Matthew, who was a disreputable person and made him the faithful recorder of the Gsopel. Christ found for His fellowship and made a model of faithfulness Mary Magdalene who had proved her infidelity previously. Christ called a profane fisherman from the Sea of Galilee and made him the foremost and most faithful preacher on the day of Pentecost. So Christ down through the centuries called multitudes of men and women, people who were faithless, untrustworthy, and shiftless and made them, through His Holy Spirit, into persons of loyalty and truthfulness. So also He makes us faithful in fulfilling our duties and unwavering in our adherence to veracity and honesty.

52. Faithful in Little Things

My small son and I were taking a walk. In the far corner of the field we found a patch of beautiful and fragrant flowers. They were in the middle of weeds, almost completely hidden and unnoticed. Yet these flowers were blooming in full beauty, and we sensed their fresh fragrance.

All of us have met persons unnoticed by many, but who, in the middle of struggle and unlikely surroundings, far from the center of attention, have lived lives of beauty and fragrance. In living lives which seemed obscure they faithfully fulfilled God's calling for them.

God's question on the last day will not be, how much were you noticed? or even, How much did you do? Rather His question will be, Were you faithful in fulfilling your calling where I placed you? The question with God is not how obscure or prominent a place we occupy but how faithful we are.

The longer I live, the more I am led to believe that many who go little noticed today will occupy the finest seats in glory because they were faithful in the place where they served.

An unknown servant faithful to God in a small struggling mountain country may well receive a greater reward than a preacher in the most prominent pulpit in the land. A mother who proves faithful to her family, though she may seem unnoticed, shall not lack for rich reward.

So it is good to remember that God is more interested in faithfulness than in fanfare.

Jesus said: "He who is faithful in a very little is faithful also in much" (Luke 16:10).

Remembered by Small Things

In a small group discussion we were reminded again of the importance of small things. We took a few minutes to try to imagine what our families would remember about us after we are gone. What would the children remember? What would husband or wife think about when a departed partner is recalled?

It was a good question to consider. We soon decided that none of us will likely be remembered for great acts or words. But, as we looked at each other's lives, we soon thought of things which will be remembered. They are small things like taking time to read or tell a story, making something for the other, a favorite dish prepared from time to time, the remembrance of special days by a gift or surprise.

We saw again that our small daily actions and words are part of a larger pattern which affects the lives of others. In these, faithfulness is important if life is to have meaning. Yet it is on these we fail most often and these are the areas we overlook so easily.

Here then is our challenge. We must strive to be more faithful one day at a time in taking time for others, in doing deeds of kindness, in performing the small everyday run of things faithfully. We must see such as our primary responsibility. Then says Jesus the big things will also be taken care of. By the faithfulness with which we fulfill the common daily duties we make the character which we will have to spend in eternity.

F. W. Faber wrote: "Little faithfulnesses are not only the preparation for great ones, but little faithfulnesses are

are in themselves the great ones. . . . The essential fidelity of the heart is the same whether it be exercised in two mites or in a regal treasury; the genuine faithfulness of the life is equally beautiful whether it be displayed in governing an empire or in writing an exercise. . . . It has been quaintly said that if God were to send two angels to earth, the one to occupy a throne, and the other to clear a road, they would each regard their employment as equally distinguished and equally happy."

Mosquitoes and Mountains

Dr. Roy S. Nicholson illustrated the importance of little things in recalling the history of the Panama Canal. The first attempt to dig a canal across the Isthmus of Panama was made by a French company. Men and machinery tackled mountains and jungles. The project was abandoned, however, not because of the mountains, but because of mosquitoes. Yellow fever, from mosquitoes, killed thousands.

American doctors found ways of protecting persons against the mosquitoes. When the mosquitoes were taken care of the mountains soon succumbed. There is a great difference between the size of mountains and mosquitoes. Yet the small mosquitoes did more damage. More men perished from the bite of mosquitoes than from dangers in the mountains.

No one succeeds in the big opportunities of life who has not been faithful in small obligations. "He who is faithful in a very little is faithful also in much: and he who is dishonest in a very little is dishonest also in much" (Luke 16: 10).

Thomas Carlyle wrote, "Do the duty which lies nearest thee." In other words, if we do the duty which we know now, the next duty has already become clearer. If, however, we refuse to do what we know we ought, the next step remains unrevealed and we walk in darkness.

Faithful fulfillment of the will of God was the great desire of Jesus. The psalmist also knew God in such a personal way that God's will was his highest and clearest desire. Why? Because of the kind of God he had. Different from heathen gods, whose desire is to punish, his God always, and in all ways, desires to give His very best and to guide in ways which are only for His children's good.

Thus we cannot be happy until we develop a disposition to do promptly and faithfully God's will for us.

Charles Wesley wrote:

Lo! I come with joy to do
   The Master's blessed will;
Him in outward works pursue,
   And serve His pleasure still.
Faithful to my Lord's commands,
   I still would choose the better part;
Serve with careful Martha's hands
   And loving Mary's heart.

John Oxenham in his poem, "Your Place," points out the importance of faithfulness:

Is your place a small place?
Tend it with care;
He set you there.

Is your place a large place?
Guard it with care!
He set you there.

Whate'er your place, it is,
Not yours alone, but His
Who set you there. [1]

---

1. Used by permission.

53. Successful or Faithful?

Lionel Whiston wrote, "The Christian is not called to be successful, but to be faithful. He is set free from the fear of failure or the compulsion to succeed. God can use his mistakes and turn apparent failures into the means of advancing His kingdom, even as He turned Calvary into Easter."

W. T. Purkiser, editor of *Herald of Holiness*, commenting on Whiston's words, says, "Words such as these must never be taken to excuse needless failure. Pious platitudes about good intentions will never forward the church nor save the world.

"Yet there is one important truth here. In an imperfect world shot through with evil, faithfulness and 'success' are not necessarily related one to another. We have to think of a multitude of Bible examples to see that this is so."

Purkiser then goes on to give a tremendous panorama of victories of the faithful in Hebrews eleven. Right in the middle of all the great successes listed in this chapter of Hebrews the faithfulness that succeeds suddenly turns to the faithfulness that suffers. Yet even in the middle of failure according to the natural eye, the truth remains that faithfulness is itself the highest kind of success.

Paul writes his letter to Rome, declaring that it is not enough to be enthusiastic about Christianity. The important thing is to continue to feed the flame of devotion. Moffatt's translation of the familiar statement seems to express it more satisfactorily by saying, "Maintain the spiritual glow." It is the radiance of faith which we are never to permit the storms of sordid living to snuff out. By constant cultivation of a great affection for God, a passionate loyalty to Jesus Christ, and a walking in the Spirit, we will be able to maintain a radiance of the heart. Keeping the flame constantly burning counts for more than a thousand deeds of effective service which are not characterized by love.

God's Heroes

It is the continuous and abiding quality of any person's magnetic Christian character which wins our approval and stimulates our admiration. A skyrocket is lovely to watch, but it is the steady light upon which mariners depend. There are people who have Christian experience as brilliant as skyrockets or like giant Roman candles. They fairly dazzle our eyes for a little while. But then they sputter and go out. This is the sickening disappointment.

All of us know that it is the people who through the years *maintain* the spiritual glow who make us believe in the genuineness of Christianity. This devotion is deep and constant because it is real.

In *Treasure Thoughts* by F. W. Faber, edited by Rose Porter, Faber says, "There is a greatness in unknown names, there is an immortality in quiet duties, attainable by the meanest of human kind; and when the judge shall reverse the tables many of these last shall be first. . . .

"To fill a little space because God wills it; to go on cheerfully with the petty round of little duties, little avocations; to accept unmurmuringly a low position; to be misunderstood, misrepresented, maligned, without complaint, to smile for the joys of others when the heart is aching; to banish all ambition, all pride, and all restlessness, in a single regard to our Savior's work; he who does this is a greater hero than he who for one hour storms a breach, or for one day rushes onward undaunted in the flaming front of shot and shell. His works will follow him. He may be no hero to the world, but he is one of God's heroes."

So it is that faithfulness to truth and right stands out in a world full of broken promises, discarded obligations, and forgotten vows. In God's book the one who is not shaken even when it is apparent it will hurt the pocketbook or mean a lost opportunity for personal advancement is really the successful one. In the home, the church, the community the one who cannot be bribed or bought and who will not cheat, lie, or misrepresent the facts is called faithful by the Lord.

Faltering in Faithfulness

Faithfulness, the fruit of the Spirit, should indeed describe the church of Christ and His servant. Laodicea was one of the most prosperous Asian cities. It had great wealth from its industry of glossy black wool and rich linens. A famous medical school, known for its eye salve, was situated in the city. The early church at Laodicea, established by Epaphras, was an immediate success.

However, in the middle of great prosperity the church faltered. It became faithless. Christ, in the Revelation, warns them of the lack of devotion and tells them to seek spiritual gold, godly raiment, and the eye salve God has so that they might see.

Paul gave his charge to Timothy and tells him to seek out faithful men to share the gospel. "You then, my son, be strong in the grace that is in Christ Jesus, and what you have heard from me before many witnesses entrust to faithful men who will be able to teach others also. Take your share of suffering as a good soldier of Christ Jesus. No soldier on service gets entangled in civilian pursuits, since his aim is to satisfy the one who enlisted him. An athlete is not crowned unless he competes according to the rules. It is the hard-working farmer who ought to have the first share of the crops. Think over what I say, for the Lord will grant you understanding in everything" (2 Tim. 2:1-7).

Again in 1 Timothy 6:11-16 the apostle gives the call to faithfulness: "But as for you, man of God, shun all this; aim at righteousness, godliness, faith, love, steadfastness, gentleness. Fight the good fight of the faith; take hold of the eternal life to which you were called when you made the good confession in the presence of many witnesses. In the presence of God who gives life to all things, and of Christ Jesus who in his testimony before Pontius Pilate made the good confession, I charge you to keep the commandment unstained and free from reproach until the appearing of our Lord Jesus Christ; and this will be made manifest at the proper time by the blessed and only Sovereign, the King of kings and Lord of lords, who alone has immortality and dwells in unapproachable light, whom no man has ever seen or can see. To him be honor and eternal dominion."

We must always remember that God calls us to faithfulness. This call does not lead to what the world considers success. Faith that endures and proves true, although it suffers, is still in God's record the highest kind of success.

54. Rewards of Faithfulness

An interesting story is shared in 1 Samuel 30 concerning faithfulness. King David and his men were away at the battle front. While away, their foes came in and laid the city of Ziklag in ashes, carrying away the wives and sons and daughters of the absent soldiers. When the men returned they were overwhelmed with grief. The Scripture says they "lifted up their voice and wept until they had no more power to weep." They began to blame David. Then David selected six hundred men and set out to rescue the captives.

When they came to the brook Besor, two hundred were so faint they could not cross over the brook. "Very well," said David, "You two hundred men stay here and mind the baggage and the others of us who are stronger will go on."

They went on, made a great recovery and returned with the spoil. When they returned to the brook Besor a protest arose on the part of those who went to battle. They did not want to share the spoil. Then it was that David fashioned a statement about faithfulness to stand for all, "As his part is that goeth down to the battle, so shall his part be that tarried by the stuff, they shall part alike."

What David said was that although not all are equally strong yet all can be equally faithful. The two hundred who did the best they could were just as worthy of the reward. The principle that we find in all the Scriptures such as the parable of the pounds, the parable of the talents, and elsewhere is that those who are faithful in their duty shall share equally. So a little obscure, inconspicuous, unknown Christian, faithful at his or her post, shall share equally with Paul, Spurgeon, Livingstone provided he is faithful.

Long-Range Results

When D. L. Moody's mother was buried, people came from various sections of the United States to pay honor to that noble woman. After different speakers had paid their generous tributes to her, the honored son, who had moved continents closer to God, came forward and said, "I want to say a word." Looking down on the placid face of the sainted mother, Moody said, "Oh, Mother, you have done more for me than everybody else in the world. You believed in me when I was a wild boy. You followed me and prayed for me and loved me. Mother, I owe more to you than I owe to everybody else in the world."

When the time comes to reward that noble son, the dear old mother shall share equally with her son.

Evelyn Underhill writing about the continued need to be faithful regardless of seeing results says: "I can well believe that the greatest part of what you achieve will be unseen by you now and will bear fruit later. It needs much faith and love to accept that and carry on all the same in a spirit of loving confidence. But that is the way, I fancy, that God's hardest jobs are done."

Jesus in Matthew 24:45 ff. contrasts the faithful and wise servant with the "evil servant." The faithful servant is obediently following his master's instructions. When the master returns he rewards him for his faithfulness. And the evil servant is punished for his unfaithfulness. In Matthew 25:14 ff. two servants were found faithful to their trust and they entered into the joy of their lord. They were rewarded by being entrusted with greater responsibility.

But the unfaithful was called a "wicked and slothful" servant and thrown into outer darkness.

God's "well done, good and faithful servant" should be our most coveted decoration.

Hugh Latimer, who was martyred in Oxford for his faith, was frequently invited to preach before the king of England. "One Sunday morning," he writes, "as I was in my study preparing myself by prayer and meditation before the service I heard a voice saying to me, 'Latimer, Latimer, be careful what you preach today, because you are going to preach before the king of England.'

"After a little I heard another voice saying to me, 'Latimer, Latimer, be careful what you preach today, because you are going to preach before the King of kings!'"

So "Let us not grow weary in well-doing: for in due season we shall reap, if we do not lose heart" (Galatians 6:9).

Charles Wesley wrote:

> The task Thy wisdom hath assigned,
> Oh, let me cheerfully fulfill;
> In all my works Thy presence find,
> And prove Thy good and perfect will.

Faithful in What We Can Do

A ten-year-old boy in Bismarck, North Dakota, who was born without arms and legs, spoke words of wisdom: "I know there are some things I cannot do. But I think of all the things I can do and I don't worry so much about the rest of it."

Sometimes we become weary because we cannot do everything in facing the problems of life. Our next duty is to do the next thing we can do without worrying too much about the rest. When we learn to faithfully do the next duty, we know somehow we receive comfort and the unknown fountains of life open up.

Sometimes we become weary in fulfilling opportunities to do good. We wonder if what is accomplished is worth all the effort. Our small contribution seems of little worth. In these moments we feel as the Scripture says, "Do not be weary in doing good, for we shall know the blessings which accompany doing good at the proper time."

An anonymous author shared this good reminder:

I am only one, but I am one.
I can't do everything, but I can do something.
And what I can do, that I ought to do,
And what I ought to do,
By the grace of God, I will do.

Finally it can be said that faithfulness has its own reward in satisfaction of work well done.

During World War II two young men became bosom buddies. One day in a fierce battle the one was struck by a bullet while the rest retreated for the night. Jim pleaded with the commander for permission to go back and bring his buddy to safety. The commander did not give permission at first because of the danger but because of the persistent pleading of Jim he finally allowed him to go.

Jim went, found his friend, who was near death. Jim put him on his shoulders and carried him back. When he entered his camp his friend died. "There," said the commander, "I told you it wasn't worth the risk. He's dead." "No," said Jim, "I have my reward. Just as I came to him, he said, 'Jim, I knew you'd be back. I just knew you'd be back.'"

Paul the apostle penned precious words giving his grand testimony in 2 Timothy 4:6-8. "For I am already on the point of being sacrificed; the time of my departure has come. I have fought the good fight, I have finished the race, I have kept the faith. Henceforth there is laid up for me the crown of righteousness, which the Lord, the righteous judge, will award to me on that Day, and not only to me but also to all who have loved his appearing."

55. Faithful unto Death

In Bunyan's *Pilgrim's Progress*, Christian met one called Faithful. As they traveled together through Vanity Fair, a great antagonism arose because Christian and Faithful did not take part in the goods for sale at Vanity Fair. They were beaten and brought bleeding to have their feet put in stocks while they awaited trial. But they bore their griefs and woes with joy, for they saw in them a pledge that all would be well in the end.

After the trial before the witnesses, Envy, Superstition, and Pick-think, Faithful was put to death. And Christian says, "Now I saw that there stood near the crowd a strange car with two bright steeds, which as soon as his foes had slain him, took Faithful up through the clouds straight to The Celestial City, with the sound of the harp and flute."

"Be faithful unto death, and I will give you the crown of life," says Jesus in Revelation 2:10. Note carefully these words. It does not say, "faithful until death." That is, be faithful to the dying point. Die before you would be unfaithful! Die before you would be false! Whatever the cost, wherever it leads, be faithful. Thus comes the reward, "I will give you the crown of life."

279

Faithfulness Costs

Faithfulness cost Abraham a willingness to give up his only son. It cost Esther to risk her life. Daniel was put in a den of lions. Shadrach, Meshach, and Abednego were put in a fiery furnace because they were faithful. Stephen was stoned to death. Peter and all the other apostles, except one, suffered a martyr's death.

God asks for faithfulness. True followers of Christ never ask what will faithfulness cost, what will happen if we are faithful, what will result if we do the right thing? These are the questions of those who follow afar off. Whenever we have an understanding of God's will and find ourselves questioning what the following of God's will might mean we are failing and unfaithful. Esther, when she knew the will of God, said, "I will go . . . and if I perish, I perish." The three Hebrew children simply said, "We know our God is able to deliver us but if not that is okay also." The faithful cannot have a primary concern about their own reputation, or even life itself.

One of the marks of mature character is the pain that comes with moral courage. Dr. John Bowman once said he felt that the Beatitudes were rungs of the ladder to perfection; the farther you read, the higher you went. "Blessed are the pure in heart. . . ." "Blessed are the peacemakers. . . ." It is quite commendable to live in harmony with others, but that too can be passive. Then you come to the last Beatitude, "Blessed are they which are persecuted for righteousness' sake: for theirs is the kingdom of heaven." Is this the greatest test of devotion, the willingness to suffer for our faithfulness to the truth?

Says Bowman, "The song of the Christian is not the song of sparrows, who fly in flocks and sing 'cheep, cheep.' It is rather the flight of eagles high in the blue, who know the loneliness of the heights of courage."

Regardless of the Cost

On a small unpretentious tombstone, which marks the burial place of the great Greek scholar, J. Gresham Machen, are the words from Revelation 2:10 "Faithful unto death."

Another character in Bunyan's *Pilgrim's Progress* is called the man with the "Strong Countenance." Looking at the difficulties of living the Christian life he boldly said, "Set my name down, sir. For I have looked this whole thing in the face; and cost what it may, I mean to have Christlikeness and I will."

Here is the kind of loyalty of which faithfulness speaks. We are more concerned about God's will than our security. We will not be content to be bargain hunters in the basement of pale piety and moldy morals. A watered-down religion that offers little and demands less will not do. There dare not be a halfhearted desire for God and truth or a mere tinge of Christianity.

In *The Constant Fire*, A. K. Chalmers retells a story illustrating faithfulness. Two men in China were interested in China's becoming a republic. One was a writer of great ability, the other a working man whose devotion to the cause made him a trusted leader. These two men were rounded up by the existing government, put under torture to make them speak their secrets. Released, they were soon again under suspicion and sought by the authorities. They escaped and eventually reached the seacoast, where a boat was waiting to carry them to safety. There at the water's edge, the worker stopped, held out his hand to the writer and said "Good-bye."

"Why good-bye?" asked the writer.

"Because," said the other, "I've decided not to go with you. You must go on to America, England, Europe, and that is your part, to interpret to the world by your understanding mind and brilliant pen the meaning of our struggle. But I must go back to face whatever I must with the rest, so that you, dipping your pen into my blood, can make the world understand that we mean what we say."

Whether his cause was worthy or not does not matter here. However, here is an example of commitment. So under Christ we must say, "Set my name down, sir, I've thought the whole thing through and I will serve Christ fully, come what may." Then we will know true freedom to fulfill our purpose in life, and the future will demand this kind of commitment.

Meekness Fruit

56. The Mighty Meek

When George Washington Carver, who was born a slave and later called the greatest scientist in America in his time, entered Iowa State College he was given a seat at the servants' table. When he graduated with distinction and wrote the class poem, he was accorded a place at the table with the faculty and remained on to teach.

George Washington Carver, his real age unknown, born in obscurity and poverty, is today one of America's immortals. This orphaned slave of Diamond, Missouri, the waif of the Missouri prairies, ransomed with the money obtained by the sale of a horse, is an example of the mighty meek. Throughout his life he gave God the complete credit for all his accomplishments and as servant of both black and white throughout the world he demonstrated a godliness in quietness and love seldom surpassed.

When Booker T. Washington was president of Tuskegee Institute in Alabama a woman one day saw him walk down the street. She did not recognize him and yelled, "Hey, you, come in here and chop some wood!" Washington gladly went in the walk, took off his coat, chopped the wood, carried it into the house and left again. A servant girl recognized him and told her mistress. The woman was horrified at what she had done. She went to apologize. "It's entirely all right, Madam," the great Negro replied, "I delight to do favors for my friends." She learned a lesson she never forgot and with her wealth she became one of the strong financial supporters of the college.

Jesus said, "Blessed are the meek, for they shall inherit the earth" (Matthew 5:5). Peter writes about "the ornament of a meek and quiet spirit, which is in the sight of God of great price" (1 Peter 3:4, KJV). "The fruit of the Spirit is . . . meekness."

Meekness Misunderstood

In modern thinking, meekness is not a coveted quality, while there is hardly a characteristic which better distinguishes Christianity. Meekness to many means spinelessness, lack of courage or strength. It is the opposite. Most of the precious promises of the Scripture are to the meek.

We like to think, Blessed are the strong, the shrewd, those who stand up for their rights, those who refuse to be taken advantage of; those who always look out for slights; those who strike it rich and make a success. We have a tendency to set high value on self-assertion. The natural standpoint is that a strong person is one who not only does what he wills but also bends others to do his will.

Meekness is not native to the natural soil of the heart. It is not a natural disposition or psychological makeup. It grows in the garden of the Holy Spirit. Meekness is meant to characterize every Christian regardless of temperament.

Meekness has a twofold expression. Toward God it issues in complete trust and submission to God. Meekness is to be mastered by the will of God. John 6:38; 26:39. It results in gentleness, consideration, courtesy. It is strength under control. Meekness is the character of the one who has the power to retaliate yet remains kind. It is from such a spirit that the expression gentle-man or gentleman arises.

Meekness in the Greek is used to describe an animal which has been trained by its master. Wild and unruly animals are worthless. But when trained they become meek (teachable and quiet). If we remember this background of the term, we will see that meekness is strength under the control of God and that gentleness is power.

Mastered by God

Meekness is an attitude toward God which manifests itself in gentleness toward others. It is an attitude of submission and yieldedness to God which results in the harnessing of our strength in godly ways toward our fellowmen. It is love which seeks first not its own but the things of God and others. The meek accept God's will and dealings without sulking, murmuring, rebellion, or resistance.

Meekness means a willingness to leave everything — ourselves, our rights, our case, our whole future in the hands of God and especially if we think we are suffering unjustly. Meekness means we learn to say, with the Apostle Paul, that our position is to put our situation in the hands of God who says, "Vengeance is mine; I will repay," says the Lord. Meekness follows the death of self-righteousness or self-assertion before God.

I Pet. 3:13

D. Martyn Lloyd Jones writes, "The man who is truly meek is the one who is amazed that God and man can think of him as well as they do and treat him as well as they do." The meek's concern is not himself, his claims, his dignity, or position. His concern is to discharge his duty to God and to turn again and again to God for help, direction, and the sheer joy of it. Thus meekness does not seek compliments in order to continue a good work. He has the strength to continue because of a deep commitment to God and truth.

A meek man thinks of what he enjoys rather than what is denied him. He believes he receives better than he deserves rather than thinking others get the advantage. The meek are willing to be injured rather than to injure. This is the true character of God. 1 Peter 2:23.

Men of meekness are marked by a confidence that both earth and heaven are God's. They have learned that

287

the men who would truly inherit the earth do so through the God who owns it. Meekness is the character of childlikeness. It is the mark of the "little one" who has a Father, and being weak and small, trusts all to the Father's care.

When one has an **attitude** of meekness toward God, he is constantly mindful of the great amount of sin and sinfulness God has forgiven him. This prepares his heart for the kind of forgiving spirit toward others that God seeks in His children according to Ephesians 4:2 and Colossians 3:18.

Moved by Gentleness

Because of confidence, trust, and submission before God the meek man can control his actions and reactions to others. The way to success for the meek man is not the slaying of his rival but the slaying of himself, that is, his own selfish ego. When Jesus said, "Blessed are the meek," He did not mean, "Blessed are the weak," but rather blessed are the strong and courageous who are not easily provoked, and "blessed are those who are so strong they do not need to assert themselves and are not threatened at every point." The person who is not meek toward God will be strong in his self-life, grasping at power and position and striking out against others.

F. B. Meyer calls us to "be lowly before God, allowing His love to enter and fill thy heart, and thou wilt find it easy to be meek before men."

Meekness is not a refuge for the weak, the flabby, the wishy-washy. It is a stronger thing for a man of vehement and impetuous temper to speak and act gently in the face of great provocation than to blurt out indignant words and bluster like a northeast wind. Ainsworth says, "The man who does not smite back because the man who smote him is a head taller than himself is not a meek man. He is a coward." The meek man is so strong that he has no need to strike back to defend himself. *Meekness is strength under control.*

Meekness means the complete absence of the spirit of retaliation. We are patient and long-suffering, especially when we suffer wrong. Peter put it this way in speaking of Christ, "Ye should follow in his steps: who did no sin, neither was guile found in his mouth: who, when he was reviled, reviled not again; when he suffered, he threatened not; but committed himself to him that judgeth righteously." Peter further says that if we are blamed for our faults and take it patiently that proves nothing. But if we do well and suffer for it and take it patiently, that is praiseworthy in the sight of God. That is meekness.

No Defense of Dignity

The meek do not defend their dignity or worry about their rights. They do not draw attention to themselves. They do not project themselves, cherish petty personal grievances, or harbor resentment over injury. The meek will not use the weapons of the weak such as slander, fists, and gossip.

God promises guidance to the meek (Psalm 25:9). The proud are always unable to detect God's guiding pillar. He promises provisions for the meek (Psalm 22:26). The proud have all they need already. He gives joy to the meek (Isaiah 29:19). No joy is like that which comes when we do not need to be self-defensive and carry ill-will toward others. The meek will be exalted (Psalm 147:6). Only those who will lower themselves God can exalt.

The world in popular opinion belongs to the bold, daring, self-assertive person. Mastery belongs to the one who succeeds in gaining power or wealth. Success comes to him who tramples all obstacles under his feet.

The meek do not push, trample, shout, and retaliate. Chappell says that the meek do not "seek to push others to the rear of the procession in the rush of life." Thus the meek can be elbowed out of the way in the world's mad pursuit of fame and fortune. They can be treated with contempt and viewed as worthless. Such evaluation is for time only. The world sees what meekness misses and fails entirely to see what it possesses. The meek, those who count for so little in this world, are designed to possess all things.

Meekness produces strength and courage. The meek man will not hesitate to assert himself when righteousness demands action. The meek man's knowledge that God has acted and is acting on the part of men gives him patience where needed and courage to act if necessary.

The way of meekness is a hard way. It is no refuge for the weak. It is no easy alternative for those who do not dare to fight in the world's arenas of success and master the things of time by trampling others underfoot. In fact, it is a road to be trod only by the strongest in faith, those who are willing to strive toward the city which God is preparing for the faithful. No, the inheritance prepared by God is not a consolation prize for the timid.

William Barclay in *Flesh and Spirit* concludes an excellent discussion of the meaning of meekness by saying that meekness "is the complete control of the passionate part of our nature. It is when we have *prautes* (meekness) that we treat all men with perfect courtesy, that we can rebuke without rancour, that we can argue without intolerance, that we can face the truth without resentment, that we can be angry and yet sin not, that we can be gentle and yet not weak." [1]

Because we cannot be meek of ourselves is precisely why meekness is the fruit of the Spirit. It comes only as the Spirit controls our lives.

---

1. William Barclay, *op. cit.*, p. 21.

57. The Meekness of Jesus

Andrew Murray wrote concerning Christ, "His humility was simply the surrender of Himself to God, to allow God to do in Him what He pleased, whatever men around might say of Him, or do to Him."

In Matthew 11:29, KJV, Jesus calls us to the life of meekness. "Learn of me; for I am meek and lowly in heart." It is John's Gospel, however, which lays open the inner life of our Lord. He speaks about His relation to God, the motives which guide Him, and the circumstances of the power in which He performs His work. In John's Gospel we see the surrendered Christ who "humbled himself . . . therefore God has highly exalted him." Notice a few of His words. And if they sound foreign to us it simply shows how little we know the secret of the meek spirit.

"The Son can do nothing of himself" (John 5:19, KJV).

"I can of mine own self do nothing; . . . my judgment is just, because I seek not mine own will" (John 5:30, KJV).

"I do not receive glory from men" (John 5:41).

"I came . . . not to do mine own will" (John 6:38, KJV).

"I am not come of myself" (John 7:28, KJV).

"I do nothing of myself" (John 8:28, KJV).

"I do not seek my own glory" (John 8:50).

"The words that I speak unto you I speak not of myself" (John 14:10, KJV).

No wonder God could do the mightiest works of all creation through Christ. The secret is that He was willing to be nothing so God could be all. He gave Himself with His will and His power entirely for the Father's work. Concerning His own power, will, glory, mission, and work He said, "It is not I; I am nothing; I have given myself to the Father at work; I am nothing; the Father is all."

Not Self-Exaltation

Christ's life of complete surrender, dependence, trust, obedience and the desire to glorify God, was the life of perfect peace and joy. We think that the secret of peace and joy is in self-exaltation and getting great glory for ourselves.

In Christ we see another way. And the more the Holy Spirit works in our lives the more we see that in this we are made partakers of Christ. The more we yield to the Holy Spirit the more we acknowledge that in ourselves there is nothing good. We are only empty vessels for God to fill.

Life takes on power, peace, and joy as we experience that, as in the life of Jesus, the root and nature of true meekness consists of being and doing nothing in ourselves or for our own glory so that God may be everything.

Paul, the apostle, caught it clearly when he said, "It is no longer I, but Christ." This is the reason for his power. This is what he means when he said, "For to me to live is Christ." Paul had given himself so completely to God that Christ was continually living His life through him.

The spirit of obedience and trust was the spirit of the whole life of Christ. Thus He felt no need to defend or vindicate Himself. Peter pointed Christ's Spirit out in 1 Peter 4.

As Christ's followers we need to learn that this same spirit is the essence of the redemptive life of Christ and our own. It is the secret to spiritual power and witness. It is the source and spring of joy and peace. Then will Christ be known, seen, and heard, and we will know the new life Christ came to bring. The Holy Spirit helps us to be clothed with humility.

Christ's Example

What does it mean then to learn of Christ, the meek and lowly one? It means to learn to surrender to God as He surrendered, to trust in God as He trusted, to depend on God as He depended, to not assert our own power but let God take care of the consequences of following Him, to live a life which receives its work completely from God and gives all glory to God.

The desire for independence was the temptation in paradise, and it is the temptation in each human heart.

Christ's life demonstrated a daily dependence on God. This was the secret of His prayer life when He told His Father everything and committed Himself to do the Father's will. Thus God hid nothing from Him. "The Father loves the Son, and shows him all that he himself is doing."

In His lowly birth, His submission to His earthly parents, His seclusion for thirty years, His service to the poor and despised, His dependence upon God, and His death on the cross — through these His great meekness shines forth.

How hard the lesson of meekness. Jesus' disciples, as many today, were concerned on the way to Capernaum as to who would be the greatest. Jesus placed a child before them and said, "If you want to be great, take that little child for your example." Until Christ's crucifixion the disciples were still concerned, not with meekness, but with might, power, and position.

293

Changed Persons

But when the Holy Spirit came there was a great difference. Matthew wrote his Gospel, calling himself "the publican." Jerome points out that Mark's Gospel is to be regarded as memoirs of Peter's message and published by his authority. Be that as it may, look at the dangerous truths pointed out about Peter. The denial and fall of Peter take precedence over the venture of walking on the sea. Dr. Luke writes his masterpieces of the Gospel and Acts without as much as signing his name. This is the ring of the Holy Spirit. How much we need to learn of the Spirit of meekness.

From the strength Christ had in His complete faith, dependence, and obedience to the Father, He could give Himself fully and freely on behalf of others. He never needed to retaliate by word or act when treated unjustly. Rather He mourned the misery of those who treated Him wrong. He knew the anguish of God's heart when He saw the wrong in the world. He could be gentle to the erring and pray forgiveness for His enemies even while they crucified Him. This is the strength of meekness.

When Jesus came to earth, He came as a strong advocate of gentleness. He called Himself the Good Shepherd. This metaphor pictures the tender care of Jesus for persons. On one occasion some people brought an immoral woman to Jesus and placed her before Him with the hope that Jesus would get tough with her. Instead Jesus forgave her and said, "Go and do not sin again." After Peter raised his sword to defend Jesus, He warned, "Put your sword back into its place; for all who take the sword will perish by the sword" (Matthew 26:52).

In 2 Corinthians 10:1 Paul makes his appeal to the Corinthians by saying, "I, Paul, myself entreat you, by the meekness and gentleness of Christ. . . ." At times it is suggested that the church should practice what James and

John advocated in Luke 9:54. They said, "Lord, do you want us to bid fire come down from heaven and consume them?" Get-tough advocates take things in their own hand. They have simple solutions for our problem. They are quick to deal with difficult problems by getting tough. But this should not be mistaken for the Christian way. Jesus, who is the personification of gentleness, continues to call His followers to a get-gentle policy.

58. Everlastingly Insignificant

A brilliant man, George Bowen, after a striking conversion, went to India as a missionary more than a century ago. In a letter to his sisters in his old age he said, "I told the Lord that I am content to be everlastingly insignificant."

This was a marked contrast to his diary early in life in which he boasted he would become a second Apostle Paul and move about the bazaars of Bombay as "Christ Himself." In later years he realized what a failure he was and only then did he become effective as Christ's ambassador.

F. B. Meyer said, "I used to think that God's gifts were on shelves one above the other and that the taller we grew in Christian character the easier we could reach them. I now find that God's gifts are on shelves one beneath the other; and that it is not a question of growing taller but of stooping lower; and that we have to go down, always down, to get His best gifts."

Although meekness usually is not sought after, yet when Jesus gave the reason for learning of Him, He said "Learn of me, for I am meek and lowly in heart" (Matthew 11:29, KJV). He might have said, "Learn of me because I am the great teacher. I have performed miracles. Look at the crowds that clamor for me every day." No, the reason He gave was that He was "meek and lowly."

Decreasing of Self

One of the meekest men of history was John the Baptist. He was such a powerful figure that Josephus, the great Jewish historian, reports many years later when John's name was mentioned people still trembled at the thought of him. Jesus' eulogy of John was that he was "greater than any man born of woman." Yet when he saw the Christ, instead of giving a speech about his own great accomplishments he sent his disciples to Jesus telling them, "He must increase, but I must decrease." When asked who he was he simply said, "I am nobody. I am to be heard not to be seen. I am a voice."

Did you ever notice that David never describes his victory over Goliath in all the Psalms? We live at a time of superlatives — the greatest evangelist, the greatest preacher, the greatest theologian, and the greatest actor. We desire dignity and position. We want some title and to be addressed properly. No wonder Christ cannot be seen.

Early in Paul's life he calls himself the "least of all the apostles." Halfway through he claims to be "less than the least of all saints." Just before his death he humbly calls himself the "chief of sinners." A man who prided himself in his position said one time in the presence of the great pioneer missionary Carey, "I believe Carey was a shoemaker, wasn't he, before he took up the profession of a missionary?"

Carey spoke up, "Oh, no, I was only a cobbler."

"A certain French marquis was raised to his grand and exalted state from very humble surroundings. He was a shepherd in his early days, and so, in his palace, he kept one room known as "the Shepherd room." In that room were reproductions of hills and valleys and running streams and rocks and sheepfolds. Here were the staff he carried and the clothes he wore as a lad when herding his sheep.

297

When asked one day the meaning of this, he replied, "If ever my heart is tempted to haughtiness and pride, I go into that room and remind myself of what I once was."

Certainly one of the reasons Christ is not seen as He should be is that it is so hard for us to decrease, to grow smaller so that Christ may increase. Yet the morning star fades away when the sun rises. In "Beside the Bonnie Briar Bush" Ian Maclaren describes John Carmichael's first sermon at Drumtochty, "I have been in Mr. Spurgeon's tabernacle, where the people wept one minute and laughed the next; have heard Canon Liddon in St. Paul's, and the sound of that high, clear voice is still with me, 'Awake, awake, put on thy strength, O Zion'; have stood in the dusk of the Duomo at Florence when Padre Agostino thundered against the evils of the day. But I never realized the unseen world as I did that day in the Free Kirk of Drumtochty. . . . The subject was Jesus Christ, and before he had spoken five minutes I was convinced that Jesus was present. The preacher faded before one's eyes, and there arose the figure of the Nazarene. . . . His voice might be heard any moment, as I have imagined it in my lonely hours by the winter fire or on the solitary hills. . . . 'Come unto me . . . and I will give you rest.' "

Mark of Christ's Follower

"Love," says Paul, "vaunteth not itself, is not puffed up." "Is not puffed up" refers to inward disposition. "Vaunteth not itself" refers to the outward conduct and behavior. It is when we have an exaggerated sense of our own importance that we swagger and boast. The apostle was speaking to the Corinthian Christians. Some were quarrelsome and disagreeable. Some were "puffed up" with a sense of the importance of their gift and prided themselves over another with a different gift. And the self-importance and the boasting led to friction and strife. Paul says the mark of love is a beautiful modesty and humility.

It is always the smaller things that strut and insist upon their own importance. Remember the frog in Aesop's Fables? He realized how small he was so he tried to blow himself up to the size of a cow. The small man needs to stand on his dignity. The person who is third cousin to the Duke never allows you to forget it.

Jesus did great deeds of mercy, but He never advertised Himself. He did not shout in the streets. When He healed the leper He told him to tell no man. He was satisfied to serve the sick and the afflicted.

How different was Jesus from those who will not serve or give in any cause unless they are given proper place, unless their names are trumpeted abroad and placed on placards. Love seeks not to be superior but to serve.

Today we would schedule Peter for a speaking tour and open our pulpits for him to tell us how it was that he walked on the water. We'd laud him for his great faith and lift him before people as a pious example of a miracle worker today. We'd scratch from his biography the lines about his lying and the notation of his denial. No wonder people do not see Jesus and His power to save. Have we lost the Spirit of meekness?

Today we would make Matthew move among the church to tell how he was once in a very lucrative business and how (can we imagine it) he left it all to follow Christ. The fact that he left a good paying job, with a lot of promise for promotion, would take precedence over the fact that it was Jesus who called him. No wonder people still see money as so important and the call of Christ as a secondary thing. Have we lost the Spirit of meekness?

Today we would introduce Paul as author of sixteen best sellers, the best known theologian of the day, and have him discuss his Damascus conversion experience. We would finally feel that perhaps Christ must be rather important if so great a man as Paul believes on Him. If such a star, along with several movie, baseball, and football stars, follow Christ, He certainly must have something going. But we would still see the stars instead of the Savior. Have we lost the Spirit of meekness?

Need of Humility

In order to witness to Christ we need meekness, a great deal more humility. We must be ready to remind people of our own inadequacy to accomplish any good thing or do what we ought to do. We might declare that what we are we are by the grace of God and that Christ is the Savior. But not only, or even primarily, do we declare it. We must live in the Spirit of meekness. This is what the Holy Spirit does when He comes to indwell us. The fruit of meekness grows in our lives. The Holy Spirit leads us as He led Paul, to realize that all our good heritage, good position, good education, good religion, and good works are as garbage when it comes to our standing before God.

In the middle of the seventeenth century Thomas Washbourne wrote:

Though heaven be high, the gate is low,
And he that comes in there must bow:
    The lofty looks shall ne'er
      Have entrance there.

O God! since Thou delightest to rest
In the humble contrite breast,
    First make me so to be,
      Then dwell with me.

EVERLASTINGLY INSIGNIFICANT

A father and his small son strolled down a street in Chicago, past the place where a skyscraper was being constructed. Glancing up, they saw men at work on a high story of the building.

"Father," said the little boy, "What are those little boys doing up there?"

"Those are not little boys; those are grown men, Son."

"But why do they look so small?"

"Because they are so high," his father answered.

After a pause the lad asked, "Then, Father, when they get to heaven, there won't be anything left of them, will there?"

It is true. The nearer we come to Christ, the less others see of us and the more they see of Christ.

59. The Gift of Gentleness

A medieval king, despotic and cruel, was persistently annoyed by rebellious outbreaks in certain provinces. He sent his army first to one province and then another to put down the rebellion. But his captains were no sooner returned from one area than they had to be dispatched to another, then to return to the first again. Executions and brutal punishment did not stop the trouble.

One day, after a new uprising, the king called in his captain of the guard. He was desperate. Terrorism only angered the people and created far more determined opposition. The king stared at the floor.

Presently he lifted his head and looked at his captain with a strange gleam in his eyes. "All our force has failed," he declared. "Who knows but there may be some power in gentleness that we dream not of."

So the king sent messengers of good will and peace to the people of the provinces and invited them into his councils, and the nation became peaceful and prosperous.

Robert Eyton wrote in 1895, "Gentleness does win its way when violence only provokes hostility. Moral power is real power. No doubt for a time it may have to yield to brute force. It is no match immediately for the bloodthirsty battalions; but all history and all experience prove that the victory of violence is short-lived and the triumph of gentleness is enduring. Even while gentleness is under the yoke it does not lose its sovereign attitudes. None feel its essential enduring superiority more keenly than those who, for a time, overwhelm it by brute force. 'It is John the Baptist whom I beheaded,' cried Herod. 'Why does he plague me still?' So mere force pays involuntary homage to the moral majesty of the meek and gentle."

Love's Winning Armor

Alexander Maclaren said, "Gentleness is the strongest force in the world, and the soldiers of Christ are to be priests, and to fight the battle of the kingdom, robed, not in jingling shining armor or with sharp swords, nor with fierce and eager bitterness of controversy, but in the meekness which overcomes. You may take all the steam hammers that were ever forged and battle at an iceberg, and except for the comparatively little heat that is developed by the blows and melts some small portion, it will be ice still, though pulverized instead of whole. But let it move gently down to the southward, there the sunbeams smite the coldness to death, and it is dissipated in the warm ocean. Meekness is conquering."

"Lead a life worthy of the calling to which you have been called," says the Apostle Paul, "with all lowliness and meekness, with patience, forbearing one another in love" (Ephesians 4:1, 2). Paul further tells Titus to encourage all Christians "to speak evil of no one, to avoid quarreling, to be gentle, and to show perfect courtesy toward all men" (Titus 3:2). Gentleness is love's sweet voice and manner.

Many striking stories surround the life of D. L. Moody. One of the most moving I've heard was told by a minister of a church Moody visited years before. The fame of Moody was far and wide and when it was announced that the well-known evangelist was coming thousands came to hear.

One evening a little boy came alone to the door of the large church. The usher at the door stopped the small, dirty, ragged boy and told him he should be at home in bed. Even when the boy explained that he wanted to see Mr. Moody the usher refused to allow him to enter. Downcast and disappointed, the little lad walked to the side of the building and began to weep.

Just then a carriage came to the church entrance and Moody moved toward the door. He heard the crying and saw the boy leaning against the wall. Moody walked over to him and asked his trouble. And the lad looked up and explained how he wanted to hear Mr. Moody but was not allowed inside.

Moody smiled and said, "Do you really want to hear Mr. Moody?" "Yes sir." "Well, my boy, I know how to get you in. I know how you can pass that big fellow at the door. But mind, you will need to do all that I tell you. Are you willing?" "Yes sir," the little fellow responded.

Putting his coattails in the hands of the boy, Moody told him to hold on to them and not let loose until he told him to.

Moody entered the building and walked to the platform. Reaching the pulpit he said, "Well done. I told you that if you would only hold on you would get in. Now, my boy, you sit there." Moody put him on the chair reserved for himself and for the evening the boy listened to the great preacher.

The minister who told this story said, "I know that story is true, for it happened in my church. Yes, I know it is true, because I was that little boy. I heard the great D. L. Moody preach, but little did I know, when I clung to his coattails, that someday I would become the minister of that same church."

What a lesson in gentleness!

Touch of Gentleness

In the long and eventful history of Athens, Denys of Halicarnassus says if he were to name the chief contribution which Athens had made to mankind — this city which produced Plato and his philosophy, Socrates and his wisdom, Euripides and his drama, Philidias and his statues — the answer would be, "She made more gentle the life of the whole world."

If there is one thing which should be said about the Christian in any country it is that every life Jesus met He touched with the touch of gentleness.

An unknown poet prayed:

Give me Thy gift of gentleness, most gracious Lord;
For whom the way was rough, and darkly black,
For clouds of sorrow hung about life's track,
Till tears and anguish seemed my double part —
It was Thy gentleness that healed my heart!
And there are others — walking weary years,
With bleeding feet, the stony track of tears.
Oh, make me gentle, Lord; through me express
The healing grace of Thine own gentleness.

Finally only the meek can do restorative work. "Brethren, if a man is overtaken in any trespass, you who are spiritual should restore him in a spirit of gentleness" (Galatians 6:1). And Paul instructs the young preacher, Timothy, to be gentle especially toward those who oppose him. "And the Lord's servant must not be quarrelsome but kindly to every one, an apt teacher, forbearing, correcting his opponents with gentleness" (2 Timothy 2:24, 25). It is possible to be intensely jealous of one's ecclesiastical position while actually out of touch with the living Lord. In fact, the less place the Lord has, the more important one's own place and position becomes.

The Strong Are Gentle

Insecure, weak leaders, in the world or church, usually try to rule with an iron hand. They cannot afford to have their opinions and conclusions challenged. They develop a dogmatic disposition and delight in docile disciples. Such are afraid of free discussion or trusting the group in decisions because they fear the weakness of their own viewpoints. Or they quickly label other viewpoints in order to escape dealing with contrasting concerns.

On the other hand, one who is strong is gentle and gracious. This does not mean he has no firm beliefs. It does not mean he is spineless or wishy-washy. Persons who have spiritual strength and assurance and know what they believe and why, can most easily stand differences of opinion and voices which challenge their own viewpoint. They can be gentle because they, like God, are strong in love and the desire to help.

The gentleness of God enables us to become better persons. When we sense how strong God is, we see how gentle He is to us in all our sinfulness and helplessness. When we sense this great gentleness we rise to new spiritual stature and strength. As the psalmist expressed it in some of his last words, "Thy gentleness hath made me great" (2 Samuel 22:36, KJV; Psalm 18:35, KJV).

So also it is the gentle Christian who restores the erring, who helps others to God, who brings out the best in others. "Only such meek people, who are anything but weak people, can do restorative work. The severe, the sharp-tongued, the suspicious, the brittle, the irritable only make healing more difficult. Theirs is not the mind of Christ; theirs is not His method of love." [1]

Correction can be given in a way which discourages and

---

1. George Arthur Buttrick, ed., *The Interpreter's Bible,* Vol. 10 (Nashville: Abingdon, 1953), p. 574.

drives a person to depression and despair. Correction can also be given in the spirit of gentleness which sets a person upon his feet with new courage and determination to do better. Meekness is the spirit which makes correction a stimulant and not a depressant.

"Meekness is a heavenly principle," wrote Chauncey Giles in 1877, "brought down in the natural. It is the sweetness and gentleness, the mildness, humility, and kindness of angelic life brought down into the duties of natural life, into the activities of business, the pursuits of pleasure; into all social, civil, and domestic relations, molding them into heavenly forms, and communicating to them heavenly blessings."

60. The Mother of Meekness

Gregory of Myssa called humility, "the mother of meekness." Rambach said that meekness "grows out of the ashes of self-love and on the grace of pride."

Meekness is usually contrasted with pride and so meekness and humility are sometimes spoken of as the same. The feet of the meek and lowly shall trample upon the proud. God will vindicate the meek as opposed to the arrogant hypocrite. So meekness is the opposite of pride and arrogance.

In any definition of Christian maturity the trait of humility must be mentioned. Chrysostom said, "Humility is the root, mother, nurse, foundation, and bond of all nurture."

But what is humility? A quotation from the excellent article on "Humility" in the *International Standard Bible Encyclopedia* will help us.

"It by no means implies slavishness or servility; nor is it inconsistent with a right estimate of oneself, one's gifts and calling of God, or with proper self-assertion when called for. But the habitual frame of mind of a child of God is that of one who feels not only that he owes all his natural gifts, etc., to God, but that he has been the object of undeserved redeeming love, and who regards himself as being not his own, but God's in Christ. He cannot exalt himself, for he knows that he has nothing of himself. The humble mind is thus at the root of all other graces and

THE MOTHER OF MEEKNESS

virtues. Self-exaltation spoils everything. There can be no real
love without humility. 'Love,' said Paul, 'vaunteth not itself,
is not puffed up' (1 Corinthians 13:4). As Augustine said,
humility is first, second, and third in Christianity."

Inner Restfulness

Andrew Murray speaks of the spirit of humility this way,
"Humility is perfect quietness of heart. It is for me to have
no trouble: never to be fretted or vexed or irritated or sore
or disappointed. It is to expect nothing, to wonder at nothing that is done to me, to feel nothing done against me. It
is to be at rest when nobody praises me, and when I am
blamed or despised. It is to have a blessed home in the
Lord, where I can go in and shut the door, and kneel to my
Father in secret, and am at peace as in a deep sea of calm-
ness when all around and above is trouble. It is the fruit
of the Lord Jesus Christ's redemptive work on Calvary's
cross, manifest in those of His own who are definitely
subjected to the Holy Spirit."

Trees loaded with fruit bend lowest. The riper wheat
becomes, the more lowly it bends its heads. Ships carrying
the greatest cargoes sink deepest. Miners go deep into the
earth for precious metals. Niagara Falls is the result of the
difference in altitude of Lake Ontario and Lake Erie. The
greatest flow of water makes the deepest riverbed. People
are fond of exalting the virtues of humility, but they crucify
it rather than submit to it.

It is said that once President Washington was riding
with a party of gentlemen when their horses leaped a rock
fence. The last steed over kicked off several stones. "Better
replace those," suggested the General. "Oh, someone will do
that," was the careless reply. When the riding party dis-
banded, Washington turned his horse, rode back the way
they had come, dismounted, and carefully replaced the

stones. "Oh, General," chattered a friend who had gone along, "you are too big to be doing that." "Oh, no," replied Washington, as he stood gravely inspecting his work, "I am just the right size."

Right Attitudes Toward Ourselves

A number of things begin to stand out in our understanding of humility. One is that humility consists in maintaining a right attitude toward ourselves. It is not abject self-depreciation. It does not mean the surrender of the dignity of our nature, given by God. "Genuine humility," said Alistair Maclean, "does not arise from the sense of our pitiable kinship with the dust that is unworthy of us but from the realization of an awful nearness to a magnificence of which we are unworthy."

Someone asked the great preacher Joseph Parker, "Why did Jesus choose Judas?" Dr. Parker replied, "I don't know, but I have a harder question. Why did Jesus choose me?"

Humility and meekness then are hooked with an honest evaluation of our strengths and our weaknesses. No one appreciates the faked humility which denies one's talents and abilities.

Use your gifts, said Paul. Quit shortchanging yourself, blaming your parents, your environment, your circumstances, your bad luck, your frailties, your foolishness, your mistakes, and the animosities of others for the emptiness of your life and for the fact that you don't seem to be getting anywhere.

Don't spend your time envying others the gifts they have while you fail or refuse to use the gifts God has given to you. It could be that you don't have the gifts of others because you have not cultivated them. On the other hand, it could very well be that you will never have their gifts because you have your own — all your own to use in the service of God as a member of Christ's body.

To be humble means that we are in earnest about God's glory rather than our own. Humility is a by-product, a result of seeking the glory and majesty of God, and a realization of our weakness and worthlessness before Him. An old preacher said regarding the great striving for higher seats on the part of many, "How astonished those people will be, if they arrive in heaven, to find the angels, who are so much wiser than they, are laying no schemes to be made archangels."

It is good to remember we cannot make other persons humble. In spite of criticism or indignities heaped upon us, we can remain proud. But we can humble ourselves. This is God's command, "Humble yourselves." "For whosoever exalteth himself shall be abased, and he that humbleth himself shall be exalted."

A Teachable Spirit

The meek, the humble spirit is a teachable spirit. The Holy Spirit, in operation in our lives, releases us and opens us to receive spiritual help, whatever the source. One who is not humble can hardly be helped. Pride causes a person to react, to analyze, and to build up resistance to the contribution of others. The proud intellectual cannot receive truth from the less intellectual.

In pride we wall up our minds so we cannot receive edification. But when the Spirit puts within us a meek and humble attitude we will not despise people who seem below or above us in capabilities and capacities. We will be able to learn from all with thanksgiving.

E. Stanley Jones testified to this truth. He said, "May I add a word of personal testimony? No one in public work can escape criticism. I have had my share. It used to cut me to the quick. But now when criticism comes I find myself asking, is it true? If so, I will take it, will profit by it. My critics thus become 'the unpaid watchmen of my soul.' If the criticism isn't true, I can still use it. I can make these fires of unjust criticism serve to burn up my fetters and make me free."

Is the ease with which we are offended related to our lack of humility?

William Law in *Serious Call to a Devout and Holy Life* writes concerning the cultivation of humility: "Let every day be a day of humility; condescend to all the weaknesses and infirmities of your fellow creatures, cover their frailties, love their excellencies, encourage their virtues, relieve their wants, rejoice in their prosperities, be compassionate in their distress, receive their friendship, overlook their unkindness, forgive their malice, be a servant of servants and condescend to do the lowest offices to the lowest of mankind."

61. The Inheritance of the Meek

When the great Japanese Christian Kagawa was living in the slums of Kobe, helping the despised and destitute, he invited a distinguished preacher to speak at a public meeting. Wearing the garments of the poor with whom he lived, Kagawa met his guest at the train. But the guest mistaking him for a porter, ordered, "Here, fellow, carry my bags. I'm looking for Kagawa."

Kagawa obediently carried the bags of this leader whose outlook upon greatness was so far from the Spirit of Christ that he could not recognize the Christian article when he saw it.

Jesus says, "The meek shall inherit the earth." Kagawa, in obedience to God and in love for his fellowmen, forgot himself. Today he is remembered throughout the world. The important man who met him that day at the train is forgotten. So the great Herod is remembered today because he happened to reign during the days of the "meek and lowly Jesus."

Only to the spiritually minded does meekness become a luminous affirmation. To all others it is blind contradiction. As Percy C. Ainsworth puts it, "And so it comes to pass that the things at which the marketplace laughs are the things by which the saint lives. When the world hears about the inheritance of the meek, the rights of the gentle-hearted, it feels itself challenged at a point where it isn't quite able to make reply. The prize of the meek is not heaven but earth."

This is a direct contradiction to all the world believes.

The world has a beatitude, "Blessed are the proud, the passionate, and the self-assertive, for they shall get everything they ask for." Materialism must trust in its hands, feet, and forces, for it has no heart.

We need not get excited when some clamor for Christ by using the same methods of the world in advertisement, noise, theater, or political platform. Such methods seem to succeed for a while. But the demands for novelty, excitement soon exhaust themselves. It's the quiet, self-restrained integrity of the meek which has lasting success. Big things do not need to be shouted about.

The Promise Is Not Revoked

As a new type of character is being evolved in an age of competition and advertisement, it is worthwhile to remember that the promise to the meek is not revoked in the twentieth century. Persons who advance by push and power will soon be forgotten, while ideas foreign to them go on stamping their mark on society and principles they could not grasp go on changing the face of the world.

Knights of the cross are not clad in steel or iron but in the soft garments of holiness and gentleness. They do not go forth with force and earthly power but they conquer the strongest squadrons of sin.

The world knows the meek as those who do not push, trample, or shout for retaliation. They can be elbowed out of the way and often become martyrs. They seem to count for so little. Yet Jesus promises that they will inherit everything. Someone is making a mistake. The world sees what meekness misses but not what it possesses. It sees what meekness gives up but not what it secures. It takes note of its sufferings but not of its victories.

Meekness is so positive it does not need to assert itself because it has something better to assert. It knows that

314

spiritual inheritance comes not by slaying one's rivals but by slaying one's self. The heirs of the earth are they who are learning to think as God thinks and to see and feel as heaven sees and feels.

In Bunyan's *Pilgrim's Progress* we read the interesting story which shows the counterpart of meekness, "Now as they were going along and talking, they espied a boy feeding his father's sheep. The boy had on very mean clothes but of a fresh and well-favored countenance; and as he sat by himself he sang:

He that is down, need fear no fall;
He that is low, no pride
He that is humble ever shall
Have God to be his guide.

"Then said Mr. Greatheart to Christian, 'Do you hear him? I will dare to say this boy lives a merrier life, and wears more of that herb called heartsease in his bosom than he that is clad in silk and velvet.' "

So the meek already inherit the earth. The meek are already satisfied, content as Goldsmith expressed it, "Having nothing, yet hath all," or as Paul said it, "Having nothing, yet possessing all things."

False and True Inheritance

Men buy and build, place deeds in safety vaults, amass wealth in bank ledgers, and call that possessing the earth. They fight, strive, and elbow for honor and fame and call that possessing the earth. In all this they fail to realize that the earth can never be won by grabbing; it must be inherited.

Even nature teaches the meek shall inherit the earth. The huge aggressive reptiles which seemed at one time to rule the earth are today stuffed, museum pieces. On the other hand the sheep, the cow, the horse, and other animals which go on serving and refreshing mankind by what they give, still inherit the earth.

Napoleon, Herod the Great, and Alexander the Great seemed to inherit the earth. But today the One who called Himself "the meek one" is all through the earth.

Inheriting the earth does not mean that we increase happiness by the acre. It does not speak of outward proprietary power. Inheritance is always a matter of relationship.

Heirs of this world in a physical sense get the title deed to an area of land. The man, however, with the spirit of the other world actually enters into real possession of the earth even though he can call none of it in the physical sense his own, for true possession of the earth does not involve money and deeds to property. A man who had made money very rapidly was one day showing a poor relative of his a fine park that he had bought. Hoping to impress him with the vastness of the domain, with a sweep of the hand, he said, "All this is my land." "Yes," came the quiet reply, "but it is my landscape." This world's success gets the title deeds; but the other world's success, the lowly, gentle, teachable spirit, enters into the real possession. A man might buy up a continent and never possess a square foot of it.

Men seek to possess the earth through money, fame, and power. They seek to inherit the earth and all it offers. But real inheritance of the earth will never come through such means. Chappell said, "Those inherit it who find in it the richest and fullest and freest life. The selfish man cannot inherit the earth. The small bit of the earth that he wins rather possesses him, and makes him, in some measure, its slave, while the wealth that is not his tends to make him restless by exciting his desire or his envy." The man who truly possesses the earth is he who can admire without coveting and enjoy without owning.

Self-Control Fruit

62. Self-Control — Love in Charge

Adlai Stevenson once visited Dr. Albert Schweitzer in his primitive jungle hospital in French Equatorial Africa. Dr. Schweitzer told Mr. Stevenson that he considered this the most dangerous period in all human history. Why? "Because," he said, "heretofore nature controlled man. But now man has learned to control nature's elemental forces before he has learned to control himself."

An automobile out of control endangers those on the highway. A fire out of control destroys everything in its path. A person out of control is even worse because our world is destroyed, relationships are broken, and everything noble, right, and true is destroyed.

James Denny pointed out one of the striking things of life is that the beautiful and most helpful traits, when restrained and in their proper place and question, become also the worst corruptible and destructive when uncontrolled. "As a fire, when it breaks loose and rages on its own account, carries swift destruction in its course, but, when restricted within certain bounds, warms our rooms and cooks our food, illuminates our towns and drives our locomotives; or as water when in flood, roots up trees, carries away houses and sweeps crops from the fields, but when confined within its banks, drives the wheel and floats the barge and rejoices the eye either by its placid flow or by the splendors of the cataract, so the very qualities which,

319

when unregulated, waste and brutalize life may, when subjected to the control of temperance, be its fairest ornament."

So it is that one gifted in conversation, can become a bore. Temper which can be a fine sensitive thing can become madness. Sex, beautiful in its proper place, can brutalize quickly and completely.

Divorce statistics, crime reports, the erosion of honesty, race relations, the collapse of sex morals, the materialistic outlook, drug abuse, overeating, alcohol and tobacco consumption — these and a thousand other proofs are constant reminders of modern man's inability to cope with himself or his environment, his inability to control himself.

Enemies Within

Temperance or self-control is last in the list of the fruit of the Spirit, not because it is least, but because it binds all the rest. Temperance, often applied almost exclusively to intoxicating drinks, is really a word which covers the whole field of emotions and passion, control of spirit, body, and mind. It has to do with the enemies within, the lusts and passions which war against the soul. A whole army storming on the outside is less than a single enemy within the walls which gives over the key to attacking forces.

One of the old Italian masters left us his conception of self-control. On the walls of a small chapel he painted a heroic, female figure with a bridle upon her lips and her right hand holding the hilt of a sheathed sword to its scabbard. That conveys, in symbol, the idea of self-command which restrains the utterance of emotion and sheaths the sword of passion.

Moralists have always placed importance on self-control but they have not realized its deepest and noblest forms in the Christian concept. From the beginning moral teachers of all lands have said, "Rule yourself" and from the beginning the attempt to govern ourselves by unaided self is doomed to failure. Self-control is not just control of wrong desires, but even more, it is control so that power is released to do right and realize full freedom.

Among the works of the flesh in Galatians 5:19-21, the Scripture lists illustrations of lack of self-control such as unrestrainedness, drunkenness, carousings. One of the chief purposes of the Holy Spirit is to make us whole persons. To do this He helps us establish the habit of having all our faculties under control, especially our inclinations and emotions. Self-control is mastery of self.

Self-control is not merely getting a hold of ourselves, shaping ourselves by our own strength. It is more than a stoic stance which refuses to be under the power of passion. Such sheer determination can do a lot. But even with such success pride can be pampered. Self-control, for our good and God's glory, comes only as we surrender ourselves first to God and commit ourselves to His way. Then His Spirit puts within us both the desire and the power to control our appetites, impulses, imaginations, and desires.

Paul says, "For God did not give us a spirit of timidity but a spirit of power and love and self-control" (2 Timothy 1:7). Peter says a person is a slave to whatever controls him. 2 Peter 2:19.

What Self-Control Includes

Self-control means then at least three things. First it means to refrain from all known wrong. There is no area of life excluded from the will of God for us. We are told to be "temperate in all things." This means we are to discover and apply the will of God to the whole scope of life.

Temperance does not mean that all things are good if one is temperate in using them. To experiment cautiously with sin is wrong. To be temperate or practice self-control means to control our lives so that what we do or do not do is in line with the divine will. We are to avoid all experiences, relationships, and attitudes contrary to the way of Christ. As Frances E. Willard wrote, "Temperance is moderation in the things that are good and total abstinence from the things that are foul."

Second, self-control or temperance does more than police wrong desires and hungers. It means we weigh what is best and abstain from the rest. It helps us know how to sacrifice the lesser for the higher good, how to discern between the good and the best. In these we find the signs of spiritual maturity.

The writer to the Hebrew Christians told them to "lay aside every weight" (Hebrews 12:1). What is a weight? It is anything in life which keeps us from being our best for God. So a weight may be something easily justified as right and good in the sense that it is not outright sin. But it may keep us from winning the Christian race.

Suppose some morning we go to a race. Runners are lined up, stripped to bare essentials. All is ready for the race when suddenly we see another fellow coming to the starting line. But, strange as it seems, he is fully dressed. He has on a full suit, a heavy overcoat, hip boots, and a heavy woolen cap. In his hands he carries his lunch bucket, an umbrella, and his pockets are filled with medication.

Everyone is surprised that such a person would try to win the race. Finally we approach him and ask him about it. "Of course," he says, "I'm running the race. What's wrong with what I wear? Is anything wrong with a coat or cap or medications? After all, the race is long, the terrain is treacherous and I may become ill. I'm going prepared for whatever may lie ahead."

We cannot tell him what he carries is sin. But we

know he will never win the race. Why? Because he is loaded with weights.

So self-control requires us not only to avoid sin but also demands the discipline to give up good things that will keep us from being and doing our best for God. Self-control means moderation and restraint in the things which are legitimate and the elimination of those things which tear down or destroy spiritual life.

Jenny Lind once expressed it well. She saw the choice clearly. Approached by a friend one evening as she sat on the beach with the Bible in her lap, she was asked the question, "Why did you give up the stage when you were enjoying such wonderful triumphs?" She replied pointing toward the mellow beauty of the golden sunset, 'When every day it made me think less of that and (laying her hand on the open Bible as she did it) nothing at all of this, what else could I do?"

Athletic Discipline

Third, self-control involves discipline. The Apostle Paul compares the moral struggle to the games so renowned in ancient Greece. He says that everyone taking part in these games was temperate in all things. Ten months of hard training was required. Discipline in everything was most severe. It could not be relaxed a single day. Otherwise a rival would get to the front.

But the candidates did not go around each day, complaining how hard their lot was. They chose to enter the game. They talked of the prize they expected to win. They spoke of the special privileges which were theirs should they win. Temperance becomes easy and exciting when we see not a corruptible but an incorruptible crown.

Finally self-control is possible when we realize that we are human and that the Holy Spirit is the power to help us

SPIRIT FRUIT

overcome. Caesar of Rome had a slave as his constant
companion. The slave's duty was to whisper in his
monarch's ear, "You are human." We all need this reminder.

But we also need the reminder that the Holy Spirit
lives in us.

We gain self-control when we have the glory of God
as our goal, not merely the good of others. Most people
who live evil lives do not want evil to destroy them. But
they are overcome because they do not have a higher
goal than self-enjoyment and self-gratification.

We also can seek to keep from sin simply because of
what sin does to us personally and to others. That may be
of some worth. But the strength to exercise self-control
over the second best will not be possible until we see that
our calling is to the very best in Christ. Johann Friedrich
Lobstein said it well, "If you would learn self-mastery, begin by yielding yourself to the One Great Master."

63. Jesus and Self-Control

The great preacher Dr. J. Wallace Hamilton tells the wonderful story of Roland Hayes. "As a boy the gifted Negro singer, Roland Hayes, heard his old Negro minister preach a sermon on Christ before Pilate. The preacher contrasted two kinds of power confronting each other. Pilate, irked by the silence of Jesus, cried, 'Why don't you answer me? Don't you know I have power?' The illiterate old preacher went on to say, 'No matter how angry the crowd got, He never said a mumberlin' word, not a word.'

"Years later, at the peak of fame with his golden voice, Roland Hayes stood before a Nazi audience in Berlin's Beethoven Hall. The audience was hostile, ugly, scornful of a Negro daring to sing at the center of Aryan culture. He was greeted with a chorus of Nazi hisses, growing louder and more ominous; for ten minutes Hayes stood there in silence at the piano, resentment swelling up in him like an irresistible tide.

"And then he remembered the sermon of long ago: 'He never said a mumberlin' word, not a word.' He shouted back no words born of anger; he kept his head, for he knew that the ultimate power was on his side, not theirs. He stood there and prayed, silently, and the quiet dignity of his courage conquered the savage spirits in his audience, and in hushed pianissimo he began to sing a song of Schubert's. He won without so much as 'a mumberlin' word.'" [1]

---

1. J. Wallace Hamilton, *Ride the Wild Horses: The Christian Use of Our Untamed Impulses.* (Old Tappan, N.J.: Fleming H. Revell, 1952), pp. 117-118.

self-control
with temper...

No one ever demonstrated more self-control than Christ. How many the opportunities He had to lash back and to vent ill feelings against those who treated Him wrong. He is our pattern and power. How did He react under difficult circumstances? He was tempted in all points like we are, yet without sin.

One young lady said that she would learn to control herself by thinking of her deceased father whom she adored. She would ask, "How would Father react under such circumstances?" This helped her to win the battle. There is value in this.

However, this is not enough. The Christian can go further than this. He can certainly be helped by asking, How would Jesus react under these circumstances? But Jesus still walks with us and lives in us by His Holy Spirit to help us gain the victory. The self-control is not a grim and dreary battle, but the surrender of self to Him. Here is the secret of self-control.

Another word to describe the balance and power of self-control is poise. Next to love, poise was the outstanding characteristic of Christ's emotional life. All His emotions were intense yet always in perfect equilibrium without straining frustration or fear. He was never upset by anything.

Christ's composure, His self-control, came from His commitment to God's purpose for Him. He always lived and acted with an end in view. The qualities and abilities of His life were given direction through His sense of purpose under God. His bearing, timing, intent, and program of action all show His discipline and commitment to God. He ordered His life in light of the Father's will. This was the secret of His self-control and it is the secret of ours as well.

64. Tame Your Tongue

A quaint story in the Talmud tells of a king who gave his jester a command, "Go out and buy the very best thing in the world." In a short time the jester was back with a package in which he had a tongue.

The king praised the jester for having chosen so wisely. "Truly," said the king, "the tongue is the best thing in the world."

Before the jester left, the king gave him a second assignment. "Now go and find the worst thing in the world." This search was also short for soon the jester returned with another package. The king unwrapped it and found a tongue.

This ancient legend supports what the Apostle James emphasizes, when he points out that we use the tongue to say the praises of God and we use it to invoke curses upon our fellowmen. James 3:9, 10. The gift of speech is both man's glory and his downfall.

Control of the tongue is one of the greatest necessities in the Christian life. There is no finer test of true Christianity than the ability to control the tongue. "The tongue is a fire," says James, "the world of iniquity among our members is the tongue, which defiles the whole body." The tongue of criticism and gossip has ruined more lives, churches, and family relationships than anything else.

The tremendous destruction through rumor, gossip, half truth, and evil speaking can hardly be overemphasized.

James uses the picture of a great fire, started by a spark, to show the awful effects of an evil tongue.

A little word dropped carelessly is like a lighted match. A thoughtless remark can start a big fire. A tiny expression of malice can begin a huge argument. A huge stack of timber can be set ablaze by the tiniest spark.

Words Divide and Kill

With the tongue, wars begin; reputations are destroyed; and wounds are made which are hard to heal. Cruel, sarcastic, sharp, and icy words are a curse. The Scripture says that if we cannot control our tongues, we will never be able to control the rest of our body or life. We start with the tongue and putting a bridle on the tongue we control the whole body.

If we put bits into horses' mouths to make them obey our will, we can direct their whole body. Or think of ships, says James. They are very large and driven by strong gales, yet they are directed by a tiny rudder. So with the tongue.

Further the tongue carries the venom which kills. Words kill. They kill love, once bright and true. They kill joy, peace, and trust. They kill ambition and a good name.

To learn another example from nature look at a spring of water. Does a spring gush forth both fresh and brackish water from the same opening? It's either going to be one or the other. Therefore, we should not think we can spout forth from the same tongue words that are both foul and clean, hateful and kind, false and true, salty and fresh.

So the Scripture recognizes the tongue as a terrible instrument for good or evil. For it to be good that which controls it needs to be corrected. Everything that is in the heart of man comes rapidly out of his mouth. The tongue must be tamed, controlled.

Shakespeare in *Othello*, Act III, speaks of ill words about another as stealing:

> Good name in man and woman, dear my lord,
> Is the immediate jewel of their souls:
> Who steals my purse steals trash: 'tis something,
>   nothing:
> 'Twas mine, 'tis his, and has been slave to
>   thousands;
> But he that filches from me my good name
> Robs me of that which not enriches him
> And makes me poor indeed.

Charlotte Bronte in *Shirley* spoke of a censorious spirit and how it nullifies the good both in the conscientious Miss Mann and in others. "Miss Mann was a perfectly honest, conscientious woman, who had passed along through protracted scenes of suffering, exercised rigid self-denial, made large sacrifices of time, money, health, for those who repaid her only by ingratitude; and now her main — almost her sole — fault was that she was censorious. Censorious she certainly was. . . . She dissected impartially almost all her acquaintances, she made few distinctions; she allowed scarcely any one to be good."

Guard the Door

So the psalmist said, "I will take heed to my ways, that I sin not with my tongue." We must watch the door of our lips. The Spirit gives the self-control which holds back the harsh answer and which refuses to repeat the hurtful rumor. The Spirit puts on our lips the law of kindness.

No other area of nonconformity to the world or self-control is spoken more about in the New Testament than

329

that which deals with the way we talk. We seem to lose control here more than any other. And, without a doubt, we grieve the Holy Spirit more by the way we speak about others than in any other way.

Sometime ago I was part of a small group studying Ephesians. In meditating on the fourth chapter I suddenly became aware that the statement about grieving the Holy Spirit was placed squarely between admonitions on how we speak about other people. I read, "Therefore, putting away falsehood, let every one speak the truth with his neighbor, for we are members one of another. . . . Let no evil talk come out of your mouths, but only such as is good for edifying, as fits the occasion, that it may impart grace to those who hear. And do not grieve the Holy Spirit of God, in whom you were sealed for the day of redemption. Let all bitterness and wrath and anger and clamor and slander be put away from you, with all malice, and be kind to one another, tenderhearted, forgiving one another, as God in Christ forgave you" (Ephesians 4:25, 29-32).

One clear sign that the Spirit is at work in our lives is that we sense His leading clearly in our speech. He shows us how sinful we are when we speak ill of others. He gives us inner control over this sin and takes away our desire to excuse ourselves for evil speaking. The Apostle Peter says that as Christians we are to put away all malice, guile, insincerity, envy, and evil speaking. 1 Peter 2:1.

A woman one day came to her pastor. After she had spilled out a lot of words about another person her pastor said, "I wish you wouldn't speak evil of others like this." She replied, "I'm not speaking evil. I'm telling the truth!" "Yes," said the pastor, "if it were untrue God would call it lying. God calls it evil speaking. When we talk about others without a loving spirit it is evil speaking."

Another person came to the preacher and said, "I have got so in the habit of exaggerating that my friends accuse me of exaggerating so that they don't understand me." He asked, "Can you help me? What can I do to overcome it?"

"Well," he said, "the next time you catch yourself lying, go right to the person and say you have lied and tell him you are sorry. Say it is a lie; stamp it out, root and branch; that is what you need to do."

"Oh," he said, "I wouldn't like to call it lying." But that is what exaggeration is.

Some years ago, the private secretary to Former President Hoover told an editor friend of mine that in the forty years she worked for him she had never heard him say an unkind word about anyone. What an example of self-control.

Probably no president experienced more slander and unfounded criticism than Hoover. No president was blamed more for things he was not responsible for than he. The opposite political party made him bear the brunt and blame for the depression years long after he left office.

Few men did more creative work in building a foundation for financial and final recovery. During all the years of unfair charges and attempts by his opponents to make Hoover look bad, while hiding the tremendous good he did, this man would not stoop to retaliatory speech. Today his life tells the story of inner strength of character and commitment hard to be equaled anywhere.

65. Control Your Thoughts

Douglas V. Steere wrote: "The greatest evidence of man's freedom lies in his power to focus his attention on what he chooses." And an unknown writer of many years ago said, "I do not know that there is anything that wants a tighter rein, or that more needs to have a line laid down like a tramrail, by which to keep it from vagrancy, than what ordinary people call their thinking."

God calls us to bring into captivity every thought to the obedience of Christ. 2 Corinthians 10:5. Paul points out how we can control our thinking, "Finally, brethren, whatever is true, whatever is honorable, whatever is just, whatever is pure, whatever is lovely, whatever is gracious, if there is any excellence, if there is anything worthy of praise, think about these things. What you have learned and received and heard and seen in me, do; and the God of peace will be with you." (Philippians 4:8, 9).

Thoughts are the material by which we live and work. Before anything is accomplished of good or evil it is thought in the mind. Thoughts are important, for "As . . . [a man] thinketh in his heart, so is he." We are told to control our thoughts.

We Can Choose

We can fill our minds with the drab and lowly or the rich and noble, the impure and coarse or the pure and refined. We control our thoughts by what we read and what we look at. The "soul is dyed by the color of our thoughts." The psalmist prayed, "Search me, O God, and know my heart! Try me and know my thoughts," and "Let . . . the meditation of my heart be acceptable in thy sight."

Alexander Maclaren asks, "What did God put a will into you for, but that you ought to be able to say *not* 'I like' or 'I was tempted, and I could not help it,' but that you might, before each action, be able to say 'I will'; and that passions, and the strings of lust and sense, of appetite and flesh, and emotions and affections, and vagrant fancies and wandering thoughts, and virtues that were running to seed, and weaknesses that might be cultivated into strength, might all know the master touch of a governing will, and might obey as becomes them. . . .

"And what did God give you a conscience for, but that the will, which commands all the rest, might take its orders from it? There are parts of your nature which are intended to be slaves, and there are parts which are intended to be masters."

Sexual lust in our thoughts is one of the most difficult forces to bring under control. Jesus described the danger of lust which destroys the best within. The Holy Spirit points out this evil and He gives us the power to keep our minds from the pornographic page and the lust which destroys all spiritual beauty and insight. The pure in heart and thought are those who see God — here and hereafter — while the impure blind themselves to spiritual reality and put God far away.

Augustine fought like a man fighting another for his life in order to be free from sins that had fastened themselves so tightly to him. By the Spirit he conquered and God made him a saint in purity of thought and life.

Unless above himself he can
Erect himself, how mean a thing is man.

This is what God does. He gives us His own Holy Spirit to rise above the low to the pure, the holy, and the right, starting in our thought life. Paul asks, "Do you not know that you are God's temple and that God's Spirit dwells in you?" (1 Corinthians 3:16).

Why was the place where Moses one day stood holy ground? Why did God tell Moses to take off his shoes because he was on holy ground? What made that ground more holy than any other? The answer to all these questions is that whatever God touches becomes holy. The ground was holy because God was there.

Wonder of wonders. We are, as Christians, the dwelling place of God. We are His temple. Where He dwells is a holy place. What limitations this puts upon our lives! What possibilities!

A full realization of the fact of God's living within means that His Spirit is quick to remind us of anything which is unholy. Like God to Moses, the Spirit says, "Remove that from your life, for you are the temple of God." The Holy Spirit lives within us and anything which is unholy cannot knowingly be allowed.

Power from Within

But what possibilities are present also! To believe that God Himself indwells us by His Holy Spirit means that we can now live and walk in new power. This is a power not our own. This is a power far beyond us. This is a power to live a life of purity and purpose which cannot be even imagined otherwise. Jesus said His Spirit shall be in us and "abide with us." This means that we are never without His guidance and power. In every thought or act or decision He is with us. He guides our thinking.

To be aware of God's Spirit within, by obedience to His leading, means to be changed from glory to glory even into the likeness of Christ. Also the Spirit of God will make me alive to spiritual truth unknown otherwise. This mortal body suddenly takes on new meaning, majesty, and magnitude. What privilege and what possibility is in the truth, "The Spirit of God dwelleth in you"!

Catherine of Siena one time spent three days in a solitary retreat, praying for a greater fullness and joy of the Divine Presence. Instead of this it seemed as though legions of wicked spirits assailed her with blasphemous thoughts and evil suggestions.

At length a great light appeared to descend from above. The devils fled, and the Lord Jesus seemed to converse with her. Catherine asked Him, "Lord, where were You when my heart was so tormented?" "I was in your heart." "O Lord," she said, "You are everlasting truth and I humbly bow before Your Word; but how can I believe You were in my heart when it was filled with such detestable thoughts?"

"Did these thoughts give you pleasure or pain?" He asked.

"An exceeding pain and sadness," was Catherine's reply.

"You were in woe and sadness because I was in the midst of your heart. My presence it was which rendered those thoughts insupportable to you. When the period I had determined for the duration of the combat had elapsed, I sent forth the beams of My light, and the shadows of hell were dispelled, because they cannot resist the light."

66. Manage Your Money

Phillip Guedella, writer and biographer, tells how in writing biographies, among the things he examines carefully is the way a man spends his money. In writing the biography of the Duke of Wellington he found a pack of receipted bills, a "fruitful source of information." Mr. Guedella says, "Show me how a man spends his money and you will show me what kind of man he is." The use of money is a dead giveaway as to what people really are.

Jesus recognized that money is no surface matter. He saw that the deepest convictions and controls of our lives are all tied up with material things. He said more about the use of money than about any other ethical or moral question. The Bible has more to say about the sin of covetousness than about drunkenness.

"Mortify therefore your members . . . covetousness, which is idolatry" says the Scripture. And again, "Nor covetous man . . . hath any inheritance in the kingdom of Christ." "They that will be [desire to be] rich fall into temptation and a snare, and into many foolish and hurtful lusts, which drown men in destruction and perdition. For the love of money is the root of all evil: which while some coveted after, they have erred from the faith, and pierced themselves through with many sorrows."

This covetous spirit fastens upon the old rather than the

young. It is most dangerous because persons do not think it to be the heinous thing it is. "The wicked . . . blesseth the covetous, whom the Lord abhorreth." John Ruskin wrote, "We do great injustice to Iscariot in thinking him wicked above all common wickedness. He was only a common money-lover, and like all money-lovers, did not understand Christ."

One need not have much to be covetous. Self-control so often gives way to money control. Instead of self-mastery money and things become the master.

A Different Standard

Following conversion to Christ persons often become ascetic. The new Christian may deplore and despise, and sometimes dispose of material things. Soon, however, he sees that things are needed to exist. Now a severe test of spiritual maturity and spiritual values arises. Material things can easily become uppermost. Here self-control is important. Self-control always puts Christ and His way first and keeps material things in their proper place. Stewardship includes all we are and have. What we give to others or spend on ourselves really belongs to God.

Anna Mow writes, "Throughout church history there has been a swinging back and forth between 'beauty' and 'austerity' in dress and architecture. Pride has just as free rein in austerity as it does in beauty. Simplicity is the balanced virtue. In simplicity there is no room for ostentation or ugliness, in fact simplicity is beauty." [1]

This is the day of the easy payment, the credit card, the status symbol, the great drive to promote the importance of things and the "buy now, pay later" push. TV programs, advertisements, and the great sweepstake campaigns promote a spirit of greediness. If we are not com-

---

1. Anna B. Mow, *Say Yes to Life* (Grand Rapids: Zondervan, 1961), p. 98.

mitted to a different standard and if we are not careful we are caught in the spirit of covetousness. One of the greatest opportunities of self-control is the way we use our money. It includes our entire attitude toward material things.

How do we check the covetous spirit? By beginning to scatter, to give away what we have. The only way to overcome covetousness is to strangle it. It ought to be destroyed root and branch. It dare not have dominion.

Most of what we are able to acquire is limited. Though the world is filled with air we can only inhale a lungful at a time. Though the earth is filled with food we can fill only one stomach at a time. Though the universe is covered with vegetation we can walk only on the grass where we are.

The Richness of Contentment

Strange as it sounds today the Scripture still says, "But if we have food and clothing, with these we shall be content" (1 Timothy 6:8). The moment we move beyond our capacity to use what we have we are possessed rather than possessing. Our wealth has us instead of us having it. Our property owns us instead of us owning it. We become slaves instead of masters. We become discontented rather than contented.

That's about it. There is a universal law that the greater controls the lesser. Put a person and his possessions side by side. Depending which grows the faster certain things happen. As wealth becomes greater than the person, it masters the man. So much so that it can completely monetize him so that it possesses his thinking in dollars and cents. Instead of warm human terms he thinks and deals in terms of cold coins on the counter. Coins determine concern and conduct. Will it pay? Is the ointment wasted? What will I get?

When we move beyond our capacity to use the godly

contentment Paul puts before us, we begin to build bigger. It is the repetition of the story told by Jesus concerning the rich man who could not be content with sufficient barns. He must have bigger barns. He was not content with a comfortable and ample house in a good neighborhood. He must have a house bigger than he needed in an aristocratic community.

So the coat we have must be cast aside for a better coat. The table we eat at must be tossed out for a better table. The shoes we wear must be thrown aside for the current style. The car, which is adequate, must be traded for a more up-to-date model.

All this is the evil spirit of discontent. Grasping discontent seeks more for self instead of more for Christ and others. Discontent drives us to desire more than we can use. This evil spirit must be cast out or it will reign and ruin us for time and eternity.

67. Conquer Yourself

Peter the Great struck his gardener a violent blow, which sent him to his bed, and a few days afterward he died. On hearing it Peter burst into tears, saying, "Alas! I have civilized my own subjects. I have conquered other nations, yet I have not been able to civilize nor conquer myself." No wonder the Scripture says, "He that ruleth his spirit [is better] than he that taketh a city." Some of the most tragic pages of history have to do with people who did not have self-control.

Temper

When one's temper controls him, it makes him a terrible slave. Someone said the preacher will never miss anyone when he speaks of temper. "Many Christians," said an old divine, "who bore the loss of a child or all their property with the most heroic Christian fortitude, are entirely vanquished by the breaking of a dish or the blunders of a servant."

Ralph Heynen, in *The Art of Christian Living* writes, "People have often said to me, 'I used to have a terrible temper but I have learned that when I count to ten before I speak, I don't say anything rash.' Such a person has not really learned to control his temper; he has only learned to control the symptoms. Self-control means that we master the anger itself.

340

"This is where we must put our Christian faith into practice. The man of the world will speak about adjusting to life's frustrations; the Christian speaks about conquering them. . . .

"Then self-control is not a grim and dreary battle, but the surrender of self to Him, so that even every thought is brought into captivity to Christ."

Wallace Hamilton points out that some people say, "If only something would abolish my temper — if I could only kill my temper and abolish it from my life, then I could be a Christian. We imagine that is the way God wants us. But you see, God doesn't want you without your temper. He has too many disciples now who won't get angry, even at the liquor traffic."

God doesn't want a person without passion, feeling, and desire. He wants persons who can control themselves, who are masters and not slaves.

Another writer tells of a young woman making her confession at church. "I've got so many sins I don't know where to begin," she said. "Every time I go out with George I quarrel. And when he gets mad, then, to try to snap him out of it, I drink. And that only makes him madder. I smoke too much; look at my fingers! I really don't care about anyone but myself. I spend all my money on clothes. I try to outdo the other girls at the office to attract the attention of the boss. I am a slave. . . . I am dragging my chains around with me."

You see, the best things in life are preserved for the person who can control his powers, his passions, his tongue, his actions.

H. A. Ironside told of a woman who came to a minister to request that he talk to her husband. She said that he never stayed home at nights, set a bad example for the children, and slammed the door if she talked to him. "Before we pray for your husband," the minister said, "there is something I want to talk to you about. What about your vile temper?" He urged her to pray, confessing her vile temper that was driving her husband away from home and alienating her children, and bringing dishonor on the name of the Lord. He urged her to pray for deliverance and to receive sweetness and graciousness. She jumped to her feet and ran out the door in another fit of anger. Her own lack of self-control was a hindrance to the salvation of her husband.

Appetite

Appetite can become a great enemy if we cannot control it. Whether it is overeating, the use of tobacco, alcohol, or drugs, or any other habit to satisfy our appetites, God will give to us the strength to eliminate all that is harmful and to be temperate in all that is good. The Apostle Paul speaks of his freedom in Christ, but Paul's freedom did not consist in giving free rein to his impulses and desires. Even when these were lawful and not harmful, he subjected each to three tests: Is it helpful? Is it constructive? Is it to the glory of God? 1 Corinthians 10:23, 31.

License will not lead to liberty but to bondage when it comes to our inner appetites. Those who endanger their health because of lack of self-control are slaves to something outside themselves. The smoker is controlled by a harmful weed; the drinker is controlled by the depressant alcohol; and the glutton is a slave to food.

Think of the suffering and the early deaths due to overeating. Think of the misery today because of the use of tobacco and alcohol. Not only do the users suffer but all those who come in contact with them.

The Bible also teaches certain standards of self-control with regard to our sexual drives. "Do you not know that the unrighteous will not inherit the kingdom of God? Do not be deceived; neither the immoral, nor idolators, nor adulterers, nor homosexuals" (1 Corinthians 6:9). Today sex is the topic everywhere and more and more people are finding themselves in trouble and in need of help. An incredible commercialization of sex has taken place in the past years. With drastically changing sex attitudes, the Christian realizes God's purpose for sex has not changed and those who do not control sex will suffer here as well as hereafter.

Self-control is the fruit of the Spirit. "But I say, walk by the Spirit, and do not gratify the desires of the flesh. For the desires of the flesh are against the Spirit, and the desires of the Spirit are against the flesh. . . . And those who belong to Christ Jesus have crucified the flesh with its passions and desires. If we live by the Spirit, let us also walk by the Spirit" (Galatians 5:16, 24, 25).

68. Discipline and Discipleship

During the days that Knute Rockne was coaching Notre Dame, a sports columnist in a South Bend newspaper earned the reputation of being the meanest, most cutting writer in the country. The anonymous writer, who knew Notre Dame well, wrote about the team's weaknesses. He pointed out the mistakes of individual| players. He told about those who were lazy, about those who broke training and didn't discipline themselves.

Of course this column made the players roaring mad. The truth hurt, and players complained to Rockne. He listened with sympathy but said he could not stop the writer. He advised that the only way the players could do so was to go out and play the game so well that they would prove otherwise.

Later it became known that the writer of the column was Knute Rockne himself. As coach of his team he was best acquainted with their weaknesses. The critical column was his ingenious device to develop a better team.

Sometimes the Scripture speaks so sharply about us it is uncomfortable. But God tells the truth because He loves us and wants to make us winners. He knows that we cannot win unless we discipline ourselves to obey the rules of life.

On a television program a small boy was asked if he had any pets. "Well," he replied, "I did have some goldfish, but some water softener got in the water, and they softened to death." So also self-indulgence, laziness, indifference, and lack of self-discipline can become a part of our lives. Our spiritual muscles become flabby and we are easy prey to temptation and sin.

Nothing good is possible in life without self-control which results in disciplined living. The writer, the musician, the Christian achieve success only through disciplines. When the Apostle Paul illustrated Christian discipline he spoke of the athlete in Greek games. "Every athlete exercises self-control in all things."

When Mark Spitz, the five gold medal winner in the 1972 Olympics, was asked about his discipline and how much he practiced he replied that he swam the distance of several times around the world. Athletic excellence is achieved only by voluntary discipline. A person must obey training rules if he is to succeed. He cannot do whatever he happens to like to do. He cannot be free to excel unless he lives by a rigorous rule.

Discipline is adherence to training with a sense of purpose. It is more than cold obedience to rules. It is determination with an end in view. A disciple is one who submits to training and follows the path to a given goal. This discipline is so often missing and yet is so absolutely essential in living the Christian life. Yet as important as discipline is in athletic and cultural pursuits, it is even more important in the spiritual life.

Daily Dogged Discipline

John R. W. Stott, the great English expositor and scholar, shared his own observation, "I'm a great believer in what I have sometimes called 'the daily dogged discipline' of the Christian life. The greatest enemies of discipline are laziness and emotionalism. Lazy people can't be bothered to acquire disciplined habits, and emotional or temperamental

345

people prefer to live by their feelings. The 'I'll see what I feel like' attitude is certain to end in disaster. We do not read God's Word and pray only on days when we feel like it, but every day (better twice a day) whether we feel like it or not. We do not join the Lord's people for worship on those Sundays when we feel like it, but every Sunday, whether we feel like it or not, because it is the Lord's Day. Do we only come to work when we feel like it? Then why should we give our heavenly Lord a service inferior to what we give our earthly employer? 'We serve the Lord Christ' (Colossians 3:24). Then let's give Him better service, greater faithfulness, and more discipline than to any human master."

Self-Destructive Freedom

There is no slave like the man free to do as he pleases, because what he pleases is self-destructive.

A California psychiatrist recently complained that four out of every ten teenagers and young adults who visit his medical center have a psychological sickness he can do nothing about.

According to the *Los Angeles Times*, it is simply this: "Each of them demands that his world conform to his uncontrolled desires. Society has provided him with so many escape routes that he never has had to stand his ground against disappointment, postponement of pleasure, and the weight of responsibility — all forces which shape character."

The psychiatrist adds, "If the personality disorder persists far into adulthood," there will be a "society of pleasure-driven people, hopelessly insecure and dependent."

The *Times* article concluded, "When you take controls of constraint off a youngster, he never learns to slow down or control his drive to demand and do what he wants." So there is a place for law!

Aaron was an eleven-year-old boy whose behavior was

346

described by Dr. William Glasser, his psychiatrist, as horrible. In his book *Reality Therapy*, Glasser says Aaron was the most obnoxious child he had ever met; the boy would kick, scream, run away and hide, become withdrawn, disrupt his classes, and make everyone disgusted with him.

Dr. Glasser saw one problem with Aaron that no one else observed: "No one had ever told him he was doing wrong." No one had ever set limits on what he could and could not do. The psychiatrist decided to try a completely new tack. The boy would have to behave, to act reasonable, or be punished. He responded remarkably. "Probably because he had been anxious for so long to be treated in a realistic way." He became courteous, well-behaved, and his miserable grades went to straight A's. For the first time in his life Aaron began to play constructively with other children, to enjoy honest relationships with others, and to stop blaming his troubles on his mother or other people.

Dr. Glasser calls this "reality therapy" and says one of an individual's greatest needs is to be made to realize that he is personally responsible for what he does, and that right behavior accomplishes more than wrong behavior.

Thus the fruit of the Spirit, self-control, is not the last of the fruit listed because it is least important. It is the fruit of the Spirit in that we cannot experience it until we yield ourselves to the Holy Spirit. It is important, particularly in a period of casualness and laxity because it is at the center of all the other fruit, giving inner firmness which makes fruit delicious and salable.

Bibliography

Allen, Charles L. *The Miracle of Love*. Old Tappan, N.J.: Fleming H. Revell Co., 1972.

Ainslie, Peter. *Cultivating the Fruit of the Spirit*. St. Louis, Mo.: The Bethany Press, 1968.

Augsburger, Myron S. *Quench Not the Spirit*. Scottdale, Pa.: Herald Press, 1962.

Barclay, William. *Flesh and Spirit*. Nashville, Tenn.: Abingdon Press, 1962.

——————. *Promise of the Spirit*. Philadelphia, Pa.: Westminster Press, 1961.

Barker, Harold P. *The Vicar of Christ*. Chicago, Ill.: Good News Publishers, 1947.

Bittinger, A. *Gifts and Grace*. Grand Rapids, Mich.: William B. Eerdmans Publishing Co., 1968.

Candlesh, J. S. *The Work of the Holy Spirit*. Edinburgh: University Press, n.d.

Chafer, L. S. *He That Is Spiritual*. Grand Rapids, Mich.: Zondervan Publishing House, 1918.

Chambers, Oswald. *He Shall Glorify Me*. Fort Washington, Pa.: Christian Literature Crusade, 1965.

Cummings, James E. *Through the Eternal Spirit*. Minneapolis, Minn.: Bethany Fellowship Inc.

Daily, Starr. *The Way of the Holy Affection*. St. Paul, Minn.: Macalester Park Publishing Co., 1951.

Denio, F. B. *The Supreme Leader*. Boston, 1900.

Dickson, W. P. *St. Paul's Use of the Term Flesh and Spirit*. Glasgow, 1883.

Draper, Maurice L. *The Gifts and Fruit of the Spirit*. Independence, Mo.: Herald Publishing House, 1969.

Edwards, J. *Charity, Its Fruits*. Banner of Faith, 1969.

Evans, Louis H. *Life's Hidden Power*. Old Tappan, N.J.: Fleming H. Revell Co., 1959.

Forodsham, S. H. *The Spirit-Filled Life*. Grand Rapids, Mich.: William B. Eerdmans Publishing Co., 1948.

Frost, Robert C. *Overflowing Life: Everyday Living in the Spirit*. Plainfield, N.J.: Logos International, 1971.

Gordon, A. J. *The Ministry of the Spirit.* Minneapolis, Minn.: Bethany Fellowship Inc., 1964.

Greeley, Andrew. *Touch of the Spirit, Virtues for Today's Christians.* New York: Herder & Herder Inc., 1971.

Green, Peter. *The Holy Spirit, the Comforter.* New York: Longmans, Green & Co., 1933.

Gruber, Eileen. *To Live in Love.* Grand Rapids, Mich.: Zondervan Publishing House, 1967.

Hambree, Charles R. *Fruits of the Spirit.* Grand Rapids, Mich.: Baker, 1969.

Harkness, Georgia. *Fellowship of the Holy Spirit.* Nashville, Tenn.: Abingdon Press.

Harrison, Norman B. *His Indwelling: The Inliving Holy Spirit.* Minneapolis, Minn.: Harrison Series, 1928.

Holden, G. F. *The Holy Ghost, the Comforter.* London, 1908.

Horton, R. F. *The Holy Spirit.* New York, 1902.

Humphries, A. Lewis. *The Holy Spirit in Faith and Experience.* London: W. A. Hammond, Primitive Methodist Publishing House, 1911.

Joy, Donald M. *Holy Spirit and You.* Nashville, Tenn.: Abingdon, 1965.

Kuyper, A. *The Work of the Holy Spirit.* Grand Rapids, Mich.: William B. Eerdmans Publishing Co., 1956.

Lehman, C. K. *Holy Spirit and the Holy Life.* Scottdale, Pa.: Herald Press, 1959.

Lewis, C. S. *Life in the Spirit.* Grand Rapids, Mich.: William B. Eerdmans Publishing Co., 1955.

NacNeil, Jóhn. *The Spirit-filled Life.* Old Tappan, N.J.: Fleming H. Revell Co., 1896.

McConkey, James H. *The Threefold Secret of the Holy Spirit.* Chicago, Ill.: Moody Press, 1897.

Maclaren, Alexander, *A Rosary of Christian Graces.* London, 1899.

Miller, J. W. *The Christian Way.* Scottdale, Pa.: Herald Press, 1969.

Morgan, G. Campbell. *The Spirit of God.* Old Tappan, N.J.: Fleming H. Revell Co., 1971.

Moule, H. C. G. *Thoughts on Christian Sanctity.* Chicago, Ill.: Moody Press, n.d.

————. *Veni Creator.* London: Pickering and Inglis, n.d.

Mow, Anna B. *Say Yes to Life*. Grand Rapids, Mich.: Zondervan Publishing House, 1961.

Murray, J. *Principles of Conduct*. Grand Rapids, Mich.: Eerdmans Publishing Co., 1957.

Nee, Watchman. *The Release of the Spirit*. Indianapolis, Ind.: Sure Foundation, 1965.

Owen, John. *Holy Spirit, His Gifts and Power*. Grand Rapids, Mich.: Kregel, 1967.

Price, Eugenia. *Make Love Your Aim*. Grand Rapids, Mich.: Zondervan Publishing House, 1967.

Raven, Charles E. *Jesus and the Gospel of Love*. London: Hodder & Stoughton, 1931.

Rees, Tom. *The Holy Spirit in Thought and Experience*. London: Duckworth & Co., 1915.

————— *The Spirit of Life*. Chicago, Ill.: Moody Press, n.d.

Robinson, H. Wheeler. *The Christian Experience of the Holy Spirit*. London: Nesbit & Co., 1944.

Sanders, J. Oswald. *The Holy Spirit of Promise*. London: Marshall, Morgan & Scott, 1954.

Sanderson, John W. *The Fruit of the Spirit*. Grand Rapids, Mich.: Zondervan Publishing House, 1972.

Shoemaker, Samuel M. *With the Holy Spirit and with Fire*. Chicago, Ill.: Word Books, 1970.

Stalker, James. *The Seven Cardinal Virtues*. New York: Dodd, Mead & Co., 1902.

Stiles, J. E. *Gift of the Holy Spirit*. Old Tappan, N.J.: Fleming H. Revell Co., 1971.

Stott, J. R. *Baptism and Fullness of the Holy Spirit*. Downers Grove, Ill.: Inter-Varsity, 1965.

Swete, H. B. *The Holy Spirit in the New Testament*. London, 1909.

Wierwille, Victor P. *Receiving the Holy Spirit Today*. New Knoxville, Ohio: Am Christian Press, 1972.

Wunderlich, Lorenz C. *Half-Known God, the Lord and Giver of Life*. St. Louis, Mo.: Concordia Publishing House, 1963.

The Author

John M. Drescher, Scottdale, Pennsylvania, was born at Manheim, Pennsylvania, and grew up at Mt. Joy, Pennsylvania. He attended Elizabethtown College, Elizabethtown, Pennsylvania, and Eastern Mennonite College, Harrisonburg, Virginia, where he received an AB degree and a ThB degree in 1951 and 1953 respectively. In 1954 he received the BD degree from Goshen Biblical Seminary, Goshen, Indiana.

Drescher has served as pastor and bishop in Ohio 1954-62, and from 1962 to 1973 as editor of the *Gospel Herald*, the official organ of the Mennonite Church. He has served on the Board of the Associated Church Press. He recently completed a two-year term as moderator of the Mennonite Church and presently serves on its General Board.

Drescher is author of four other books: *Meditations for the Newly Married, Heartbeats, Now Is the Time to Love, Follow Me,* and ten visitation pamphlets. Drescher has written for more than 85 different journals and magazines and contributed chapters to four additional books.

In September, 1973, he became pastor of the Scottdale Mennonite Church, Scottdale, Pennsylvania.